A GENERAL REPORT ON THE YUSUFZAIS

H.W. Bellew

SANG-E-MEEL PUBLICATIONS
25, Shahrah-e-Pakistan (Lower Mall) Lahore.

954.912 Bellow, H. W.
A General Report on the Yusufzais/
H. W. Bellow.-Lahore: Sang-e-Meel
Publications, 2013.
xi, 265pp.
1. Civilization. 2. N.W.F.P - History.
I. Title.

2013
Published by:
Niaz Ahmad
Sang-e-Meel Publications,
Lahore.

ISBN-10: 969-35-0545-X
ISBN-13: 978-969-35-0545-0

Sang-e-Meel Publications
25 Shahrah-e-Pakistan (Lower Mall), Lahore-54000 PAKISTAN
Phones: 92-423-722-0100 / 92-423-722-8143 Fax: 92-423-724-5101
http://www.sang-e-meel.com e-mail: smp@sang-e-meel.com

PRINTED AT: HAJI HANIF & SONS PRINTERS, LAHORE.

INTRODUCTION.

In the spring of last year I commenced a general report on the Yusufzai district, compiled from notes and observations made during a residence of several years in the country. The subjects for consideration being varied and extensive, they were classed under separate chapters, and arranged much in the form of the present report; and, being well advanced towards completion, I had hoped to submit the whole in complete form by the end of the year.

In September, however, disturbances having broken out on the frontier, the Corps of Guides moved out on service, and I was for the time being prevented from completing the work; but on the conclusion of the war, and the return of the regiment to quarters, on the 11th January, I at once resumed my original work; and, as the recent events in this district had brought us in contact with the different tribes around and beyond the British border in this direction, I purposed to incorporate a notice of them and their countries with the original report on the Yusufzai plain.

This, however, I found was not easily managed without producing confusion, and I, therefore, deemed it preferable to re-write the report, maintaining the original plan, and to extend the description to the whole Yusufzai tribe and the country possessed by them, regarding both of which I had already a considerable collection of notes.

In compiling this report, I have derived assistance from "Mills History of India" and "Cunningham's Sikhs," as regard some historical dates and facts, and from "Speede's Indian Gardener" for the names of many of the plants mentioned. For the rest, where the authority is not mentioned in the text, I have written from personal observation, or from native information. To accompany the report, I have prepared a map of the country to which it alludes; the whole has been compiled from native information compared and corrected. The plain portion of the country of the Yusufzais is left blank, an excellent map of this tract by Major Walker being published already. For the appearance of my map, in the clear and finished style it now possesses, I am indebted to the kindness of Major H. C. Johnstone, of the Revenue Survey, to whom my best thanks are due.

In the main, I believe the details of this map, as well as the information brought together in the report, are reliable, for considerable pains have been taken to test, and, as far as practicable, verify all points on which any doubt arose. In conclusion, I would express a hope that the report may prove acceptable; and, if not interesting, at least instructive.

H. W. Bellew, *Assistant Surgeon,*
Corps of Guides.

Murdan, 18*th March* 1864.

CONTENTS.

CHAPTER I.—TOPOGRAHY.

PAGES.

CHAPTER II.—HISTORY.

CHAPTER III.—ANTIQUITIES.

CHAPTER IV.—INHABITANTS.

CHAPTER V. GOVERNMENT AND CUSTOMS.

CHAPTER VI.—CLIMATE AND PRODUCTIONS.

APPENDICES.

CHAPTER I.

TOPOGRAPHY.

Designation.

YUSUFZAI is the name of a large and powerful tribe of Afghans. It is also used by them to designate the country they live in; but by us the term is only applied to that plain portion of their country now under British rule.

Limits.

The true Yusufzai country comprises all that diversified stretch of territory contained between the Lâorai and Laspisar mountains on the north, and the river Indus on the south, and bounded by Bajawar and the terminal portion of the Swat river on the west, and the Kohistan of Ghorband and Yassan on the east.

Mountains.

The major portion of the tract thus limited, is a rough mountain region throughout, and is drained to the Indus by direct and indirect channels. The separate courses of these give to the country its peculiar physical formation and natural divisions into districts.

Plains.

The lesser, or south-western portion of the Yusufzai country, is an extensive and open plain, forming a part of the great Peshawar basin, but separated from the rest of its extent by terminal portions of the Swat and

Kabul rivers. It is the only portion of the Yusufzai country within the red line of the British border.

Description.

A topographical description of this tract only is the subject of the following pages; but some information regarding the rest of the country beyond the border, and for the most part gathered from native travellers, will also be added, in the hope that it may prove interesting, if not useful.

Boundaries.

The plain, or *samah* of Yusufzai, as it is generally styled, occupies the eastern portion of the Peshawar valley, and is bounded as follows, viz:—

North.

On the north, by a continuous and lofty range of mountains, which, extending east and west, separate it from Swat. The principal peaks on this range are, in succession from west to east, Sapraisar, Sîlaipatti, Khânorah, Hâzârnâo, Malakand, Shâhkot, Charhât and Morah.

East.

From mount Morah, an extensive range diverges directly southward; and, terminating at the river Indus, in the lofty and massive Mahâban, forms the eastern boundary of the plain, and separates it from the adjacent districts of Buhnair, Chamlah, and Amâzai; or, as they are sometimes collectively called, Barhand. The principal peaks on this range between mounts Morah and Mahâban, are Sînawar, Pajah, Alishair, Garrû, and Sarpatai.

South.

On the south, the boundary is formed by the Indus from Mahâban to Attak, and from that point up to the junction of the Swat and Kabul rivers by the united streams of both. The first portion of this boundary separates the plain from the Hazâra country, and the latter from that of the Khattaks.

West.

The western boundary is formed by the Swat river from Nisattah, where it joins the Kabul stream, up to Abâzai, where it passes into the Hatmânkhail hills. This boundary separates the plain from the Dâûdzai doâba, the tract included in the angle formed by the junction of the Swat and Kabul rivers, which, in this part of their courses, are locally known as the Landai and Nâgûmân, respectively. The term *Landai*, which signifies "short," also applies to all that portion of the stream from the point of union of the Swat and Malîzai or Panjkora rivers in Arang Barang, down to its junction with the Indus at Attak. The latter term, *Nâgûmân*, only applies to that portion of the Kabul river between its passage through the Khaibar hills and its junction with the Swat stream or Landai, at Nisattah, and very appropriately expresses the devious and unreliable character of the stream in this part of its course.

Landai.

Nâgûmân.

Geographical position.

Length.

Breadth.

Area.

Population.

Aspect.

The Yusufzai plain within the limits defined, extends between 33° 55′ and 34° 35′ north latitude, and 71° 40′ and 72° 45′ of east longitude. In its greatest length it is 64 miles from south-east to north-west; and in its greatest breadth from north to south, it is 46 miles. Its area, including the tract at the foot of the hills, is about 3,200 square miles. Population about 140,000. The country is an unbroken plain, with an undulating surface gently sloping to the south. It comprises the following local divisions or districts, viz., Rânîzai, Lûnkhwar, Mandar, Gadûn, Khattak, and Hashtnaggar.

Divisions.

Rânîzai is a tract of plain at the foot of the hills on the north border between Hashtnaggar and Lûnkhwar. It is named, as is usual with this people, after the tribe holding it. Rânîzai is an extensive district, and, stretching over the Totai hills, includes the whole of the lower end of the Swat valley. The portion on the plain, and at the foot of the hills, contains about twenty-five villages, of which the chief are Harrichand, Skhâkot, Irozshâh, and Totai.

Rânîzai.

Lûnkhwar, or Lâmdakhwar, so named on account of its ravines always containing water, is an extensive gulf in the hills between Malakand and Pajah. It is mainly occupied by the Bâîzai clan, and is frequently named after them. It contains also a small colony of Khattaks. It contains about thirty villages, of which the chief are Lunkher, about 800 houses, the market town for the Swat valley and countries to the north, Katlang, Palli, and Kharkai.

Lûnkhwar.

Mandar, or Mandanr, named from the clan possessing it, is the largest district of all, and occupies the whole of the central and eastern portion of the plain south of Pajah ridge, and is the name by which the whole of the tract east of Hashtnaggar is generally described in native books. This district comprises six sub-districts, according to the tribes composing the Mandar clan. They are Kamâlzaif Amâzai, Razar, Khodokhail, Utmânzai, and Gadûn.

Mandanr.

Each of these is further sub-divided, according to the divi-

Tappas. sions of the tribes. Thus Kamâlzai comprises the lesser districts of Mishrânzai, chief town Torû, and Kishrânzai, chief towns Hoti and Mardân.

Kamâlzai.

Amâzai. Amâzai comprises the lesser districts of Dowlatzai or Sûdhûm, chief town Rustam, which is the market for Buhnair and the countries to the east, and Ismailzai, chief town Kâpûrdagarrhi.

Razar. Razar comprises the five lesser districts of Akokhail. Malikzai, Manîzai, Khidarzai, and Mâmûzai. The chief towns are Smailah, Yârhusain, Kâlûkhân, Shiwah and Nowikila. Khodokhail comprises the Bisâtkhail and Bâmkhail, chief towns Chinglai and Totallai. Utmânzai comprises the lesser districts of Sadozai, Zalozai, and Dorâzai; chief towns are Kotah and Topi, Zihdah, and Hund, and Kilâbat.

Gadûn. Gadûn comprises the lesser districts of Sâlâr and Mansûr; chief towns Gandaf and Bîsak. This last district is not properly in the Mulk-i-Mandar; the Gadûns not being Yusufzais at all, but a clan of the Kâkar tribe, whose settlements are in the Hâzârah country across the Indus. This remark applies also to the two next districts, as will be presently noted. The Gadûn country occupies the western slopes of the Mahâban, and the small strips of plain enclosed between its spurs. It is an extensive district, and beyond the border.

Khattak. Khattak is a tract of wavy ravine-cut country along the banks of the Indus and Kabul rivers, between Hund on the former and Nowshaira on the latter, and marked off from Mandan by a low ridge of desert waste. This district, as the name implies, is occupied by the Khattak tribe, whose main settlements are in the hill tract on the other side of the Kabul river. Its chief towns are Jahângira and Nowshaira. Hashtnaggar, or, as it is written in native books, 'Ashnaghar, is an extensive tract along the banks of the Kabul and Swat rivers from Nowshaira to Abâzai. It is a populous and fertile tract, and contains many flourishing villages. It is inhabited by Mahmandzais and Mians. The latter are the merchants, who carry on most of the trade with the countries to the north. Their chief imports are, timber from Swat and Panjkora, iron from Bajawar, hawks and ponies from Kâshkâr, &c. The chief villages are Prâng, Chârsadda, Turrangzai, and Tangi. This district is separated from Mandan by a wide expanse of waste land, known as the *mairah*.

Hashtnaggar.

On referring to the boundaries of Yusufzai, it will be observed that they cut off the plain from the surrounding countries either by a chain of mountain ranges difficult of passage, or by a barrier of rivers connected one with the other, and with a few exceptional points, unfordable throughout.

Isolation.

The former enclose it on the north and east, and the latter on the south and west.

Such being the isolation of the Yusufzai plain, we may here profitably note the means by which it communicates with the countries around; and these are naturally of two kinds, by mountain passes and ferries.

Communications.

Before enumerating these, it is necessary here to note that the British border by no means corresponds with the natural boundaries already detailed. On the

British border.

contrary, the boundary in some parts is an undefined line across the open plain, in others it is marked by spurs projecting into the plain from the main mountain range, whilst, in some localities, it runs along the base of this mountain range, but in no instance extends up to the natural water shed line.

Passes.

In describing the hill passes leading out of the Yusufzai plain, it will be convenient to take them in order, according to the local divisions of the district, and commencing at the Swat river on the west, to conclude at the Indus on the east, thus including between these two points all the practicable or commonly used passes through the mountain ranges forming its northern and eastern limits.

Note.

With this order in view, the passes are as follows, premising only that the distances are approximate, and the result of information from natives compared and checked :—

Hashtnaggar to Hatmânkhail.

I.—From Hashtnaggar to the Hatmânkhail country, there are four passes.

Spai-darrah.

1. The Spaidarrah pass. From Tangi, over a plain but ravine-cut country, eight miles. On to Rangmiana, four miles; to Nâswar, four miles; to Ziârat Yusuf Baba, eight miles; and to bank of Swat river, eight miles—between and over low hills all the way. From Yusuf Baba Ziârat, the road leads along the river bank through the *Spaidarrah* or "Dale of dogs," seven miles, where is a ferry for crossing the river by swing ropes, and then goes on to Targhâo, nine miles, and to base of Koh-i-mor, twelve miles.

Tor Kamar.

2. The Tor Kamar pass. From Tangi to Nawadand, eight miles; to *Tor Kamar*, or "the black ridge," six miles; to Gholam Kili, five miles; to Kalandai ferry,

three miles; cross river by raft, and on to Targhâo in Arang Barang, nine miles.

Khanora.

3. The Khanora pass. From Tangi to Prangarh, ten miles, over open plain intersected by ravines; on to Uchalgat in the hills, five miles; then between and over low spurs of Khanora mountain to Dabbar, six miles, on to Soimianah, two miles; cross river by skins or raft, and on to Targhâo, six miles.

Sînâzai.

4. The Sînâzai pass. From Tangi to Gandairai, seven miles, along the course of a ravine over the open plain; on to Totai in the hills, nine miles; then over a high ridge of Hazarnâo mountain, and down to Sînâzai, seven miles; cross the river by raft, and on to Targhâo, six miles.

Difficulties.

The last of these routes is described as the easiest and most frequented. None of them, however, are much used even by men of the country, owing as much to the difficulties of the roads, which are only practicable for footmen, as to the want of shelter and supplies, and the danger from robbers who infest the country. By the first route the river is crossed by swing ropes. At the usual place for crossing, the river is described as flowing tumultuously in a narrow channel, between precipitous rocky banks.

Ranizai to Swat.

II.—From Ranizai to Swat, there are four passes.

Digarr.

1. The Digarr pass. From Skhâkot by Mírdih and Usmânkhailogarrhi to Ariânkot, seven miles, over a rough country at the foot of the hills. From Ariânkot, four miles, through a glen to Digarr hill; then up its side and down to Maikhband in the Ranizai division of

Swat, five miles; and on by Pirkhail to Totakân Matkana, four miles, over a plain country traversed by ravines. This route is only frequented by footmen, but horses can travel by it.

Kâl-darrah.

2. The Kâl-darrah pass. From Skhâkot by Mirdih to Kharkai of Ranizai (there is another of Baizai), eight miles over a rough ravine-cut country, overrun by low rocky heights. From Kharkai, along a narrow glen, to the Kâldarrah hill, and up to Chapal, a small hamlet at its top, three miles; then down to Dairi Jolagrâm in Swat, four miles. This is a steep and difficult pass, and is only used by footmen.

Malakand.

3. The Malakand pass. From Skhâkot by Mirdih to Dargai, seven miles, through rough country at foot of the hills; then through the Jabbânrdarrah glen to foot of Malakand hill, where there is a well and camping ground, four miles. From this, up the hill side to the hamlet of Pirânokorûna at its top, then down by a road to the right to another hamlet at the foot of the hill, about five miles; then on over a rough plain to Batkhailah, two miles. This is described as a good and easy road for laden cattle, is well wooded, and abundantly supplied with water.

Branch road.

From the Pirânokorûna hamlet, on the top of the hill, two other roads lead off to the left. One of these leads to Dairi Jolagram, and the other to Batkhailah. Though shorter than the main road, both are very rough and difficult, and only used by footmen.

Chârghotai.

4. The Chârghotai-ghâkhi pass. From Skhâkot and Mirdih to Dobandi, at foot of hills, eleven miles. Thence through narrow winding defiles to the Châr-

ghotai-ghâkhi or "four peaked ridge," over this and down to Batkhailah, seven miles. This is a very difficult pass, and only used by footmen.

Lunkhwar to Swat.

III. From Lunkhwar, or Baizai, to Swat, there are three passes.

Shâhkot.

1. The Shâhkot pass. From Palli of Baizai through the defile, over the Shâhkot hill, and down to Dairi and Allahdand in Swat, about eighteen miles. This is a steep, rough, and difficult road, but is well-supplied with wood and water, and is frequently traversed by laden cattle.

Charhât.

2. The Charhât pass. From Palli by Shairkhâna to Morah-bândah, then northward over the Charhât hill, and down to Thânnah in Swat, about sixteen miles. This is a steep and difficult road, and is only used by footmen.

Morah.

3. The Morah pass. From Palli by Morah-bândah, and over a spur from Mount Morah down to Thânnah in Swat, eighteen miles. This is the pass mostly used by merchants and travellers. It is described as a good and easy road for laden cattle, and is well supplied with wood and water.

Baizai to Buhnair.

IV.—From Baizai to Buhnair, Sâlârzai, there are two passes.

Bâz-darrah.

1. The Bâzdarrah pass. From Palli by Shairkhana to Bâz-darrah six miles; then through a narrow gorge and over a low ridge, and down to Girarrai in the Sâlârzai district of Buhnair, five miles; then along a plain to Jowar, three miles. A difficult path, only used by footmen.

2. The Kohitanga pass. From Miankhan through a long and narrow defile, over a high ridge and down to Kingargalli in Buhnair, ten miles. This is a difficult pass, but is used by laden cattle. It is well wooded, and water from springs is abundant. From Kingargalli the road is easy, and winds over an open but ravine-cut plain to Nansair and Pampokha, three miles.

Kohitanga.

Sudhum to Buhnair.

V.—From Sudhum to Buhnair of Sâlârzai, there are two passes.

1. The Sînâwar pass. From Chargholai along a ravine-cut tract to Pîrsai, at the foot of the hills, eight miles; then eastward, through the rocky defile of Khoana-darrah to the foot of Alishair mountain, six miles; and south-eastward round its base to the Waikhbândah hamlet; five miles. Not an easy road, but practicable for laden cattle, water from springs is in plenty.

Sînâwar.

2. The Sulaisar pass. From Chargholai by Pîrsai, through Khoana-darrah, to foot of Alishair hill, fourteen miles; then up the Sulaisar spur to Sarbândah, at its top, five miles; and down to Waikhbândah, three miles. A steep mountain path only used by footmen. From Waikhbândah the road winds along deep ravines to Kuhai, four miles.

Sulaisar.

Sudhum to Buhnair.

VI.—From Sudhum to Buhnair of Nûrîzai, there are two passes.

1. The Malan-darrah pass. From Rustam to the Malan-darrah village, at the foot of the hill, seven miles; through a gorge, over Malan-darrah ridge and down by Mian Yusuf to Nowikila in Buhnair of Nûrîzai, seven miles. From this point two roads lead across the plain, one

Malan-darrah.

to Bagra, and the other to Bajkatta. This is described as a good road for laden cattle, and well supplied with wood and water.

Ambailah.

2. The Ambailah pass. From Rustam by Surkhawai, through the Panj-darrah defile to Ambailah in Chamlah, about sixteen miles; then north, over a low spur of Garrû hill, the Buhnair Kandâo, and down to Dairi, seven miles. From Dairi, the road leads by Chîna across the plain and the Barhandû stream to Daggar. This is a good pass for laden cattle, and much frequented. It is well supplied with wood and water.

Sudhum to Chamlah.

VII.—From Sudhum to Chamlah, there are two passes.

Ambailah.

1. The Ambailah pass. From Rustam to the hamlet of Surkhawai, over a plain but ravine-cut country, five miles; then through the narrow Panj-darrah defile, over an easy ridge, and down to Ambailah in Chamlah, eleven miles, and on over an open plain, four miles to Kogah, the chief village of Chamlah. This pass is the route by which the produce of Chamlah and the countries beyond reaches Yusufzai.

Narinji.

2. The Narinji pass. From Rustam by Machai to Parmûli, ten miles, over a plain with ridges of hill on either side; on to Narinji, six miles; then through narrow winding glens by Mîrshâhi to Shpol-bândah, and up a steep hill to Lâlû-bândah on its top, eight miles; then down to Kogah through a gorge, four miles. This route is mostly used by footmen only, but horses and camels can go by it, but not without risk.

Razar to Khodokhail.

VIII.—From Razar to Khodokhail, there are four passes.

Bâghoch.

1. The Bâghoch pass. From Narinji to Mrîshâhi, then eastward over the Baghoch hill, a spur of the Sarpattai range, and down to Chinglai in an open glen, eight miles. This is a difficult track, and only used by footmen. From Chinglai, two roads lead off. One due north to Sûrâh in Chamlah, eight miles. It leads over the Sarpattai range by the Shaikhâno-darrah pass, is well wooded and watered at the foot of the hill, but is very difficult for laden cattle. The other road leads eastward from Chinglai, over a rough and ravine-cut country, past the village of Kalân to Kandgalli, at the foot of Mahaban, where it is joined by Sarpattai, five miles. From Kandgalli, the road leads up a steep hill into a long and narrow defile, the Jan Mahomad Kandao, which winds down between the Sarpattai and Mahaban mountains to Lângâ and Nagrai, nine miles. From this, the road descends through narrow and steep gorges to Charorai, the chief town of the Amazais, near the river Barhandu. This is not an easy road, but laden cattle can traverse it. The country is covered with pine forests, and abounds in springs of clear water.

Dârrân.

2. The Dârrân pass. From Parmûli eastward, over an open plain, traversed by ravines, to mouth of the pass, seven miles; through the narrow defile or pass, and by Bâgh and Swâwai to Chinglai, ten miles. This is a short pass, and practicable for laden cattle.

Jahângîr-darrah.

3. The Jahângîr-darrah pass. From Manairi, along the hill skirt to Salîmkhan, three miles; then along a dry rocky ravine in the Jahângîr-darrah or glen, and past the villages of Bâmkhail Totâlai, Khalli-kila, Ghûrghûshti, and Dandar, to Kandgalli, fourteen miles. This is a rough road, and badly supplied with water, but is practicable for laden cattle.

4. The Dakârah pass. From Manairi to Ghûrghûshti, seven miles; thence eastward by Shaidoh, Ghlodarrah and Kadrah, six miles; then north by Dakârah and Ramcharkot, over hills, and up to Mangalthannah, eight miles. This road winds along narrow glens and deep ravines; and, though very rough, is practicable for laden cattle. From Mangalthannah, which is on a high spur of Mahaban, a road leads into the Jan Mahomad Kandâo, and thence to the Amazai country. It is only used by footmen.

Dakârah.

From this point, eastward to the Indus, and on the western and southern slopes of Mahaban, is the country of the Gadûn tribe, and a portion of the Utmânzais. They communicate with the plain by two main routes, which, following the courses of the two great ravines draining the hills, conduct to Maini on the one hand and Topi on the other.

Gadûn.

From the foregoing particulars, it will be observed that the various hill passes conduct through narrow defiles, either between or else over the lower spurs emanating from the higher mountain peaks, which at intervals project from the main range bounding the Yusufzai plain on the north and east. Of these peaks, or higher mountain masses, only a few are of sufficient elevation to receive a covering of snow for a shorter or longer period during the winter months, and then only on or about their summits, where for the most part they support dense and extensive forests of pines—trees which are entirely absent from the lower spurs. The most notable peaks on this bounding range, are, in order of succession, from west to east Khânorah, Hâzârnâo, Malakand, Morah, Pajah, 'Alishair, Sinâwar, Garrû, Sarpattai, and Mahaban.

Note.

Mountains.

Hazarnao, Morah, and Mahaban, are great mountain masses. They receive more snow, and keep it longer than any of the others, and support also more extensive pine forests.

Peaks.

All these passes, as well as the countries they lead to, are beyond the British border; and, with but few exceptions, have never been traversed or examined by Europeans.

Passes are all beyond the border.

On its remaining borders, the Yusufzai plain adjoins British territory, and communicates with the adjacent districts by means of a chain of ferries over the rivers severally forming its southern and western limits.

Ferries.

These we will now enumerate, commencing at the point where the hill and river boundaries meet, and, next beyond the last hill pass described; and, taking them in the order of their succession, will conclude at the last ferry next the point where the first hill pass described commences.

Order.

In doing so, it will be convenient to class the ferries with the rivers they cross, only premising in this place that the exact spots here indicated are not always constant. Changes are sometimes necessitated by alterations either in the river banks or currents, or else by changes in the volume and velocity of their waters, results dependent on the succession of the seasons and their accompanying climatic and atmospheric phenomena. Changes such as these, however, seldom necessitate a greater removal than a few hundred yards up or down the stream; and the ferries, when thus changed, often again revert to their original sites after intervals of a few years or months.

Sites change.

I.—The Indus river ferries.

Indus river. There are five ferries over the Indus, in that part of its course bounding the Yusufzai plain.

1. From Kabbal to Torbailah. From two to four boats are procurable at this ferry in case of need, but one only is usually plied.

Kabbal.

2. Paihur to Dall Mohatt. There are two boats at this ferry. It is only used in the hot weather; in the cold season it is moved down to the next ferry.

Paihur.

3. Gallah to Ghâzi. There are two boats here, only used in the cold weather and moved up to Paihur in the hot.

Gallah.

4. Hund to Yâsînzai and Amîn. One boat used all the year round. In case of need, four or five boats can be produced.

Hund.

5. Jabarbâzar to Hazroh. One boat. This ferry is not now worked, the traffic crossing by Hund.

Jabarbâzar.

II.—The Kabul river ferries. There are six ferries over this stream, between its points of junction with the Indus and Swat rivers at Attak and Nisattah.

Kabul river.

1. Jahângîra to Shaidoh. Two boats. In case of need, eight or a dozen can be procured from Attak.

Jahângîra.

2. Misrîbândah to Akorah. Two boats. This is the

Akorah. favorite ferry between the eastern portion of the Yusufzai plain and the Khattaks.

Pîrsabâk. 3. Pîrsabâk and Badrakai. This ferry has been closed of late years.

Nowshaira. 4. New Nowshaira to old Nowshaira. This is the largest ferry in connection with Yusufzai. In the hot weather it employs from six to eight boats. In the cold weather, and sometimes throughout the year, there is a bridge of boats below this ferry, the property of Government.

Khaishki. 5. Khaishki to Pîrpai and Zâkhail. There are two boats here, but the ferry is little frequented.

Shâh Alam. 6. Zardâd-dairi to Shâh Alam, two boats. This ferry also is but little frequented.

Swat river. III.—The Swat river ferries. There are ten ferries over the Swat river, in that part of its course bounding the Yusufzai plain, from Nisattah to Abâzai.

Nisattah. 1. Nisattah to Khalîl or Mângânro-bandah. From two to six boats are employed here. It is the principal ferry between Peshawar and Yusufzai, through Hashtnaggar. More correctly it belongs to the preceding set.

Prâng. 2. Prâng to Agrah, two boats. There is a boat building yard here. The boats go down to Kurâchi with country produce, and are there sold.

3. Charsaddah to Gidar, two boats. From Gidar, over a strip of island, to Shahi, and then across a second stream by boat to Kharki. This is towards the north. From Gidar, southward across the island to Gulâbâd, then by boat across a second stream to Nowikila. One boat at each place.

Charsaddah.

Kâzikhail.

4. Kâzikhail to Kot, two boats.

Hissâr.

5. Hamîdgul Mian-garrhi to Hissâr, two boats.

6. Razar to Shaikhân, two boats. From Shaikhân by Tarnâo to Dildâr-garrhi, and across a second stream to Srîkh Mârozai, two boats.

Razar.

7. Utmânzai to Spînkai, two boats.

Utmânzai.

Turangzai.

8. Turangzai to Fazaldîn Mian-dairi, four boats.

Umarzai.

9. Umarzai to Chînah, two boats.

Abâzai.

10. Abâzai to Mattah, four boats.

At none of these ferries, excepting Attak and Nowshaira, can more than from two to four boats be procured without previous notice, and time allowed for their collection. At Attak, Nowshaira, and Charsaddah, there are extensive timber yards, and a considerable number of boats are turned out annually from the building yards.

Boats.

Besides these ferries, the natives are in the habit of crossing the river by swimming on a *shinâs*, or inflated ox hide, from bank to bank, at any point.

Shinâs.

Jâlah.

They also cross at any point on the *jâlah*, or portable raft, formed by placing planks or charpoys on a platform of inflated skins fastened together, and ferried across by men paddling on *shinâses* at each corner. In former years, the *shinâs* and *jâlah* were much used by robbers, who, crossing singly on their own shinâses, brought back the fruits of their plunder on jâlahs, made by fastening their inflated hides together as described above. The use of the shinâs is now prohibited, except by license.

Such are the means of communication between the Yusufzai plain and the countries around.

Surface of the plain.

The tract thus isolated, presents a gently undulating surface, plain throughout in its central, western, and southern tracts; but, to the northward and eastward, it is more or less overrun by low rocky ridges, jutting out from the main mountain ranges in those directions.

Central and south-west tracts.

In the former tracts, the country is a vast open expanse; and, except in the immediate vicinity of the rivers, along whose banks are many villages and much cultivation, presents at the first glance a singularly uninviting aspect, owing to the paucity or entire absence of trees on large tracts, and the uninteresting level of the surface. On closer inspection, however, it is found to possess more variation of scene than is discovered at first view. The country is traversed by some great ravines or vicarious river channels, along the courses of which are planted a number of villages with their trees, gardens, and cultivated lands, though still the greatest portion by far is an extensive stretch of waste land, termed in the colloquial *Mairah*. The mairah is more or less covered with a stunted brushwood, composed mostly of *bair* bushes. Be-

Mairah.

tween the detached patches of these, are strips of cultivation along the borders of the waste, and the general surface supports a growth of grasses and herbs that suffice to pasture the cattle and flocks of the district. The nature of this vegetation will be the subject of a future chapter.

The *mairah* is not one unbroken spread of waste land, but is divided by the great central *nallah* or ravine of Yusufzai, and the cultivation of the population settled along its course, into two main tracts, named according to their relative local positions. That on the west is the Hashtnaggar-mairah, and that on the south-east is the Khattak-mairah.

Former state.

In former times, these desert tracts were constantly traversed by armed and mounted bands of robbers, who lived by the plunder of unwary travellers, or of cattle straying too far from their village grazing grounds; but, since the establishment of the British rule, all this has been put a stop to, and now travellers and cattle cross and wander over its wide and lonely wastes without let or hindrance.

Present state.

The best proof of the present security of these formerly dangerous tracts, is in the fact of the progressive extension of cultivation on its surface, far away from protection for the crop under other circumstances. Year by year, by steady degrees, the waste is being reclaimed and brought under cultivation; and, since my first arrival at this station, in 1856, must have advanced fully two miles into the mairah, at a low calculation.

Mounds.

One other object deserves note in this place, as being connected with the aspect of the country. I allude to the numerous mounds of bare earth that dot the country all over, and which, from their singular appearance, magnitude, and numbers, at once attract the attention and excite curiosity as to their origin, history, and meaning. They will be more particularly noticed in a future chapter; here it will suffice to state that they are artificial heaps, abounding in fragments of red pottery and the remains of old walls, &c., and are evidently the sites of the habitations of men of bygone ages.

Lateral tracts.

In its lateral tracts, the Yusufzai plain presents a more diversified aspect than that of the central tract just described; and, though of opposite kinds on the different sides, much more interesting and grateful to the eye.

Western.

The tract on the western side is occupied by the separate district of Hashtnaggar. Here the land lies low in a strip along the left bank of the Swat and Kabul rivers, contains many villages, is highly cultivated, freely irrigated, and well stocked with large trees, such as the mulberry, sissu, tamarisk, jujube, &c.; and willows, along the water-courses. Away from the river, the land rises into the mairah, which is used as a common grazing ground for the cattle of the district.

Eastern.

The tract along the eastern side of the plain, as well as along the whole extent of its northern boundary, presents a picturesque mountain scenery. Here dell and dale succeed each other in every variety of arrangement. At distant intervals, great spurs project on to the plain and gulf off the mountain skirts into a series of close vallies, which, by varying combinations of glen and gorge, rock and precipice, meadow and water-course, scattered groves and compact villages, present a variety of scenery seldom met with in one district; and which, to be duly appreciated, must be seen.

Cultivation.

The general surface along this tract, although very stony, and much cut up by the drainage off the hills, is, nevertheless, well cultivated. Not unfrequently the cultivation is carried high up the hill slopes, on which for the most part the cattle are dependent for pasture. On the lower spurs this is at best but scanty; for such ridges are mostly bare ledges of rock in their lower heights, though more or less well covered with a stunted brushwood and varied herbage at their higher elevations. The very general absence of large trees, and of pines especially, on these spurs, is a notable feature; for on the highest ranges the splendid and extensive pine forests form an essential element in the beauty of the scenery, as well as in the virtues of the climate.

Streams.

There is no perennial stream flowing all through the Yusufzai plain; but the drainage from the hills, as well as that from the plain itself, is carried off by a number of ravines, the extent, magnitude, and ramifications of which constitute a remarkable feature of the country, whilst they are objects of importance on account of the sudden floodings they are at certain seasons subject to, rendering them for a while obstacles to free communication between the different portions of the district they traverse. For these reasons, it will be well to describe the channels by which the plain of Yusufzai is drained. And here it may be premised that most of the ravines have one or more springs in some part or other of their course, though mostly near their origin in the hills. The water from these springs, to a limited extent, is more or less constant throughout the year; and, as a general rule, in seasons of unusual drought, when the springs disappear from the surface, water is generally to be obtained by digging down a few feet in the beds of their former streams.

Drainage.

Water.

According to native accounts, the water in all these ravines has greatly diminished during the past half century, and several permanent springs, it is reported, have entirely disappeared.

Its scarcity.

At the present day, there is certainly a scarcity of water in the district generally, and several circumstances combine to lead to the belief that this was not the case in former ages. The majority of the ruins and other remains of the former habitations of man are now desert wastes from this very cause; for those of them that still retain facilities for water-supply are at this day inhabited, new buildings having risen on the ruins of the old.

Former abundance.

History also describes this tract of country as far more populous, better wooded, and more plentifully supplied with water, than it is at the present day; as will be more particularly noted in the next chapter.

Source of supply.

At the present day the *nallah*, ravine, or natural water-course, is the only reliable source of water-supply in all that portion of the district not directly on the river's bank. To this there are but few exceptions, and it will be found as a consequence that the bulk of the population are settled along their courses, or else in their vicinity, for in such positions wells are remunerative, and supply water as well for agricultural as domestic purposes. On the flanks of the main channel of drainage, between it and the river boundaries on the other hand, as well as between its more distant branches, the land is more or less elevated and dry, as in the central tracts, the Hashtnaggar and Khattak *mairahs*, &c. In such tracts there are but few, if any, villages; whilst the cultivation is entirely dependent on the heavens for its supplies of moisture.

Ravines.

Excepting only its north-west and south-east angles, the whole extent of the Yusufzai plain is drained by one great ravine, which, coursing through its central tract, empties into the Kabul river between the villages of Pirsabâk and Nowshairah.

Chalpâni.

It is called the *Chalpáni*, or "deceitful water," on account of its sudden floodings and numerous-ever-changing quick sands. By its own branches of origin, and a succession of tributary ravines, the Chalpâni, or *Khalpáni*, as it is as often called, conveys away into the Kabul river all the drainage from the hills and plain country lying between the Totai hills on the west, and the Khodokhail hills on the east, an arc of near sixty miles of hills.

Extent and branches.

This ravine being the largest and most important in the whole district, we may conveniently commence with its description, including the ravines joining it on either side. Commencing then with those on the west of the Chalpâni ravine, are:—

Bagiârrai.

I.—The Bagiârrai-khwar. The main ravine commences above Kâldarrah, midway between the hills of Malakand and Hâzârnâo, passes by the villages of Kharkai, Dargai, Mirdih, Sangair or Khangarrhi, Skhâkot, Dobandi, Shingrai, and Shairgarh, to Jalâla. Below this last village, except after floods, it does not contain any water during the hot season. Above Skhâkot the Bagiârrai receives a number of ravines on either side. Those on the west bring down the drainage from the spurs of Hâzârnâo, and those on the east the drainage from Malakand. Between Skhâkot and Jalâla, the Bagiârrai receives from the west three or four ravines that drain the Totai hills. Of these the chief comes from Bahram-dairi by Harichand, Pirsaddah and Madbâbaziarat, and joins the Bagiârrai at Jalâla. From this point the Bagiarrai goes southward to Kot Jûngrah, there receives a small branch from the east; and then, passing through a low ridge of rocks, joins the Chalpâni on its west, about two miles above Gujargarrhi.

II.—Lunkhwar, or Lâmbdakhwar. Begins by two main branches that drain the spurs from the Shâhkot hill. They pass one on either side of the Lundkhwar town, and unite directly on its south. The western branch is the Barwazah-kandah. It comes down from Koh-Maloh, and passing by Kharkai, Kâloh, Dândiah, Dâghi, and Mian Isa, flows on to Lundkhwar, and meets below the town on the east; the other branch, called the Landai Kandah, which comes down from Koh Pir Ali, passes by Kaloh and Daghi. The united ravines then pass in one great cutting by Katigarrhi, and join the Chalpâni at Sayadabad.

Lunkhwar.

III.—The Chalpâni, or Khalpâni-khwar. Drains the Morah hill and spurs by four or five minor branches. The chief of these begins at the foot of Morah; and, passing both Bâzdarrah villages, Shairkhanah, Zormandai, Jalâlpûr, Sarobaï, Tazagram, Kasimai, Charchur, Dairai, Lîkpani, Jangidair, and Kotakai, reaches Sayadabad, above which it is joined by the Lunkhwar on the west. Beyond this, it passes on by Pîrâbâd and Arabai to Gujargarrhi, above which it is joined by the Bagiarrai on the west. It then goes on by Baghdâda, Mardan, Hoti, Mayar, Torû, Khâo, Ghaladair, Khatki, Kotarpân, Baghobânda, and Chokai, on to the Kabul river, which it joins between Pirsabak and Nowshairah. Between the villages of Kotarpân and Khatki, it receives the Hissâra Kandah, a long ravine, that drains the plain on the west. It begins near Pirsaddah, winds round Khânmai, passes between Mangâh and Dargai, and then traverses the plain south-eastward to the Chalpâni. On its east, this ravine receives a branch called Murdâra Kandah, which also drains the plain; and, winding round the Rashakai village, joins it near Khatki. It is a narrow, deep cut drain, and impassable for several hours after heavy rains. The Hissara

Chalpâni.

Kandah is the boundary between Yusufzai, or Mandan, and Hashtnaggar.

Gadar Rûd.

IV.—The Gadar Rûd. Drains the northern slopes of Sinawar and Pajah, by a number of channels, which, gathering, unite at Smailki into one channel, which goes on by Sangao, Miankhan, Kâtlang, Bilândai, Jamâlgarrhi, Kaziabad, Gadar, Hamzakhan, Bâbînî, Mohib, and Zormandai, and then spreads over the plain in a marshy track to join the Chalpâni at Ghaladair. This is an extensive ravine, and contains many springs along its course.

Mukâm Rûd.

V.—The Mukâm Rûd. Drains the western slopes of the 'Alishair, Bâroch, Malandarrah, and Garrû hills, by a number of scattered branches, which, uniting at Rustam into one wide channel, onwards take a winding course past Chînah, Hamzakot, Nawigram, Chargholai, Kotarpân, Bârîkâb, Katâkhat, Jûngra, Gûjrât, Bakhshâlî, Kaki, Shâhbâzgarrhi, and Kâpûrdagarrhi, to Mohib, beyond which it joins the marshy track of the Gadar Rûd.

Wûch Khwar.

VI.—The Wûch Khwar. Drains the Kochkand and Narinji hills by two branches, which, coming down by Shairdarrah and Narinji, respectively, unite on the plain between Mirali and Parmûli, and then passing by Jalâl, Sangbatai, Shiwah, Asotah, and Shaikhjana, to Nowikila, there turns to the west; and passing Kâlûkhan, Adînah, and Smailha, becomes spread over the nazar land common to this and the two preceding ravines. The nazar land is an extensive tract of low lying marsh between the villages of Kapurdagarrhi and Ghaladair. It contains a number of stagnant ponds, called "*dandd*" in the colloquial. Some of these are of considerable extent, and contain more or less water throughout the year. The two largest ponds are the Shahdandd and the Khânâ-dandd.

VII.—The Shagai Kandah. Drains the Loaighar hill by many small channels, which uniting near Amânkot, pass on across the Darrân defile to Hamzadair; and, winding by Mansûbdâr, Tulândai and Yar-Hosain, joins the Balar ravine near Dobiân.

Shagai Kandah.

VIII.—The Balar Kandah. Begins on the plain between Danddukali and Dâghi, passes Yakûbai, Bazar, Dobian, Gumbat, Gidar, and Kandarai, and ultimately joins the Mukâm Rûd, a couple of miles above its junction with the Chalpani.

Balar Kandah.

This completes the Chalpâni system of ravines. By it the whole of the central tract, and most of the hill border of the Yusufzai plain, is drained by one main channel into the Kabul river.

The rest of the district eastward, to the Indus, is drained by four principal ravines that convey their watêrs separately to the Indus. They are, continuing the succession as before:

IX.—The Badrai Khwar. Drains the hills of Sarpattai and Panjtar. It begins at the foot of Mahaban above Kandgalli, passes through Jahângir-darrah by the villages of Dandâr, Saidoh, Ghurghushti, Khalli Kila, Bâmkhail Totalai, Salimkhan, Manairi, Swâbi, Kala-darrah, Panjpir, Kadai, Zihdih, and Dodair, and finally falls into the Indus between Hund and Harriân.

Badrai Khwar.

X.—The Bûrai Kandah, drains Koh Ajmair; and, passing between Kilabat and Kotah by Tandkohi, Marghûz and Dodair, finally becomes lost in low marsh land, or, in times of flood, joins the Badrai ravine.

Bûrai Kandah.

XI.—The Jabahgai Kandah.

Jabahgai Kandah.

Drains the land about Bamkhail and Baja into the Kilabat marsh.

XII.—The Shahkot Kandah. Drains Mahaban and spurs of its Shahkot peak by two main channels, which meet near Topi. The one to the northward comes down by Mangalthannah, Sairi, Panjman, and Maini. That to the southward by Otlah, Kohlagar, Shnai, Bâda, Bisak, and Gandaf, on to Topi. From this point the drainage flows in one channel by Zarobai to the Indus above Mûnarah. By these four ravines, the drainage from the western slopes of Mahaban, as well as from the adjacent plain, is conveyed to the Indus. To complete this notice of the drainage, it only remains to describe the ravines in the north-west angle of the district. There are two principal ones, viz :—

Shahkot Kandah.

XIII.—The Nâswar Kandah. Drains the Sapraisar and Hatmânkhail hills, passes by Bucha, Nâswar, Tarakai, Nowadandd, Saparai, Rangmianah, Bâbai, Tangi, Kunawar, Shairpao, Umarzai, on to Turangzai, where it joins the Swat river.

Nâswar Kandah.

XIV.—The Jaindai Khwar. Drains the Khânorah and Totai hills; and, passing by Kot, Palli, and Gandairai, to Kunawar, joins the Nâswar ravine there. Both of these are very wide, deep, and boulder strewn ravines, and more or less dry in the hot season.

Jaindai Khwar.

From the above details, it will be seen, as was premised, that the greater portion of the population of Yusufzai is settled on or near the courses of the natural channels by which the country is drained. Many of the villages named as at the sources of these ravines, are beyond the British border.

Population settled on the ravines.

Cultivation.

The tracts of plain country lying between these great ravines are more or less well cultivated everywhere along their banks, where there are facilities for irrigation by means of wells; but at a distance from the ravines,—though even on these there are extensive stretches of cultivation unirrigated artificially,—the tracts are for the most part left waste as grazing grounds for the cattle. For this purpose, however, they are only available during the spring and autumn months, as during both the summer heats and winter frosts the surface is more or less barren. As a consequence, the cattle of the country are during these seasons frequently hard pushed for the means of subsistence; and the result is, that the breed,—though, perhaps, not solely from this cause,—is an inferior one, being of low height, small limbed, and more or less generally ill-favored.

Pasture.

Cattle.

Note.

Such are the chief points in the topography of the Yusufzai plain. Before proceeding to a description of the highland portion of the country, it will be well here to note its main geological features, as far as have been ascertainable.

Geology.

The plain itself consists of a fine alluvial deposit, the composition and depth of which varies in different localities and at different distances from the surface.

Surface soil.

In most parts of the plain the soil is light and porous, and contains more or less sand to a depth of from four to twenty feet. Below this the sandy admixture is much less, or even entirely absent; its place being taken by

Kankar.

clay, either soft or indurated, and often combined with beds of nodular limestone or *kankar*. This formation may extend to a depth of from four to sixteen feet or more, and is succeeded by beds of gravel and sand of unknown thickness.

Sub-soil drainage.

This last stratum contains the sub-soil drainage, and is the source of water-supply in wells. Into it sink and disappear all the springs that flow down from the hills into the ravines at their skirts. The above particulars are the results of an examination of artificial wells and the cuttings of natural water-courses.

Cultivated tracts.

It is unnecessary here to describe the surface soil in the different portions of the district; but it may be noted that the cultivated tracts consist of a rich, light, and porous soil, composed of a pretty even mixture of clay and sand. Where the former prevails in excess, the surface is either low and marshy, and abounding in reeds and rank grasses, or else it is elevated, dry, hard, and fissured, and for the most part barren, or but supporting a mean growth of hardy, stunted, and thorny bushes. In some parts, the borders of such tracts are covered with a saline efflorescence. When the latter constituent of the general surface soil or sand prevails in excess, the surface is either entirely barren, with a loose unsteady soil, or else supports a scanty vegetation in small detached and scattered tufts. Examples of the former class of soils are to be found in the marshy tracts in the east of the Chalpâni ravine, and in the wild desert tracts of the Hasht-

Barren tracts.

Sand.

Marsh.

naggar and Khattak mairahs. The latter class of soils is mainly confined to the tracts on the river's banks.

Hill skirts and rocks.

The country skirting the base of the hills, and in some parts extending some distance on to the plain, is more or less covered with coarse gravel, broken stones, or boulders of various mineral character in the different localities. Thus, for example, in the Lunkhwar district, the surface near the hills is a strong bed of limestone pebbles, mixed with boulders of conglomerate.

Lunkhwar.

Suddhum.

Manairi.

In the Suddhum district, feldspar grit predominates. At Manairi, and the adjacent hill skirts, coarse fragments of quartz and limestone cover the surface, and contain also a sprinkling of micaceous schist. Onwards, from this to the Indus, along the skirts of the Mahaban range, the surface is characterized by a variety of forms of trap and conglomerate, mixed with limestone, marble, and various combinations of mica and feldspar. The existence of these boulders far away from the present course of the river, with the fact of their identical character with those in the bed of the river, lead to the conclusion, no obstacles intervening, that they were brought down and deposited in their present sites in ages past, by the Indus river itself, which, in this part of its course, must have assumed a lake formation.

Mica schist.

Trap.

Limestone.

Erratic boulders.

Rocks little known.

The geological formation of the hills bounding the Yusufzai plain is not well known, owing to their inaccessibility. Some

Difficulties.

idea, however, of their structure and composition is derivable from an examination of the pebbles and boulders brought down in the ravines that drain their slopes, and the results of such lead to the conclusion that the hills bounding Yusufzai are all of primitive or metamorphic rocks; for the boulders washed down from their sides consist mostly of syenite and porphyry, in a variety of forms, together with pebbles and fragments of quartz, primitive limestone, mica and clay slates, trap-rock in great variety, horneblende, feldspar and gneiss. These are only to be found in the beds of the ravines, near their origin in the hills. The distant parts of the beds of these drains, as is naturally to be expected, contain only sand and gravel.

Primitive rocks.

Of the hill spurs projecting into the plain, the majority consist of non-fossiliferous limestone, overlaid apparently by a friable grey or brown mica slate. The strata in these spurs mostly lie from north-west to south-east, and dip to the north at varying angles in different localities, but everywhere very high, that is between sixty and eighty-five degrees. Amongst the Panjpir ridges, some of the strata have quite a perpendicular direction.

No fossils.

Mica schist.

Strata.

In the hills at Manairi, which are of limestone, there are veins of marble, mottled black, green, and yellow, or pure green and pure yellow. Similar veins exist in the Pajah hill. In both localities the rock is quarried by the natives and manufactured into marbles, rosary beads, amulets, charms, &c.

Marble.

Uses.

At Nawigrâm, the Ranigatt hill consists of compact

Granite.

Buildings.

granite. On its summit are the ruins of an extensive ancient Budhist or Hindu city. The buildings are of massive structure, and constructed of great blocks of the rock accurately chiselled. Their excellent preservation, though they are probably not less than 1,500 years old, would lead to the belief that they had only lately left the mason's hands.

Preservation.

Trap.

At Shiwah, the hill consists of amygdaloid trap, the layers of which rise in regular steps from beneath the Karamar hill, the base of which is slate, and the summit limestone.

Gneiss.

Uses.

The Malandarrah hill is composed of gneiss. The rock is extensively quarried for the manufacture of mill-stones, which are distributed all over the district; the article being a household necessary. At Shahbazgarrhi, Garrû and Sarpattai, the hills are of trap-rock, of very varying composition and structure; in some parts being firm and compact, in others loose and friable. As a sample of the former kind may be quoted the celebrated *lât* at Shahbazgarrhi, on which is an inscription, supposed to be one of those pillar edicts of Asoka, establishing Budhism as the state religion of his kingdom, 250 B. C., and of which there are other examples in different parts of the peninsula. On the Shahbazgarrhi rock, the inscriptions, though coated with lichens, are still in excellent preservation, and quite easily transcribable. Examples of the latter, on crumbling forms of trap, are abundant on the Garrû and Sarpattai ranges. Their detritus forms the surface soil at the foot of these hills.

Budhist *lât* of trap-rock.

Varieties of trap-rock.

The Pajah hill is limestone, and contains a splendid cave temple of the ancient Budhists. Though now in a state of ruin, its interior abounds in the remains of former temples and other buildings. Lime is burnt on this hill. The Takht-i-Bahai hill is composed of grey micaceous schist or slate. On its summit are the ruins of an extensive Budhist or Hindu city and idol temple, all built of the material of the hill.

Limestone.

Cavern.

Mica-slate, grey.

Of the hills on the northern or Swat border, I have not been able to obtain reliable informations beyond that in the Totai hills of Ranizai there are quarries of a fine, soft, blue slate. Slabs of it are used as tablets over the graves of Mahomedans here, and are for this purpose also carried to Hashtnaggar. These quarries are probably the sources whence the ancient Budhists and Hindus derived the material for the manufacture of the multitude of idols and temple decorations, &c., that at this day are found in such quantities in the many ruins of their former habitations in all parts of the district; for the stones compared together are of the same material exactly.

Blue.

Uses.

From the above particulars, it would appear that the hills around the Yusufzai plain are altogether formed of primitive or transition rocks. I have not met with a fossil derived from any one of them, nor can I hear of a fossil having ever been found in them. Though from their structure one would be led to expect the existence of the richer metallic ores, yet such are not known to have been met with. There is, nevertheless, a very popular

Deductions.

Metallic veins.

belief that these hills contain untold treasures of gold, only they are hidden from mortal ken. The toils and labours of wandering devotees in search of these treasures have hitherto been in vain.

Iron slag.

Ancient foundries.

On the Bághoch hill, near Bagh, in Chinglai vale, and on the hill Lohach, above Pihûr, are remains of some very extensive iron foundries. On both hills the surface for many hundred yards is covered with the ruins of old furnaces for the smelting of iron ore, and the ground in their neighbourhood is strewed with any quantity of slag and dross. Many of these masses appear still to contain some of the metal. Nothing is known locally as to the history of these furnaces; but, being in the immediate neighbourhood of the Budhist and Hindu ruins of Ranigatt and Mount Banj, they are probably relics of the industry of those departed races.

Iron pyrites.

Stealite.

On a detached hill near Lunkhwar, the surface is covered with small cubes of iron pyrites; and on a hill some miles further north, near Skhakot, is a quarry for soap-stone. It is indestructible in the fire, and is used as a blow hole for furnaces, and also as slabs for cooking bread upon.

Conglomerate.

Pudding stone.

In the ravines about Lunkhwar are also found handsome pebbles of conglomerate and boulders of pudding stone, which, in the hands of the stone-cutter, might be converted into a variety of articles of ornament and utility.

Note.

This completes our topographical account of the lowlands or plain of Yusufzai. We will conclude the chapter with some notes on the rest of the country beyond

Highlands. the British border, the highlands of Yusufzai, acquired from native sources of information, compared and corrected.

Extent. The highlands, as has been previously stated, comprise the greatest portion of the country of the Yusufzais, and constitute all its north-western, northern, and eastern portions, the south-western tract of plain alone forming the British territory described in the previous pages.

Divisions. By the natural formation of the country, this highland tract is divided into two main portions, separated from each other by a great mountain range, of which Ilam and Dosirrah are the prominent peaks. This range towards the west is continuous with the mountain chain, already described as forming the northern boundary of the Yusufzai plain, and Mount Morah is the connecting link. Towards the east the Ilam mountains, of which Dosirrah is only a peak, terminate in the high peak of Ghorband, which, whilst marking the limit of the Yusufzai country in this direction, mingles by its spurs with the Kohistan of Yassan.

Northern. To the north of this mountain range, the Yusufzai country, as far as the Laorai mountains, which with those of Laspisar separate their furthest district of Dîr from the Kashkar country, is characterized by a succession of long narrow valleys, which, running a more or less north-east to south-west course, drain to a common channel named the Panjkora or Malizai Sîn, a stream which, winding in a narrow channel between high mountain ridges, joins the Swat river previous to its passage through the Hatmankhail hills.

Southern. The country to the south of the Ilam range, as far as the Indus, is, on the other hand, characterized by a net work of mountain ridges, the main direction of which is more or less north and south, that enclose between them and their offshoots a number of constricted valleys and glens, the form and direction of which are as irregular as the hills bounding them, but the drainage from which flows direct to the Indus by separate channels, to be described further on.

Northern limits.

Of these two divisions, the northern extends as far as the Laorai mountains, which separate the Yusufzais from Kashkar and Chitral on the southern slopes of Hindu Kush. Its eastern limit is formed by the spurs of Ghorband, coalescing northward with the Kohistan of Hindu Kush, whilst towards the west its limit is formed by the Laspisar mountains and the Bajawar country.

Mountains.

In this extent the country is traversed by several parallel ranges of mountains, between which lie a succession of valleys, mostly coursing with the hills from north-east to south-west.

Valleys.

Of these valleys, the southernmost—most extensive, and most important—is that of Swat. Beyond it are the valleys of Tormung, Nihag, Karoh, Oshairai, and Dîr. The drainage from each of these is by a perennial stream; and, all these uniting in a common channel, produce the Panjkora river.

Each of these valleys requires a few words of separate notice.

The Swat valley.

Swat.

Boundaries.

This is a rich and fertile strip of land between the Ilam range and its extension westward, as far as Hazarnao on the south, and the Larram mountains with its western and eastern prolongations, the Kamrani and Munjai mountains, on the north. Its eastern limit is at the Ghorband peak, and towards the west at the Hatmankhail hills and Bajawar.

Extent.

In length it is about seventy miles from end to end, and in breadth, at its central or widest part, about ten miles from the base of hill to hill. At either extremity the valley is closed and overrun by spurs from the opposite boundary ranges approaching each other.

Drainage.

It is drained by the Swat river, which pursues a middle course between the hills, and receives on either side the ravines and hill streams that drain the numerous glens and gorges which open into the valley at quick intervals all along the base of its boundary hills.

Cultivation.

The Swat valley is highly cultivated and densely populated throughout its extent along the course of its river, whilst each glen and gorge has its hamlets or collections of shepherds' huts. The general surface of the ground is rough and stony, and there is a considerable slope from the foot of the hills to the bed of the river. Owing to this slope of the surface, the fields are laid out in strips of terraces one above the other, the boundary walls being formed of the stones collected from the surface. By this arrangement the soil is cleared of stones, and made level to retain the water led on to it for irrigation.

Crops.

Cultivation is general throughout the valley. The chief crops are rice and wheat, lucerne, chick peas (mattar) and beans (lobia), but the sugar-cane, barley, Indian corn, cotton, and tobacco, are also cultivated. Generally all the cultivation is irrigated, water being plentiful, and easily led off in canals and cuttings both from the river and the numerous hill streams flowing to it;

Irrigation.

and, in order to facilitate its retention in the soil, the land is laid out, as above mentioned, in flat strips of terraced fields that extend from near the river's bed to the foot of the hills.

Population.

Along the course of its river, the valley is described as being crowded with villages, hidden amongst groves of stately trees, and surrounded on all sides by an unbroken stretch of cultivation. The hills on either side are well stocked with forest trees. On the southern range they are principally pines; but on the northern are magnificent forests of the Deodar cedar.

Forest trees.

In the valley itself, the trees commonly met with are the plane, poplar and willow, the mulberry, sirrus, sissoo, bukain. acacia, olive, and jujube; and, in the higher parts of the valley, are also found the walnut, diospyrus, or *amlúk*, &c. Swat is famous for its timber, rice, and honey, all of which are exported to Peshawur in exchange for salt and cotton fabrics, &c.

Climate.

Diseases.

The climate of Swat is described as mild in winter and agreeably warm or temperate in summer. It is noted also for its extreme unhealthiness. Its peculiar vernal and autumnal intermittents, frequently, from all accounts, assuming the remittent or continued forms of fevers, and prevailing as epidemics, are in their seasons the plague of the country, and attack both sexes and all ages alike. The effects of this generally prevalent disease are plainly discernible in the physical condition of the people. Abdominal dropsies, enlarged spleen, and cataract, are described as the common diseases of the country; and, my own personal experience of the people, judging from those who come down for treatment to the Murdan dispensary, bears out the truth of the statement.

Divisions. The Swat valley is divided into three local districts, viz., Ranizai, Kûz Swat, and Barr Swat.

Ranizai. Ranizai, so named after the clan of Yusufzais inhabiting it, occupies the lowest or westernmost part of the valley. The tribal chiefs of the district are Suhbat Khan of Allahdand, and Shairdil Khan of Dairi. Both these chiefs also exercise considerable influence over the entire population of the Swat valley, there being no recognized chiefs in the other districts. In the Ranizai district of Swat, there are thirty-five villages. Of these the chief are Totakan, Matkana, Dairi, Jolagram, Khar, Nowikili, Batkhaila, Amandarra, Maikhband, Allahdand, and Amankot, on the left bank; and Dairi, Barangolah (2), Kamalai, and Badwan (2), on the right bank. Of these, Allahdand, Dairi, Khar, Batkhaila, and Totakan Matkana, each contains more than 300 houses. The country here is an open plain, in parts encroached on by low hill spurs, and generally sloping more or less rapidly to the river's bed.

Kûz Swat. Continuous with, and on the east of the Ranizai district, is lower or Kûz Swat. It extends from Allahdand to Charbagh, a distance of about thirty miles, by an average width of four or five miles. It contains along the river course thirty-two villages, between the two named as its limits, and there are others in the glens at the foot of the hills on either side. The principal villages in this district are Thanna, containing 800 houses, and the residence of the Khankhail or ruling tribe; Barrikot 300 houses, Ghaligai and Kambar each 200 houses, and Mingowra 500 houses, all on the left bank of the river.

Characters. This district is the richest, most fertile, and most unhealthy portion of the Swat valley.

Beyond Charbagh eastward to the end of the valley, where it becomes blended with the Kohistan of Ghorband, is Upper or Barr Swat. The last village in this direction, at the foot of the Kohistan, is Charrarrai, containing about 150 houses. Between this and Charbagh are twenty-three villages, in close proximity to each other, along the river course. The principal are Charbagh, 350 houses; Minglaur and Sangota, 300 houses; and Saidugan, three small hamlets, notable as the residence of the Akhûn and his murîds. In this district the ground is uneven, and much overrun by spurs from the boundary hills on each side. Cultivation, nevertheless, is abundant; and here, as elsewhere in the valley, in narrow terraced slips, in stages one above the other, from the river's bank to the foot of the hills.

Barr Swat.

Cultivation.

The Swat river is a clear, brisk, and noisy stream, and flows over a wide, firm, rocky or boulder-strewn bed, with low banks of shale on either side, or, as is more prevalent, with long strips of sloping beach covered with loose pebbles and boulders. During the winter months, the stream is fordable at most parts; but, during the summer, when it becomes swollen by rains and melting snows, the river is only passable on rafts or inflated skins. There are no boats or regular ferries across this river in any part of the Swat valley.

Swat river.

The villages mentioned above, as being planted along the river's course, are all on high ground, more or less distant from the actual channel of the water, that is to say, they are from a quarter of a mile to two miles distant from it.

Villages.

The population of the Swat valley, taking the three dis-

Population. tricts together, is estimated at about 96,000 souls. The bulk of the population are husbandmen, who live on the produce of their cattle and fields, and whose domestic wants are supplied by a minority of merchants, petty traders, mechanics, and artizans.

Cattle. Cows, buffaloes, and goats, as also mules and donkeys, are plentiful in Swat; but sheep and horses are scarce.

Inhabitants. **Clans.** The Swat valley is occupied by the Akozai division of the Yusufzais. The Akozais are in two great divisions, viz., the Baizai and the Khwazozai. Each of these contains several clans, and each of these clans has its separate portion of land.

Baizai. The Baizais have the following clans, viz :—1, Babozai; 2, Ranizai; 3, Musakhail; 4, Maturizai; 5, Abakhail; 6, Azikhail; and, 7, Zangikhail.

Babozais. 1. The Babozais are mostly settled in the north east corner of the Yusufzai plain, in the valley of Lunkhwar; but they have the following lands in Swat by their villages, viz :—

Nowikili,	Gogdarra,	Balogram,
Pajigram,	Udigram,	Kambar,
Nowikili,	Sangota,	Minglaur,
Jambîl,	Kokarai,	Dangram,
Salampur,	Sapalbandi,	Kâtaili,
Mingowra,	Saidugram,	Kukrai.

Ranizais.

2. The Ranizais are mainly settled on the north border of the Yusufzai plain, and in the Totai hills west of the Babozais; but have the following villages in Swat, viz:—

Totakan,	Matkana,	Khar,
Dairi.	Jolagram,	Nawikili,
Batkhaila,	Amandarra,	Maikhband,
Kamalai,	Baranglolah, (2),	Badwan, (2),
Dairi,	Allahdand,	Amankot.

Musakhails.

3. The Musakhails have the following villages, viz:—

Landaki,	Nowikili,	Ghoratti,
Kotai,	Abûa,	Jalala.

Maturizais.

4. The Maturizais have the villages of—

Charbagh,	Gulibagh,
Dakorak,	Alamganj.

Abakhails.

5. The Abakhails have the villages of—

Ghaligai,	Manihar,	Parrarai,
Nagua,	Shingardar,	Barikot,
Najigram,	Amlûk,	Nawagai.

Azikhails.

6. The Azikhails have the villages of—

Chaliar,	Khwazakhaila,	Tigdiarrai,
Khoûna,	Churarrai,	Pia.

Zangikhails.

The Zangikhails have no villages in Swat, they are altogether settled in the country south of the Ilam range.

By the foregoing particulars, it will be noted that the

Khwazozais.

Babozais occupy the Swat valley for the most part only south of its river; the tract on its north is in like manner occupied by the Khwazozais, who have the following clans, viz:—1, Adînzai; 2, Shamozai; 3, Naikbi-khail; 4, Shamizai; and 5, Subûjuna.

Adinzais.

1. The Adinzai lands include the villages of—

Chakdarra,	Sairsadda,	Alimast,
Ramora,	Mushmukam,	Shiwa,
Jangoh,	Taizugram,	Kitiârai,
Aotla,	Kashmir,	Kutigram,
Uchakai,	Badnumai,	Gadkalan.

Shamozai.

2. The Shamozai lands contain the villages of—

Chûngai,	Tairang,	Zarakhaila,
Didawar,	Garrari,	Khizana,

Naikbikhail.

3. The Naikbikhail lands are—

Sairsanna,	Galoch,	Nasrat,
Daiolai (2),	Tutanobanda,	Tal,
Dardial,	Chanchûdairi,	Kalakili, &c.

Ashikhail.

4. The Shamizai (Ashikhail) lands are—

Daghi,	Akhunkili,	Gadhai,
Chindakhwar,	Azarai,	Aligram,
Kanjûgan,	Danghar,	Bandai (2),
Dilai,	Nimgolai,	&c.,

Subujuna.

5. The Subujuna, a corruption of its two divisions of Sibbat and Jûnah, lands are—

Shakardarra,	Shairpalam,	Sangbat,
Bamakhaila (2),	Khararai,	Landai,
Drushkhaila (2),	Kalakot,	Paitai,
Binowrai,	Baidarra,	Shishban.
Shamgwatai,	Runigar,	Sakhara,
Nowkhara,	Shawar (2),	&c.

Note.

The villages here mentioned, as belonging to the different clans inhabiting Swat, include all but the smaller hamlets and shepherds' huts in the hills. Many of these villages are far away from the rivers' course, in the glens opening on to the main valley. Several of these glens are of considerable extent, contain from eight to sixteen villages or hamlets, and are drained by perennial streams.

Tributary glens.

The chief of these glens, on the south of the river, are the *darrahs* of Katilai (or Saidûgan) and Minglaur, on the south of the river, and those of Uchuna, Sairsannah, and Galoch (or Tal Dardial), on the north of the river.

Fruit trees.

They are all well cultivated and stocked with fruit trees, of which the apple, pear, quince, walnut, and *amlûk* are the most common. The apples and quinces are said to rival those of Kabul in the excellency of their qualities. Oranges also are produced in some parts of the valley.

Pines.

Timber trade.

The hills on the northern border of Swat are famous for their pine and deodar forests. Those in the Tal Dardial district, supply Peshawur with much of its larger sizes of timber. This trade is an important and increasing one, and is wholly in the hands of a small clique of Mians, of Hashtnaggar.

In the north-west corner of the Swat valley, north of its

river and the Ranizai district, is the Talash valley. The district lies between the Barangola mountain on the south and the Kamrani range on the north. On its west flows the Panjkora river, and on its east it is separated from Swat by the Gadkalan ridge, a low spur that connects offshoots from the Barangola and Kamrani mountains.

Talash.

The Talash valley is about sixteen miles long by four wide in its broadest part. It is drained to the Panjkora river by a main central ravine, which joins it near the collection of hamlets known as Gûrî. Between these, however, and the river is a stretch of hill country said to abound in ruins of former cities and forts. The Talash valley is hill-girt on all sides, and contains the following villages along its main ravine, viz., from east to west, Gadkalan, on the ridge between Talash valley and Uchuna in Swat, Nasafa, Saraie Kuza where resides one of the chiefs of the district, Sayad Mahomad Ali, Damdarhal, Kalomanri, Banda, Barra Saraie, Ajoh, Machoh, Bampokha, Bajowri, Amlukdarra, Gumbat, Shamshikhan where resides the chief, Mazullah Khan, Shigoh-kas, and Gûrî. The inhabitants are Malizai Afghans, and acknowledge Ghazan Khan of Dîr as their tribal chief. It is said they can provide him with 2,500 matchlock-men. Through Talash leads the common route from Swat to Dîr over the Kamrani Ghakhai pass.

Extent.

Villages.

Army.

The rest of the Yusufzai country, north of Swat, is occupied by the Malizai tribe, of whom Ghazan Khan of Dîr is the recognized chief. The limit westward of the Mâlizais is marked by the villages of Janbatai and Ayasairi, and the rock Tortigga.

Malizai.

Limit.

Beyond this boundary are the Tarkilani tribes of Barawal, famous for its iron, Jandaul and Bajawar.

Character.

All this tract, as far as the Laspisar and Laorai mountains, which separate it from Kashkar and Chitral, is a mass of most difficult mountains, the main direction of which is from north-east to south-west. Its drainage is carried off by five hill streams, which, by their union, form the Panjkora river.

Streams and vallies.

These streams take the names of the valleys or glens they flow through, and are from south to north, Turmung, Nihag, Karoh, Oshairai, and Malizai or Dîr.

Turmung.

The Turmung-darrah is described as a narrow tortuous valley, about sixteen miles long, and containing about twenty villages, large and small. Its chief town is Turmung, 250 houses, situated at the foot of a hill, and on the edge of its rivulet, where it joins the Panjkora stream.

Nihag.

The Nihag-darra is described as about thirty miles long from north-east to south-west; contains about twenty-six villages, and abounds in cultivation and fruit gardens.

Karoh.

The Karoh-darrah is described as a narow defile between high hills, is about twenty miles long, and contains eighteen villages.

Oshairai.

The Oshairai-darrah is an open valley, above thirty-five miles from end to end, and contains forty villages.

Clans. The clans inhabiting these four valleys are classed in two great divisions. Those of Turmung and Sultan. Karoh are called Sultan, and those of Nihag and Oshairai are called Paindah. Paindah. Each of these two divisions can turn out 3,000 matchlocks to join Ghazan Khan's standard.

Dîr. Dîr is the name of the furthest valley at the base of the Laorai range, and also of its chief town, which contains about 350 houses protected by a detached fort. Both are on high ground, above the river of Panjkora, which is here called the Malizai Sîn. In the Dir valley there are about twenty-four villages.

Character. All these valleys are described as narrow and hill-bound, with numerous winding glens and gorges defiling into them from the hill spurs on either side. The villages, too, are described as all in similar situations throughout this tract, viz., with a hill rising up directly behind, and a ravine streamlet flowing by directly in front and below.

Roads. There are no roads through the country, except for footmen, over the hills. The only route for travellers and merchandize is by a rough, winding and difficult path along the precipitous slope of a hill range, and directly above the rivers' bank. And this route is only practicable with safety during the winter season.

Passes. From Swat to Dîr there are three different routes, viz., the Munjai Ghakhai, the Larram Ghakhai, and the Kamrani Ghaknai.

Munjai. The Munjai Ghakhai pass is the shortest but most difficult route, and only practicable for footmen. It leads from Barrikot in Swat to Dîr, and is two days' journey for a strong highlander. From Barrikot, two roads go up to Daiolai, in the Tal Dardial hills, then over the Munjai pass and along a *tarai* at the foot of the hills to Khagram on the Panjkorah river, then along its bank twelve miles to Dîr. The distance from Barrikot to Dîr by this route is about fifty-six miles.

Larram. The Laram Ghakhai pass, is described as very difficult and dangerous, but practicable for laden mules. The route is four days journey from Thannah in Swat to Dîr. It goes through the Uchûna glen to Kotigram at the foot of the pass, then over the hill and down to Ganjilai, and Rabat on the bank of the Panjkora river. It then crosses the river to Barûn and winds along its bank by Khal, Tormung and Khagram to Dîr. Through the latter part of this route the road winds along a steep hill side immediately above the river. At parts the path is very narrow and there is the risk of falling into the river.

Kamrani. The Kamrani Ghakhaî pass is described as the easiest and most frequented route to Dîr. It is nevertheless a difficult road full of risks, and four days journey from Thannah in Swat. The road leads past Uchûna and Gadkalan over its low ridge into Talash, then across the valley to Dairi near the foot of the pass. Then over the Kamrani hill and down to Shukaoli on the bank of the Panjkora river. Cross to Diarun and past several villages, of which Konatair is the chief, to Barûn, and then along as described in the last route.

The eastern extremity of Swat beyond Churarai is occu-

Shûkâlâm.

pied by the Shûkalam district. It is a narrow, long and winding defile connecting Swat with the Yassan country by a three days journey over most difficult hills. It is occupied by Kohistanis who are not Afghans, and is celebrated for its ponies, which are here bred in great numbers, and sold mostly in the Kashkar country.

Southern.

The Yusufzai country south of the Ilam range, between it and the Indus, may be divided into two parts, an eastern and western, separated by the Dumah mountains. The former is overrun by great mountain ramifications coursing from the Ilam range to the Indus. Of the further portion of this tract I have been unable to collect any information. But the nearer portion or half is described as containing three narrow and winding valleys, parallel to each other, and draining to the Indus. They are the districts of Kana, Chakaisar and Pûran.

Divisions.

Eastern.

Kânâ.

Of these the Kânâ district is the largest, and with its tributary valley or glen of Ghorband contains about thirty villages. The population are mostly Azikhail and Zangikhail Yusufzais. The chief towns are Kormung, Kânâ and Upal. Most of the villages are on the banks of a ravine, which in the hot months has a stream capable of floating down timber from the hills to the Indus. Three kinds of pine and the deodar grow in these hills. From the head of the glen at Ghorband to the river Indus is two days journey.

Chakaisar.

The Chakaisar district is a narrow valley with branching glens on each side. It is drained by a perennial stream, which joins the Indus opposite Takot, contains about twenty-four villages, and is occupied by Azikhail and Babozai Yusufzais. The Chakaisar valley is narrower than that of Kana and is nowhere two miles broad. From end to end it is two days journey. It communicates with Swat by the Gadwa pass between Sonaili and Minglaur. The route is a day's journey for a strong footman.

Pûrân.

The Pûrân valley drains to the Indus at Kabulgram by the Itai ravine. In its upper parts it is joined by Makhozai and Chagurzai glens, and contains altogether about thirty-five villages, of which Kabulgram, Jatkûl and Sûndûî are the chief. Throughout its extent the Pûrân district is very close and hill-bound.

Western.

The western portion of the Yusufzai country south of the Ilam range consists of three districts viz., Buhnair, Chamla and Amazai.

Buhnair.

Of these Buhnair is the most open and extensive. It consists of a hill-girt plain, about eighteen miles, by twelve miles, but encroached upon by spurs on all sides from the boundary hills. It is drained by a perennial stream, at its lowest two feet deep, which also drains the adjoining districts of Chamla and Amazai, and joins the Indus at Mabrai. This is the Barhando river.

Mabrai.

Clans.

Buhnair is occupied by the Iliaszai division of the Yusufzais. Of the Iliaszais there are seven clans, viz., Aishazai, Salarzai, Nurizai, Doulatzai, or as it is generally called Panjpai, Gadaizai, Makhozai and Chagûrzai. The district occupied by these clans in Buhnair contains about ninety-four or 100 villages.

Cattle. The inhabitants are rich in cattle, especially buffaloes, and are solely occupied in the tending of their herds and the cultivation of the soil.

Passes. Buhnair communicates with Swat by three passes, viz: Karakar, from Ligianai to Nawagai, Juarai, from Bishaonai to Salampur, and Gokand, from Narbatawal to Jambil Kokarai. All these passes are very difficult and only used by footmen.

Chamla. The Chamla district is a small valley, drained by a perennial stream, winding through its centre, to the Barhando. It is about 14 miles long by 4 wide at its western end, and contains about 22 villages. Towards the east the valley is closed by the Torghûnd hill, a spur of the Aronai ridge, which joining with the Garru mountain on the west separates the Chamla valley from that of Buhnair. On the other side Chamla is separated from the Khodo Khail district by the Sarpatai ridge. Chamla is properly a tributary valley to that of Buhnair, and is mostly held by Buhnair clans, though from its central position a share of it is claimed by all the clans in its environs, and most of them have a few representatives living in it. It is a pretty little valley, with a light gravelly soil, abounding in clear rivulets, and well clothed with trees of a large size. The chief town is Kogah.

Amazai. The Amazai district occupies the eastern and north slopes of the Mahaban mountain, and is occupied by the Amazai tribe. It is a narrow and rough country, drained by many mountain torrents, all of which are perennial, to the Barhando. It contains about thirty villages along the courses of the different hill streams. Charorai is its chief town. The whole of this district is well wooded with pines. Cultivation is scanty, but as much as the surface will permit of. Cattle are plentiful, and *ghī* is the chief product of the country.

Conclusion.

Such is a brief outline of the topography of the Yusufzai country. The accompanying map will convey some idea of the relative positions of the different districts alluded to in the previous pages, as well as of the general formation of the country. Some observations regarding the climate, productions and inhabitants of these districts will form the subject for future chapters.

CHAPTER II.

HISTORY.

Imperfect knowledge.

THE ancient history, or even that up to a late date, of the country now known as Yusufzai, is but very imperfectly, if at all, known in any connected record of successive events.

Scattered records.

Casual notices relating to it are, however, occasionally met with in the different native records of the past transactions of the various sovereigns of the two great empires on the natural boundary line between which it lies—India on the one hand, and Persia on the other.

Marks of past revolutions.

The position of Yusufzai on the main road of communication between these two empires, would naturally ensure for it a participation in the political vicissitudes of each; and, of such having been the case, the ruins and antiquities which at this day abound in all parts of the country, are the mute witnesses.

Require examination.

They wait only the enquiry of the antiquary and archæologist to speak out volumes of interest regarding the hidden past.

A brief description of some of these ruins will form the

History.

subject of the next chapter. In this we may, with interest, if not profit, note some of the more notorious events of ancient history that are connected with this almost unknown corner of the British Indian empire, before proceeding to a summary relation of its recent history.

Earliest record.

Although, in all probability, it had been previously traversed by Darius Hystaspes, the earliest authentic account we have of this region dates from the time of Alexander the Great, who, as is well known, marched through it on his advance from Kabul to India, about 326 B. C.

Alexander's visit.

According to Arrian, Alexander divided his forces into two grand armies at Kabul. By some accounts, he sent one of these by the direct route through Peshawur to cross the Indus at the site of the present Attak; and, by others, to cross at the site of the present Nilab, which was in former ages the common ferry of the Indus. With the other army, himself at its head, Alexander marched towards the same river through the difficult mountain region now comprising the districts of Kunar, Bajawar, Swat, and Buhnair.

March in the hills.

Difficulties.

In their victorious passage through this country, the Macedonians endured many hardships, and encountered very serious obstacles, as much owing to the difficulties of the rugged tract they had got into, as to the stout opposition of its warlike inhabitants; but the courage and discipline of the troops, aided by the intrepidity, firmness, and prestige of their leader, enabled them to surmount all the difficulties and dangers that faced them. They everywhere

Triumphs.

drove off their opponents, destroyed, or else garrisoned with their own troops, their fortresses, and captured their war elephants, and immense herds of cattle. The latter were of a superior breed; and Alexander selected some of the finest, and sent them to his own country for the improvement of the stock there. Before leaving the hills, Alexander founded some new cities in the room of those he had destroyed. His last triumph over the enemy in this region, and before crossing the Indus, was at the celebrated rock Aornos, located, according to popular tradition, on a spur of the Mahaban mountain, in the immediate vicinity of Amb, and on the right bank of the Indus.

Aornos.

Alexander's successors.

After Alexander's death, which occurred in Babylon in 323 B. C., and on the ensuing break up of his vast conquests, the eastern provinces of his empire fell to the lot of Selencus, his first General and successor. He in turn was followed in the government of this region by a succession of Greek sovereigns and independent satraps, of whom very little is known beyond that they struck coins in their own names; and, in imitation of the Persian monarchs, assumed the title of "King of Kings." The Greek power lasted more than a century and a half, when it was replaced, first by the Bactrians and then by the Scythians, who, by the second century of the Christian era, had spread into India, and settled in its upper parts.

Greeks.

Bactrians.

Hindus.

After the Scythians, came the Hindu kings, who reigned in Kabul at the time that country was seized by Sabaktaghin, the

Mahomadans.

Tartar. In the reign of his son and successor, Mahmud, they were completely driven out of the country, or at least to the east of the Indus.

Want of information.

Of all these several dynasties and nationalities, little or nothing is known historically; but of the dates, names, and effigies of many of their sovereigns, a multitude of records are to be met with in the coins at this day, dug out of the soil around the ruins of their ancient dwellings.

Testimony of coins and relics.

From the religious emblems found on these coins, it would appear that Budhism was not known in the time of the Greeks; but during that of their successors, the Bactrians and Scythians, it was in high favor, and flourished with wonderful success, to judge from the multitude of their reli gious establishments and idols the ruins of which still exist.

Fa Hian.

The Chinese pilgrim, Fa Hian, visited this country at the commencement of the fifth century. He mentions the districts of Swat, Mahaban, &c., by name, and describes the monasteries, temples, &c., as most flourishing, and the doctrine of Foe as held in the highest reverence by all classes in most parts of this region, a few localities only calling forth a lament for the decay of their temples, and the neglect of their monasteries. A couple of centuries later, another Chinese pilgrim, Houan Thsang, followed in the steps of his predecessor; and, like him, grieves over the increasing decay of the monasteries and temples, and neglect of the priesthood in some important parts of his route. In Udianah (supposed to be the present Yusufzai), especially, the religion of the "barbarians"—the Brahmins—was already fast replacing the purer faith of Budhism.

Houan Thsang.

Brahminism continued steadily to increase, and soon after entirely superseded Budhism, and flourished unchecked for several centuries, till at length it was suddenly swept away by the flood of Islam, under Mahmud and his fanatic hordes, who rolled over this country in irresistible waves of destruction on their way to the conquest and conversion of India.

Brahmins.

It was at this time, about 1004 A. D., that the religion of the Hindus received its death blow in these parts. It was, indeed, completely annihilated, for Mahmud's ruthless soldiery only spared the lives of their victims on an immediate and unconditional adoption of Islam, whilst, with untiring exertions, they strove to wipe out every trace of heathenism from the country by a general sacking, burning, and razing of the temples and monasteries, and a complete destruction, or, where this was impracticable, the disfigurement of the idols and implements of worship. Not a temple, tope, or monastery escaped the keen scrutiny of these barbarians, and much less the dwellings of the people. Fire appears to have been the chief means of destruction; for most of the ruins that have been excavated bear marks of its action, and shew signs of the hasty flight of their former inhabitants.

Mahomadans.

Some of these unfortunates, it is probable, found a safe retreat, for a period at least, from the fury of their pursuers in the higher mountain ranges that bound the country on the north; and, although even there they were ultimately overtaken by Islam, the advance of the new faith in that direction was not uniformly smooth and successful, nor the result of a sudden revolution. Even to the present day, whilst the general advance of Islam in these parts has been slowly but steadily progressive, a considerable tract of the

Their spread.

Hindu Kush range, now known as Kafiristan, has remained completely untouched by its power.

Blank in the history.

From the time of Mahmud's reign, which closed with his death in 1027 A. D., and during which this country, except the hill districts, was completely devastated and depopulated, little or nothing is known of it for a period of several centuries, beyond that it was a deserted wilderness, the haunt of the tiger and the rhinoceros, and only occasionally visited for the sake of pasture by the shepherd tribes accustomed to roam about the neighbouring countries. By these it was gradually re-peopled, and cultivated in scattered spots, till in time other tribes of cultivators came in and settled all over the plain, much as they are at the present day.

Country deserted.

Re-peopled.

The country, however, has never properly recovered its former condition of prosperity. Now wretched mud hovels stand on the ruins of former towns and cities, the buildings of which are still in many parts traceable by the remains of their massive stone walls. The great number, and the extent, of these ruined towns, indicate the former existence here of a very much more numerous population than that of the present day, and more than in its present state of cultivation the country could support. How long it took for the "Garden of India" (for, according to M. Remusat, in his explanatory notes to Fa Hian's itinerary, the ancient name of this region *Udianah* or *Udyana*, "the garden," was expressive of its uncommon fertility and richness in the fruits of the earth) to degenerate into a desert waste, capable of sheltering the rhinoceros

Former prosperity.

Its decay.

and tiger in the marshes and thickets that grew upon the sites of former habitations and fields, it is difficult to say; but it is probable that the plain was not re-visited or inhabited by man till fully a century after its devastation by Mahmud; and even for centuries subsequently, it is probable that it was only visited occasionally as a pasture-land by migratory shepherd tribes. For Mahmud's destructive hosts were not conquerors and settlers, but passing robbers and plunderers. So were his successors, Janghiz Khan and Taimur Lang, with their untold swarms of destroying savages, who, in the thirteenth and fourteenth centuries, swept through this region on their way to India, and effectually prevented any attempt at colonizing or re-settling the country.

Successive revolutions.

It is probable that this country did not become re-peopled, on the plains at least, till after the time of Taimur Lang, and then only very thinly on its borders by shepherd tribes; for when the Afghans came to it about the middle of the fifteenth century, they found it thinly populated, and an easy conquest, as will be related hereafter.

Subsequent re-settlement.

The Emperor Babur passed through this country about 1523 A. D., some fourteen years after his first arrival at Kabul from his own country of Farghana. At the time of his visit, the plains of Yusufzai and Ashnaghar and the cantons of Swat and Buhnair, were occupied by the Yusufzai Afghans, Peshawur, or Baghram as it was then called, and the adjoining districts were held by the Ghoriakhail Afghans, whilst Bajawar and the neighbouring hills were in the possession of the Hatmânkhails and Tarkilanris. In all these districts, mixed with the Afghans, were scattered communities of the Dilazaks. All were cultivators and shepherds. Babur appears to have followed much the same route to India as that

Babur's visit.

previously pursued by Alexander. According to Akhûn Darwaiza's account, Babur's route was as follows:—

His route.

From Kabul he marched to Nachûl, where, on the day of his arrival, a tremendous earthquake occurred. It is said to have continued half an hour. In some places the earth opened out, and, again closing, swallowed up all that fell in; and in others the surface sunk down below the former level. From Nachûl his army entered Bajawar (probably by the Hinduraj pass); and, being opposed by the inhabitants, fought them and drove them to their capital, a stone fortress in the hills, after a short conflict, the Dilazaks being terrified at the effects of the till then unknown musketry used by Babur's troops. Their fortress was next assailed and carried, the defenders being massacred in its defence. Babur placed a garrison of his Mughals in the fortress under his favourite courtier, Khwajah Kalan, and then marched up the Babakara glen, where the Dilazaks had collected in force. Here he fought them on the tarai or hill skirt; and, after the battle, erected a pillar of their skulls on a rock overlooking the plain, as a warning to the other tribes inclined to oppose his progress, and as a memorial of his victory. Popular tradition points to the Tor-tigga rock as the site of this pillar of skulls. Babur next made a raid up the adjoining Chandûl valley; and, on his return, encamped on the plain where the Bajawar and Panjkora streams meet. Leaving his camp at the spot indicated, Babur spent a few days with Khwajah Kalan, and a few select companions from amongst his chiefs, in a succession of convivial meetings and wine parties. In his memoirs, Babur extols the wine of this country, which he says was mostly brought from Kafiristan, and also mentions that the Bajawaris were addicted

Bajawar.

Babakara.

Chandûl.

to the use of a strong intoxicating beer, or *bozah*, brewed from a kind of millet.

Babur's pastimes.

In the intervals of his debaucheries, Babur held public audiences, and received the submission of the tribes around, and amongst others of the Yusufzais, through their chief, Malik Shah Mansur; meanwhile his troops were pillaging and ransacking every accessible corner of the country. Babur received the Yusufzai Malik with every mark of distinction; and, by way of sealing a friendly alliance with the tribe, took his daughter to wife, she being a celebrated beauty of the country. On returning to his camp on the Chandûl stream, Babur received the submission of the Swatis, through their chief, Sultan Wais, and under his guidance made a raid into the Panjkora valley, or Maidan, by the Kahraj route.

Public duties.

Advance to

On advancing from Bajawar, Babur crossed the Panjkora river, and entered Swat by the Khwajah Khizr route. This road leads along the *tarai*, or skirt of the Kamrani hill, past Guri, (the Massaga of Alexander, in the angle of junction of the Guræus or Panjkora and Suastes, or Swat river) into the Talash valley, and on to Swat. From Swat, Babur marched to Bânra Palî, on the borders of Buhnair, and thence descending on to the plain of Yusufzai, camped at Katlang, in the Lunkhwar valley. His next march was to Shahbazgarrhi. Here his troops destroyed the *ziarat* of Shahbaz Kalandar, and ravaged the country as far as Ashnaghar.

Swat.

Yusufzai.

From this Babur marched along the Mukam stream, on

Rhinoceros hunt.

the banks of which some of his attendants started a rhinoceros, which escaped their chase, wounded, into the thickets around; and, crossing the Kabul river, moved on to Nilab, where he crossed the

Indus ferry.

Indus. At this ferry, or near it, Babur hunted a tiger, and drove it into the river, wounded.

Changes in the country.

This account conveys a very different picture of the Yusufzai plain of 300 years ago and that of to-day. There is now neither the marshy thicket nor the rhinoceros; though of the former there are yet traces in the extensive tracts of marsh land on either side of the Makam ravine, and which in the previous

Present condition.

chapter were described as *nazar* land, abounding in *dandds*, or pools of stagnant water. Of the former existence of the rhinoceros in these parts, the natives have not even any traditional knowledge. They appear, nevertheless, to have been plentiful in all this region; for Babur, in his memoirs, mentions that many were killed at the mouth of the Khaibar pass by the chiefs of his army, with whom the novel sport was a favourite pastime during their short stay in the district after their chief's return from the Jhilam expedition, and preparatory to his incursion into the Kohat, Bannû, and Dehrajat districts.

Babur's return.

After plundering the tract between the Indus and Sulaimân range, Babur returned to Kabul, and was there shortly afterwards visited by his brother-in-law, Malik Shah Mansur, Yusufzai, son of Malik Sulaiman, and eight or ten of the most important men of the tribe. This party travelled by what was then the usual route through

The Yusufzais.

Swat, Bajawar, and Kunar; and, on arrival at Kabul, were received with due honor, whilst as a mark of particular friendship, Babur decorated them all. On his brother-in-law he bestowed the "*tugh*" or "badge of honor," and to each of the others was given a *khilat*, or "robe of honor."

Territorial limit.

Before dismissing them to their homes, Babur, at their own request, settled a long standing dispute as to the limit of the Yusufzai territory, and decided that all the country up to Abua, in Swat, was Yusufzai land; with the country beyond they had no concern.

Date of settlement.

There is much uncertainty as to the exact date when the Yusufzais settled in the country that now bears their name. According to Akhûn Darwaiza, they came from the Kandahar province; and, in their migration eastward, arrived at Kabul when Mirza Ulugh Beg was governor. He succeeded his father, Shah Rukh Sultan, who was a son of Taimur Lang, in 1446 A. D. In the time of Babur, who first came to Kabul in 1504 A. D., the whole of the Peshawur district had already been colonized by different Afghan tribes; and, on his second visit, fourteen years later, he found the Yusufzais had spread well into Swat. The settlement of the Yusufzais in their present limits, on these data, must, therefore, have been between and subsequent to the dates above-mentioned.

History.

An account of the migration from Kandahar of the Yusufzais, their wanderings, and final settlement in their present limits, will be described in a future chapter. It will suffice here to note that they took their present possessions from the Dilazaks, whom, without much difficulty, they drove across the Indus to the Hazarah mountains, after a single but desperate and decisive battle fought on the plain between the villages of Gadar and Langarkot. The site of the latter village is the present Kapurdagarrhi.

Dilazaks.

It is not clear who these Dilazaks are. By some they are supposed to be Tarkilanri Pukhtuns; but the Afghans reject the relationship and assign them an Indian origin. They were a wine-bibbing and idolatrous race when the Yusufzais first came in contact with them, and possibly their name may have some connection with their origin, for Sâkî is the name by which the ancient Budhists in these parts, the disciples of Sakîa Muni, were formerly known.

Transportation.

Akhûn Darwaiza relates that Shah Salîm Badshah (who on ascending the throne assumed the title of Mahomad Jahangir, 1615 A. D.), on his return to India from a hasty visit to Kabul, took and bodily deported the Dilazaks from Peshawar and Hazara, and settled them as a colony in the Dakhan.

Yusufzais extend.

After settling themselves firmly in the plain, the Yusufzais pushed on into the hill country beyond, and in a few years became masters of Swat and Buhnair. In 1519 A. D., when Babur journeyed this way, their limit included the lower half of Swat, and it was subsequent to this that they spread into their present limits. For many years after Babur's time, the Yusufzais, under the government of Malik Ahmad and Shaikh Mali, lived in peace and prosperity, and devoted themselves to the cultivation of their newly-acquired lands, which were about this time divided into hereditary lots and distributed amongst the different clans and their respective families, by common consent, under the direction of Shaikh Mali. The division of the land then made holds good to the present day throughout the Yusufzai country.

But when Khan Kajoh succeeded to the chiefship, a feud broke out between the Yusufzais and their neighbours the Ghoriakhails, who occupied the Peshawar district. It lasted many years, and entailed serious loss and injury to both parties, till finally settled by the great clan fight at Shaikh Patûr, or, as it is as often called, Tapûr, when the whole of the Ghoriakhails were completely broken and dispersed, and lost numbers of their men and women captives to the victorious Yusufzais. Shaikh Tapûr is the ruined old fort that overlooks the village of old Nowshaira, and the scene of the battle is now occupied by the site of the dâk bangalow hard by the grand trunk road.

Feuds.

Battle of Nowshaira.

Shortly after this event, and during the early part of Akbar's long reign, the Yusufzais were further strengthened by the removal of their constant enemies, the Dilazaks. A great many of their families were deported to Hindustan, and their villages and lands in the Hazarkhani district of Peshawar were made over to the Mahmands; and in the following reign, as already mentioned, the rest of this tribe were removed far away into Hindustan by Shah Salîm.

Dilazaks bodily transported.

Whilst in this part of his extensive dominions, Akbar built the fort of Attak Banaras, and placed his son Salîm in it as governor; but, previous to his departure for Hindustan, he made it over to the custody of Raja Mân Sing, one of his most trustworthy feudal chiefs.

Attak fort.

It was about this time, viz., the commencement of the 17th century, that the tribes of Lamghan, Bajawar, and Swat, quarrelled as to the boundaries of

Tribe feuds.

their respective lands. The Yusufzais, who had never yet succeeded in occupying the whole of Swat, seized the opportunity for the advancement of their own interests, and formed an alliance with the Lamghanis, or Lughmanis, and both together ousted the Bajawaris and Barr Swatis, and appropriated their lands; the Tarkilanris of Lamghan taking Bajawar, and the Yusafzais Barr Swat and the hill country to its north.

Noted chief.

During these wars and extensions of territory, Ali Azgar was the most noted of the Yusufzai chiefs. Indeed, since the time of Malik Ahmad, who ruled them when they first came to this country, they had not seen his like. He spread the power and lands of the Yusufzais to the furthest limits; and, at his death, left them in possession of the country from Nawaghai in Bajawar to Tanawal in Hazarah. In these conquests he was aided by Malik Hindal, Akozai, Malik Yâmâh, Malizai, Malik Matah Khan, and Mullah Ibrahîm, Iliaszai, and Malik Tarki, Mandar.

Peace.

After the Yusufzais had settled down from the excitements of war, and had for a period enjoyed the peaceful cultivation of their fields, they were roused by a commotion of a different kind, owing to the rapid spread amongst their neighbours of a remarkable heresy, which only a few years before had been imported from Hindustan.

Religion.

The promulgator of this new doctrine in these parts was one Bazîd, the son of a learned priest of Kanri Kurram, named Abdullah. Bazîd had received a fair education at the hands of his father, who intended that he should in due course succeed him in the office of village priest.

Bazîd.

The son, however, had learned enough to give him a yearning to see the world beyond the narrow limits of his own wild Waziri hills. He soon found an opportunity of joining a *kafilah* going to Samarkand; and, after a stay there of some months, he joined another proceeding to Hindustan, of which country he had often heard marvellous accounts. At Kalinjar, he made the acquaintance of one Mullah Sulaiman, and soon contracted a friendship with him. This man appears to have been an odd mixture of the Hindu and Mussalman in his religious belief. He frequently argued with his new friend on religious subjects, and finally made him a convert to his own peculiar doctrine; this, in brief words, was a belief in the metempsychosis, controlled by the agency of mortal saints.

His heresy.

On his return to Kanri Kurram, Bazîd made known his conversion to the *tanasukhi mazhab*, or "doctrine of metempsychosis," and set about to gain converts amongst his own tribe and family. The father, however, was so shocked at his son's apostacy, that in a fit of rage he sought to take his life. But Bazîd managed to escape with only a few slight wounds, and straightway fled his home. After wandering about for awhile, he found an asylum amongst the Mahmands in Nangrihar with one Malik Sultan Ahmad.

Its success.

In Nangrihar.

After a rest here for awhile, and finding his doctrine was not well received, he removed to Peshawar and found shelter with the Ghoriakhails. In a short time he succeeded in converting the greater portion of the tribe, especially its Khalîl division. On his unexpected success amongst these tribes, Bazîd gave out that he was the *Pir Kamil*, or "Perfect Saint," without whom there was no road to God or Heaven. As his discipline was very lax and accommodating, the number of his converts increased with amazing rapidity.

In Peshawur.

The Mahmandzais soon followed the example of their neighbours of the Doaba, and flocked, *en masse*, to the "Perfect Saint;" and, inviting him to dwell amongst them, placed their fort at his disposal as a residence.

In Ashnaghar.

From Hashtnaggar, Bazîd issued proclamations calling on the tribes around to come to him as the accepted "Pir Kamil" for guidance and instruction in the way to heaven.

Enemies.

This measure gained Bazîd the notoriety he sought, and daily added new converts to the number of his followers, by whom he was now styled *Pir Rokhan*, or "Saint of Light;" but it also roused to activity the champions of the orthodox faith.

Akhûn Darwaiza.

Their chief was a learned mullah of Peshawar, who had long enjoyed a reputation for superior piety and wisdom. He was a man of Mughal descent, named Akhûn Darwaiza Baba. His family had for some generations been settled in Nangrihar, and there he himself had received his early education. He now brought himself prominently before the public by his active opposition and denunciation of the heresy propagated by Bazîd, and by the refutation of the false doctrines he set forth in his book entitled *Khirpan*.

Factions.

The war between the mullahs was soon joined in by their respective followers, and the people became divided into two religious factions, who viewed each other with such animosity and hatred that collisions between members of the opposed sects were of daily occurrence, and the general peace of the country became in consequence disturbed.

Their names.

The followers of the Akhûn styled their leader the *Pir Rokhan*, and Bazîd the *Pir Tarîk* or "Saint of Darkness." Their opponents also used the same distinguishing terms, styling Bazîd the *Pir Rokhan* and the Akhûn *Pir Tarîk*. The disturbed state of the country produced by this unhappy state of affairs soon roused the anxiety of Muhsan Khan, Akbar's viceroy at Kabul, and he at once determined on the capture and punishment of the author. By tact and prompt action, he surprised Bazîd in his fort in Hashtnaggar, seized and carried him off to Kabul, and there cast him into prison.

Disturbances.

Bazîd, however, before long managed to effect his escape; and, returning at once to the scene of his former successes in Hashtnaggar, soon and without difficulty again collected his followers, who now more than ever were convinced of his saintship and the truth of his doctrines; but, being again hard pressed by his enemies, Bazîd was forced to seek a more secure abode, and consequently removed to the Totai hills, accompanied by a small band of devoted disciples. In these hills, however, his doctrine did not receive the favor he anticipated, and he, therefore, removed to Tirah.

Bazîd escapes.

Asylum in the Totai hills.

Removes to Tirah.

The Afridis and Orakzais, tribes as ignorant of any religion as they are lawless in their lives, at once flocked to the standard of the saint, and were eager converts to an indulgent and easy religion just suited to their tastes.

In a short period Bazîd gained so great an influence over these tribes, that for purposes of his own he found no difficulty in raising them bodily against the Mughal rulers of the country, whom they now commenced to

Prospers.

Turns robber.

harass by a systematic plundering of the high roads between Kabul and Jalalabad. Bazîd himself often took part in these raids; and, for the safer and more convenient prosecution of his schemes, he built a fort in the hills bordering on Nangrihar, the scene of his operations.

Is punished.

These acts again roused Muhsan Khan, who attacking Bazîd in his own hills, drove him and his followers to their fort. This was next taken and levelled, many of the defenders were killed, others taken prisoners, and the band completely dispersed. Bazîd, with his usual good fortune, managed to escape with his life, and made his way back to Hashtnaggar, where he met a friendly reception from his former converts and supporters; but he had hardly

Dies.

recovered from the fatigues and hardships of his late wandering life, when he was attacked with a low fever and died. He left five sons,

His sons.

of whom the eldest, Shaikh Umar, succeeded to his "praying carpet." None of the sons, however, had the influence of the father; and the opponents of their sect, headed by Akhûn Darwaiza, soon gained the mastery over them. The eldest son and his brother Khairudin were killed on the banks of the Kabul river by the Yusufzais, who from the first were staunch supporters of

Their fate.

the orthodox faith. Another son, Nurudîn, was captured in his flight towards Hashtnaggar by some Yusufzai shepherds, and burnt at a stake. The fourth son, Jaladudin, escaped to Tirah; and, following in the steps of his father, subsisted for a time by plundering the roads in company with the band of a notorious freebooter and highway-robber of these parts, named Abdullah Khan Uzbak; but he was killed in 1592 A. D. in one of his marauding expeditions near Ghazni by Jafar Beg, who had been despatched by Akbar to concert measures with Mahomad Kasim Khan, the governor of Kabul, for the apprehension of this notorious ruffian. His head was cut off and sent down to Akbar. The fifth son was captured in Hashtnaggar, and kept close prisoner in India till his death.

Military operations.

During the time that Jafar Beg was hunting Jalaludin in the highlands, between Kabul and Ghazni, the Governor of Kabul, Mahomad Kasim Khan, sent one of his Generals, Zain Khan, Kokah, with an army to settle the adjacent districts of Bajawar, Swat, and Buhnair, and to punish the Afghans on those borders for their recent turbulence and insubordination, as well as to collect the revenues due for several years past. Zain Khan set out on this expedition by the Kunbar route, over the Hinduraj pass, into Bajawar; and, erecting a fort, left a garrison in it to keep the country, and went on by the *tarai* through Talash to Swat, where he was stoutly opposed by the Yusufzais; but, driving them off, he built the fort of Damghar in the midst of their valley, and, leaving a garrison in it, scoured the country around, and severely punished the Yusufzais for their insolence; but not without meeting some serious checks, and receiving large reinforcements from Kabul, were his operations brought to a close in this valley, and then he punished the people to an extent they had never before suffered.

Under Zain Khan.

His route.

His severities.

He plundered and burned their villages, confiscated and drove off their cattle, destroyed their crops, and massacred the inhabitants of all ages and both sexes indiscriminately. In fact, he thoroughly devastated the country.

This terrible example had the desired effect; for the rest of his progress through Buhnair, Mandanr, Hashtnaggar, and Peshawar, on to Kabul was almost unopposed. His track, nevertheless, was throughout marked by plunder, ruin, and bloodshed. The cruelties and barbarities enacted by Zain Khan's troops are described as very dreadful. Several of the Afghan tribes were so reduced by death and captivity in this expedition that they have never since recovered their former status.

Their result.

After this severe lesson, the Afghans settled in the Peshawar valley and surrounding hills had no energy left to carry on their religious controversies with the spirit and activity they had previously exhibited. They had, in fact, already had too large a dose of the sword to admit of their again appealing to it for the decision of their differences on religious subjects. And the Bazîd heresy, in these parts at least, owing to the death of its originator and his successors and the dispersion of their proselytes, died out and disappeared almost as rapidly as it arose.

Quietude.

But in Tirah it flourished with wonderful success for many years under Ihdâd, the grandson of Bazîd by his son Shaikh Umar. This man also led the life of a robber; and his bands of religious burglars and highwaymen, who for many years infested the country between Kabul and Peshawar, acquired notoriety for their success, enterprize, courage and cruelty.

Tirah.

When fairly rid of Zain Khan, Kokah, and his troops, the Yusufzais again turned to their fields and flocks, and were engaged in the care of these for many years before they recovered from the serious losses they had suffered at his hands.

Yusufzai.

Peace and plenty, however, soon made the Yusufzais forget the severe lesson they had but so lately received. They no sooner replenished their grain stores, re-stocked their cattle and sheep pens, and brought up their children to manhood, than they refused submission to the government of the empire, of which their country formed but a remote and insignificant corner.

Peace and plenty.

The governor of Peshawur had more than once sent his agents amongst them to collect the government dues, but they were ignored. He at length sent a small body of troops to enforce the claim, but these the Yusufzais attacked and drove out of their country. It was this determined show of opposition and rebellion that led the Emperor Aurangzaib Alamgir to determine on their punishment and subjection. In 1670 his troops entered the country in force, but the Yusufzais did not wait to meet them. They hurried off to the hills with their families and flocks, &c., and left only their home-steads and crops to be burnt by the enemy, in the hopes of their speedy retirement. In this, however, they were disappointed, for the imperial troops settled in the midst of their country, and for its future subjection built a fort that commanded every corner of the plain.

Insubordination.

Punishment.

Aurangzaib's army.

A curious and interesting record of this expedition was recently found in the village of Kapurdagarrhi (the site of the fort above mentioned) amidst the ruins of some old walls. It is a white marble tablet with a well-preserved Persian inscription, to the effect that "in the twelfth year of the reign of Aurangzaib Alamgir, equal to the year 1080 H., Shamshair Khan, Tarîn, on the part of the govern-

Curious record.

ment conquered this country of Mandar, and built this fort, mosque, and well." The ruins of each still exist, and are almost the only remains of red brick buildings in the whole district. The tablet was sent to the Peshawar museum by Captain Shortt, who first discovered it.

Submission.

When the Yusufzais discovered that the new comers were not the birds of passage they took them to be, they gradually came down from their hill retreats, and tendered their submission. Their lands were restored to them, and hostages were taken for their future good behaviour.

Period of quiet.

During the rest of this reign, and in the short succeeding one of Shah Alam, the Yusufzais remained quiet and peaceable, and were busy recruiting their recently exhausted resources. But in the following reign of Mahomad Shah, they again rebelled against the authority of the governor of Peshawur, and laid violent hands on his son, who had been sent amongst them to collect the revenue.

Rebellion.

These events occurred in 1725 A. D., and their success appears to have made the Yusufzais more than ever insubordinate and confident in their own strength; for, in the succeeding reign of Nadir Shah, they were the only Afghans on this border who refused submission to his authority. Nadir sent several expeditions against them; but, as usual, the Yusufzais on the approach of his troops moved with their families, flocks, and chattels, to their hill retreats in Sinawar and Mahaban, and left the plain to take care of itself.

Nadir Shah.

On Nadir's arrival at Peshawar in 1738 A. D., the Yu-

At Peshawar.

sufzai chief, Nazoh Khan, was summoned there to tender the fealty of the tribe, but proudly refusing, a force of Mughals, under Subahdar Jalair, was despatched to coerce him. On the approach of this force, the Yusufzais retreated to the recesses of their hills, only holding the Shairdarrah village as an outpost at the foot of the hills.

Expedition.

The Subahdar followed the fugitives and, *en route*, sought to establish a terror by the most cruel barbarities. The villages and crops were burned, and with them the aged and sick unable to move; other poor wretches who remained behind, trusting to the clemency of the invaders, were systematically blinded and ruthlessly hacked by an unrestrained soldiery, whilst the plain generally was devastated.

Hill retreat.

Arrived at the foot of the hills, Jalair tried to force the Ambailah pass, but was driven back with loss at the Surkhawai hamlet at its entrance. He next attempted to take it by a flank attack up Shairdarrah glen, above which the Yusufzais were encamped with their women and children; but the Yusufzais when brought to bay, fought with greater courage and determination than the Mughals gave them credit for. They rushed down the hill with loud shouts; and, sword in hand, threw themselves upon the Mughal troops with the impetuosity of desperate men.

Mughal defeat.

The Mughals became panic-struck, broke, and fled. The Yusufzais, with increased clamour, poured down the Shairdarrah defile from all sides, and pursued the retreating enemy as far as the Chalpâni ravine.

Nadir's revenge.

On learning of this disaster, Nadir at once set out in person to retrieve it. He passed by the scene of his Subahdar's defeat; and by a forced march through the Chinglai glen, established his camp on the Shakot spur of the Mahaban mountain. From this point he commanded the country on both sides, and the tribes at once tendered their submission. Nadir levied a fine, took hostages for its due payment, and then went on to Hindustan, and the Yusufzais once more returned to their sacked and ruined homesteads. Traditionary accounts, sometimes very marvellous, of Nadir's exploits in this country, may be heard from any "grey-beard" of the district. They have certainly left an impression of his invincibility on the minds of the people.

Ahmad Shah at Peshawur.

Ahmad Shah Abdal, Nadir's successor, after two ineffectual invasions of Delhi and Lahour, in 1744 and 1746 A. D., came to Peshawar in 1749, and at once the different chiefs of the country flocked to his standard.

His reception.

Samand Khan, the chief of the Mahmandzais of Hashtnaggar, was one of the first to hasten to Peshawar with the tender of allegiance of his clan. He was followed by the chief of the Mandar clan, Fattah Khan, son of Nazoh Khan, of Hoti, with whom were the Khans of Toru and Babozai. Ahmad Shah received them all with distinction; and, directing the Mandar chiefs to join his camp with a contingent of 500 horse for service in Hindustan, dismissed them honorably.

Yusufzai contingent.

The Yusufzai contingent joined Ahmad's camp at Attock, and afterwards performed good service against the Mahrattas, whose leader, Gohar, was slain by a party of them. They were also conspicuous actors in the capture of Lahour.

After his victory over the Mahrattas, Ahmad Shah suddenly retraced his steps to Kabul, leaving a strong garrison, and with it the Yusufzai contingent, to hold Lahour. On his second advance, a couple of years later, his camp was joined by the Khalil and Mahmand tribes of Peshawar, and some Yusufzais.

Other tribes.

With these, having relieved his besieged garrison at Lahour, for during his absence the Mahrattas had collected in force for the recovery of their citadel, he went on to Delhi.

Their services.

After Ahmad Shah's death, in 1773 A. D., his son Taimur ascended the throne. During his twenty years' reign, this prince made periodical visits to Peshawar in the cold weather, the better to collect his revenue from the outlying provinces of his kingdom bounded eastward by the Indus. During this reign, the Yusufzais paid their quota of the revenues regularly through Nowshair and Shahwali Khans, both sons of Fattah Khan of Hoti, and the appointed *mûájibdars* of the government.

Taimur Shah.

Taimur was succeeded by Shah Zamân, who, shortly after ascending the throne, followed the example of his predecessors and invaded Hindustan. He lacked, however, both their genius and their enterprize; and, after getting as far as the Chinab, was driven back by the Sikhs, a people of a comparatively new nationality. In this expedition many Yusufzai adventurers accompanied Shah Zamân's camp under their chief, Nowshair Khan, of Hoti.

Shah Zamân.

The ill-fated Shah Zamân had hardly made good his retreat to his own capital, when a most serious revolt, headed by Fattah Khan Barakzai, broke out.

His misfortunes.

and for the time absorbed his entire attention, for its object was no less than to dethrone himself in favor of his half-brother Mahmud.

And fate.

With his usual bad luck, all Shah Zamân's endeavours to quell the tumult, or check his enemies, proved unavailing. He himself was betrayed into the hands of his rival's son, Kamran, and by him cruelly blinded in 1803 A. D.

Mahmud.

The way thus cleared, Mahmud ascended the throne, and his first act was to eject the miserable, deposed, and sightless monarch's full brother, Shuja-ul-mulk, from the provincial government of Peshawar, and to appoint in his stead his own son, Kamran, with Fattah Khan Barakzai as confidential agent and adviser. Burning with hatred and revenge for the injuries himself and his full-brother, the rightful sovereign, had suffered, Shuja-ul-mulk canvassed his friends, and, collecting a strong party, managed with their assistance to secure the person of the usurper of his brother's throne; and, casting him into prison, himself assumed the sovereignty.

Imprisonment.

Shah Shuja.

Shah Shuja-ul-mulk's enjoyment of power, however, if indeed it could be such, was but short-lived. Fattah Khan's great power and active hostility was more than he could cope with; and, wisely for his own safety, Shah Shuja determined on abdicating what had cost him so much to acquire.

His abdication.

In 1809 he fled the capital; and, after a period spent in seclusion and vagrancy in disguise, he reached Lahour in 1813, and there sought an asylum of th

Sikhs; but, being disappointed in his hopes in this quarter, disgusted at the indignities dealt him, and the loss of his precious jewel, *Kho-i-Núr*, which he had managed hitherto to conceal about his person, and tired of the Sikh chieftain's vacillation, he effected his escape; and, finally, in 1816, threw himself on the mercy of the British Government, through their Political Agent at Ludianah, which was then the frontier station in this direction.

Flight.

Refuge.

On Shah Shuja's disappearance from the scene of contention, Mahmud, effecting his liberation from prison, at once rose to the surface; and, through the influence and exertions of his former friend and supporter, Fattah Khan Barakzai, once more secured the throne. Mahmud at once made him his Wazir; and this he did more for the purpose of controlling his power and watching his acts, than as a mark of confidence, or as a reward for his previous services; for the extensive relations and great power of this extraordinary man were now as much a cause of apprehension and suspicion to Mahmud as they were of jealousy and hatred to his son and heir-apparent, Kamran. And that this should have been the case, is not at all unnatural, if we but reflect on the position that by his own talents and energy Fattah Khan had at this time secured for himself.

Mahmud.

Liberated.

Enthroned.

His Wazir.

Talents.

Fattah Khan was the son of Sarfaraz Khan Barakzai, a man of good family, and a chief in his own tribe; and who, whilst yet a young man, had, under the name

Birth.

of Paindah Khan, acquired notoriety for his rare soldierly and administrative qualities.

Aspirations.

The son evidently inherited the father's talents and ambition; for it seems certain that during the anarchy and confusion that followed on the death of Taimur, the aim of Fattah Khan was to secure the power and position of his own large family first, preparatory to flying at higher game for himself; and he simply used Mahmud as a puppet to disguise his real designs, which were nothing short of securing the throne ultimately for himself. How he laid the foundations for his future rising will be understood at a glance on considering the distribution of the provincial governments of the kingdom at the time of Shah Shujah's abdication and flight, in the beginning of the century. The whole country, in fact, was divided between the many sons of Paindah Khan, the brothers of Fattah Khan, Mahmud's Wazir.

Schemes.

His brothers.

That celebrated Barakzai chief had a numerous and notorious family of sons by his several wives. By one wife he had the Sardars Fattah Khan, Azîm Khan, and Jabâr Khan. The first named was Mahmud's Wazir, and the other two were jointly and successively governors of Kashmir.

Kohndil Khan, Rahmdil Khan, Mihrdil Khan, Pûrdil Khan, and Shairdil Khan, were sons by a second wife. The last named died in youth, but the other four were jointly governors of the Kandahar province. They divided its revenues and shared its rule, one of the brothers being the ruler in each of its divisions of Kilat Ghilzai, Kandahar proper, Girishk and Farrah.

By a third wife, Paindah Khan had five other sons, viz.,

Their distribution.

Ata Mahomad Khan, Sultan Mahomad Khan, Pir Mahomad Khan, Yar Mahomad Khan, and Sayad Mahomad Khan. Each of these Sardars was provided with a provincial government on the Indus frontier, between the Dehrajat and Hashtnaggar.

Amir Mahomad Khan and Dost Mahomad Khan were sons by a fourth wife. They ruled the provinces of Kabul and Ghazni.

Mahmud, the puppet, meanwhile had his head quarters at Herat.

The Wazir obnoxious.

With the kingdom thus apportioned amongst his own brethren, it is not astonishing that Fattah Khan was viewed with suspicion by Mahmud, and hatred by Kamran, both of whom now felt themselves to be mere tools in his hands.

Murdered.

Kamran had determined at all hazards to get rid of his detested and formidable rival. An opportunity occurred in 1818 whilst on the march from Kabul to Ghazni, and Kamran, long on the watch, seized it. He entrapped the unsuspecting Fattah Khan into his tent at Haidar Khail, and taunting him with the discovery of his seditious schemes, had him hewed in pieces limb by limb.

Revolution.

This act at once precipitated the crisis that had for some time been impending. The whole country forthwith rose against Mahmud and his son, who, to escape the vengeance of the murdered Wazir's brothers, were forced to flee to Herat. There they were left undisturbed, for the murdered man's brothers were too busily engaged, each one in

Anarchy.

securing his own portion of the dismembered kingdom, to find time to exact the retribution which amongst Afghans is considered a sacred duty as much as a point of honor.

Dissolution.

What followed is told in a few words. Each province of the but newly constructed Durrani empire at once became an independent chiefship under the ruler who, at the time of the dissolution of the Abdal dynasty, happened to be its governor, and they were appropriated in the same disposition as that above detailed.

Weakness.

In this weak and divided state, the country continued for several years, and, exciting the cupidity of the Sikhs, who had already in 1841 possessed themselves of Attak, was becoming annexed piecemeal by them.

Losses by annexation.

They first, during the absence at Kabul of Azim Khan, attacked Kashmir, and easily took it from his brother Jabâr Khan, whom they permitted to retire to his own country. They next, in 1818, advanced on Peshawar;

The Sikhs.

and this province after a succession of struggles, terminating in 1823 with the celebrated battle of Nowshaira, they finally completely wrested from the Afghans. The Sardar Yar Mahomad Khan was, however, continued as the governor of the district, whilst a Sikh army, under Harri Sing, garrisoned Peshawar, in order to keep the country and ensure the payment of revenue.

A religious upstart.

A few years after the advance of the Sikhs in this direction; and, during the height of Afghanistan's political anarchy, a new character appeared on the scene as a *quasi* claimant of the sovereignty. This was no other than Mir Sayad Ahmad, of Bareilly, better known in these parts as Sayad Badshah. He styled himself *Amir-ul-muminin,* and for a brief period enjoyed a very successful career, while stirring up the kings and peoples of the different adjacent *Sunni* Mahomadan governments to flock to his standard, which was now unfurled to re-establish the empire of Islam, and to rid the Indian peninsula of its infidel peoples,—the British and Sikhs.

Sayad Badshah.

As this man's later career is intimately connected with the history of Yusufzai, it will not be amiss in this place to give a brief account of his antecedents and life in this recent acquisition of the British empire in India, and more especially as the band of religious enthusiasts first collected by him still flourish in this region, and have on more than one occasion been a source of annoyance and anxiety to the British authorities.

His history.

Mir Sayad Ahmad was a native and resident of the city of Bareilly, where for many years he had been distinguished among men of his own creed for his learning, piety, and zeal in support of the pure doctrines of Islam, as acknowledged by the Sunni sect, and which, since the establishment of the British rule, had suffered much from the negligence, corruption, and want of religious enthusiasm on the part of professing Mahomadans generally. He was one of a very numerous party of religious enthusiasts and bigots, scattered all over Hindustan, who, anxious for the preservation in its integrity of their religion, were by a community of interests naturally drawn towards each other, and found consolation and support in a correspondence and interchange of sentiments, deploring the flagging prospects of

Country and class.

Character and aspirations.

Islam, and sighing for the day when it would once again flourish as the paramount faith.

Conditions and schemes.

Many of this body, disgusted at the loss of their power and influence, and lamenting the cheerless stagnant prospects of their religion, found a relief from their griefs and sorrows in wandering about the country hatching schemes for a Mahomadan revival, or else in a pilgrimage to Mecca. They there enjoyed unhindered a season of fanatical devotion, spiced with the alluring pleasures of framing and discussing plots for the destruction at one swoop of the hated infidels, and the instant spread of Islam and their own interests throughout the Mahomadan world. One of this class was Mir Sayad Ahmad of Bareilly.

Pilgrimage.

Between forty and fifty years ago, he left Bareilly in company with Mullah Ismail, of the same city, on a tour through Hindustan; and, having visited the principal seats of Mahomadan learning and religion, finally left the country on a pilgrimage to Mecca. Whilst there he collected a small party of bigots, and, with himself as leader, proclaimed a *jahâd* against the infidels in India. After a while, he set out with his party of Ghazis, a mixture of fanatics of all races, but for the most part returning Hindustanis, and travelled through Balochistan to Kandahar.

Fanaticism.

Reaches Kabul.

Army of fanatics.

Here, after a short stay, he was joined by a few more followers, and proceeded to Kabul, where he met with encouraging success, the numbers of his band exceeding 300 fanatics. With these he advanced to Peshawar, where Yar Mahomad Khan was ruler. His cotemporaries were Kamran at Herat, Kohndil Khan at Kandahar, and Dost Mahomad Khan at Kabul.

At Peshawar.

At Peshawar, not meeting with the active support he anticipated, the Sayad moved on to Yusufzai, where he met a friendly reception from the chiefs of Hund and Zihdih, and was also on good terms with the Sayads of Buhnair.

In Yusufzai.

From this point he opened communications with his friends and supporters in Hindustan; and, receiving promises of assistance in men and money, at once organised a band of *Mujdhidins*, or "Warriors of the Faith," under his own leadership, and issued a proclamation for a *jahâd*, under his own seal, as *Amir-ul-muminin*.

Assumes the sovereignty.

The gauntlet thus thrown down was at once picked up, and a Sikh army marched from Peshawar to try conclusions with the self-appointed Amir-ul-muminin.

Opposed by the Sikhs.

Gathering his band together, and strengthening it with a contingent from Khadi Khan, of Hund, and another from Ashraf Khan, of Zihdih, the Sayad marched out triumphantly to give them battle. The two advancing armies met at Saidoh; but, in the first onset the Sayad's undisciplined rabble were panic struck and easily dispersed with great loss. The Sayad himself escaped with only a few body attendants, and removed to Swat, where he found shelter at Batkhaila. This first blow to his aspirations occurred in the spring of 1827.

And routed.

In Buhnair.

After a short rest in Swat, the Sayad moved over to Takhtaband, in Buhnair, a noted nursery for saints, and a perfect hot-bed of fanatics. Here he was well received by the people; and, collecting a small gathering about himself, again busied himself preaching a *jahád.* Owing, however, to the feuds and quarrels then rife amongst the Afghan tribes, and the Yusufzais especially, he met with but small success. He persevered nevertheless; and, besides circulating his proclamations throughout the adjacent districts, forwarded copies to the rulers of Kashkar, Bukhara, Kabul, and Herat; also to Khanan Khan the Ghilzai chief, to Shah Zamân, at Ludianah, and even to the Sultan-i-Rûm. His success in these quarters, however, was no better than it had been with the Yusufzais.

Schemes.

Activity.

Whilst thus engaged the Sayad discovered that his plot to seize the fort of Attak by treachery had been communicated to the Sikhs by Khadi Khan, of Hund, who, since the Sayad's disaster at Saidoh, had withdrawn his allegiance and support from him as the Amir-ul-muminin. He accordingly set out with his band to punish the offending Khan. In this enterprize he was assisted by Mir Bâbû, and Mobîn, Maliks of Chargholai, who, with their respective contingents, joined him on the march to Hund. A fight ensued, but with advantage to neither party. The Sayad on this pretended a desire to make up the quarrel; and, through the medium of a noted recluse of the neighbourhood, named Abdulghafur, and now the Akhûn of Swat, who by many years of a hermit's life had acquired great influence over the people, got the Khan to visit him. As soon as separated from his guards, the Sayad forthwith had the Khan seized and slain on the spot; and then removed up to the Khodokhail hills, where he was welcomed by Fattah Khan, the chief of Panjtar.

Is betrayed.

His revenge.

Allies.

In Khodokhail.

From this retreat, the Sayad issued his proclamations as sovereign of the Yusufzais, for by this time, he had gained many scattered adherents amongst their numerous clans. But his commands and religious discipline soon proved too rigid for the tastes of the people, whilst the Sayad further made himself obnoxious by insisting on the Yusufzais giving their daughters in marriage to his band of foreigners, a measure which was extremely distasteful to the proud Afghans, and soon resulted in the alienation of the whole tribe. His former friends of Chargholai now became his enemies, whilst the people of Hoti *tappa* entirely ignored his authority.

New allies.

His rule.

Loses favor.

And adherents.

Enraged at this shew of disrespect, the Sayad came down from Panjtar to punish the culprits. Chargholai at once submitted, begged pardon, and promised better behaviour for the future, and was, therefore, passed uninjured; but Hoti and Mardan, persisting in their obstinacy, were attacked, plundered, and burnt. These events occurred in 1829.

Coercion.

Success.

The Sayad's increasing power and boldness now alarmed Yar Mahomad Khan, the Governor of Peshawur, who lost no time in marching with an army against his rival.

Opposition.

The hostile forces met in the Zalozai tappa. The Peshawar troops, under the personal command of Yar Mahomad himself, encamped at Kundah, whilst the

Armies meet.

Sayad's camp was pitched at Zihdih, under the command of Mullah Ismail; the Sayad himself securing the shelter of Ashraf Khan's citadel in the village.

Stratagem.

The Sayad's force is said not to have exceeded 600 fighting men, mostly Hindustanis; whilst Yar Mahomad's troops were reckoned at 3000 men with six guns. During the night, Mullah Ismail, having previously surrounded Yar Mahomad's camp with parties of men in ambush, marched out to the attack with small parties of men, who held long ropes, on which lights were fixed at short intervals, stretched between them.

It success.

The artifice succeeded, the Peshawar troops seeing these parties advancing on all sides, thought they were surrounded by a superior force, became panic-struck, and broke in all directions. In the confusion that ensued, the Sayad received a report that his Hindustanis were overpowered, and being massacred. Without delay he mounted his mule and set off for Panjtar; but, at daylight, was overtaken by a messenger, who announced that his Hindustanis had gained the victory, and were in full pursuit of the enemy towards Hund, only Mullah Ismail with a small party remaining behind in charge of the captured camp and guns. This intelligence, though at first discredited, proved true; and presently Mullah Ismail, having collected his scattered troops, marched back with his trophies to Panjtar, being joined *en route* by the Sayad. During this struggle, Yar Mahomad was mortally wounded, and died on the road near the village of Lahour, but his body was carried into Peshawar for burial.

Peshawar troops routed.

Yar Mahomad killed.

The Sayad's followers, after this success, increased so

Prosperity.

rapidly that there was not room for them in Panjtar, and they also became a burthen to Fattah Khan, who, finding it difficult to feed and restrain them, more than once gave the Sayad a hint to seek other quarters.

Moves to Amb.

The Sayad consequently moved over to Amb, the chief of which town, Paindah Khan, tendered submission and offered tribute. The Sayad acknowledged the first and accepted the other at the rate fixed by the *Shariat*. Whilst at Amb the Sayad's followers, it is said, mustered over 6000 men, Hindustanis and men of the country in about equal proportions. He also at this time gained a great number of adherents throughout the Peshawur district.

Increase of followers.

Expedition from Peshawar.

As soon as Sultan Mahomad Khan succeeded to the government of Peshawar, he made arrangements for avenging the death of his brother, Yar Mahomad Khan, and was joined in the expedition by the deceased Sardar's cousin, Habîb-ul-lah Khan, a brother of Sultan Jan, the late ruler of Herat.

The Sayad's army.

The Peshawar troops had marched as far as Hoti when they came upon the Sayad's army under Mullah Ismail, encamped at the adjoining village of Mayar. The Sayad's forces who had came down from Amb were 500 footmen, all Hindustanis, and about 1,500 horsemen, mostly men of the country. The fight commenced at day-light on the banks of the Chalpâni, between Hoti and Mayar. The Hindustanis were driven back early in the struggle, and pursued as far as Kapurdagarrhi, by Habîb-ul-lah

Battle at Hoti.

Khan. Meantime, however, the Sayad with his horsemen had gained the advantage over Sultan Mahomad Khan, and was pursuing his broken forces over the plain in the opposite direction. Habîb-ul-lah Khan, afraid of being cut off at once, returned to join Sultan Mahomad's force, and thus checked the Sayad in his pursuit; but his rallied Hindustanis presently coming up, the Sayad continued the pursuit and followed the Peshawar troops as far as Hashtnaggar, without, however, catching them up.

The Sayad's success.

At Hashtnaggar, the Sayad halted some days, and sent a missive to Sultan Mahomad Khan, ordering him to come in and tender allegiance to the Amir-ul-muminin; but, receiving a defiant and threatening reply, forwarded in answer the following taunt:—

His advance on Hashtnaggar.

"In dargâh-i-ma dargâh-î-na ummaidi naist.
"Sad bâr agar bishikasti bâz â
"Har ânchi kardi bâz â, bâz â, bâz â."

Correspondence.

Receiving no rejoinder to this, the Sayad advanced, and, by a night surprize, got possession of the Michni village. At this further success of the Sayad's arms, Sultan Mahomad Khan began to fear for himself; and, receiving no aid from Kabul, as a last resource invited the Sayad to Peshawar to conclude a peace. The Sayad, however, had previously been bent on this journey without waiting the formality of an invitation; and, on arrival at the city, at once took possession of the fort and assumed the government, and, as a sop to keep him quiet, gave Sultan Mahomad Khan

Surprize of Michni.

Enters Peshawar.

Assumes the government.

the districts of Doaba and Hashtnaggar by way of *jâgir.* These events occurred at the close of 1830.

Appoints agents.

After a brief stay in Peshawar, the Sayad returned to the genial climate of the Mahaban hills, where he fixed his head quarters; but he previously established Mullah Muzhir Ali in the Gokhatri as his viceroy, and left a strong guard for his protection. The Sayad was now really an Amir-ul-minin,* but was generally styled "Sayad Badshah." From his hill retreat, by means of trusty agents in the priesthood all over the country, the Sayad circulated his decrees and collected the tithes in all the districts from Kohat to Tanawal.

Removes to the Mahaban hills.

Hard rule.

But his rule being strictly according to the *Shariat,* proved most distasteful and irksome to the people, who had hitherto, after a fashion of their own, enjoyed unusual independence in their civil and religious liberties. They were, moreover, oppressed by the Sayad's foreign agents, who, besides robbing them of their property in excess of the fixed tithes, caused a wide-spread disaffection and hatred by forcibly taking the Afghan maidens as wives. Unable through the ordinary means to ameliorate their unhappy condition, or to obtain redress of their grievances, the Afghans decided on ridding themselves of their oppressors, by some means, fair or foul. With this object a plot was formed in Peshawar, and communicated to trusty partizans throughout the country. The scheme was to massacre all the Sayad's agents, wherever posted, in all parts of the country, and the signal was "let every man kill his sacrifice at the hour of evening prayer on —— day." The conspiracy was carried out with complete

Disaffection.

Conspiracy.

success; and, in one hour, Mullah Muzhir Ali and almost all of the Sayad's *thannahdars* and agents throughout the country were treacherously murdered. Thus the Sayad lost his power at one blow as rapidly as he had acquired it, and after barely two months of its enjoyment.

Massacre.

Now, in the decline of his fortunes, the Sayad discovered that his patron and host, Fattah Khan, of Panjtar, and the Mahaban tribes generally, were not the true partizans they professed to be. He accordingly moved across the Indus with the remnant of his band of Hindustanis, and settled at Balakot, in Huzara, where he met with sympathy from an ignorant people, yet unaware of the troubles they were bringing upon themselves.

Desertions of adherents.

Removes to Hazarah.

At Balakot, the Sayad gained possession of the fort, and perseveringly set about collecting adherents, of whom the major portion were from Hindustan. He was hardly settled in this retreat, however, before the Sikhs, in 1831, marched an army against him. The fort was captured after a severe fight by the Sikh commander, Shair Sing, and both the Sayad and Mullah Ismail, together with 1,300 Hindustanis, were slain.

At Balakot.

Sikh attack.

The Sayad's death.

The remnant, barely 300 strong, escaped to the hills, where, after a while, they were joined by the small party of Meer Wali Mahomad, a son of the late Sayad's sister, who, with Ruknudin, had some time previously been despatched to Kashmir on some secret service, and the

His army destroyed.

The remnant.

united bands then retraced their steps to Takhtaband, in Buhnair, where they settled. With Meer Wali Mahomad was the late Sayad's widow, a daughter of Sulaiman Shah, king of Kashkar. She was pregnant at the time of her husband's death, and soon after gave birth to a daughter named Hajirah, or Hagar.

Desertions.

At this time the prospects of the late Sayad's kingdom, not being as bright as his followers had anticipated or hoped for, their numbers began to decrease by desertions, deaths, and he absence of recruits. Amongst the first to desert was Mir Wali Mahomad, who, with the Sayad's widow, went down to his friends in Hindustan.

New leader.

Settle at Sittanah.

The remnant, left in Buhnair, chose Moulavi Nasuridin as their leader; and, on the invitation of the Sayads of Sittanah, moved over and settled there. They were now about 300 men, and were commonly known as the "Mujahidins," but were indentified with the Sayads of Sittanah in opposition to the Utmanzais, with whom they were at issue regarding the ownership of some boundary lands. The Mujahidins remained quietly at this place for nearly three years under the leadership of Nasirudin, subsisting on funds furnished by their friends in Hindustan, when a small party of new arrivals being robbed and maltreated by the people of Munarah, a small village on the river bank (since carried away by a flood), they were roused to activity. Headed by their leader, they made a sudden attack upon the village, killed many of the inhabitants, and plundered their houses. On their return journey they visited Topi, which also they plundered.

Quarrel with the tribes.

This unexpected behaviour of the Mujahidins at once turned the Yusufzais against them. Fattah Khan, the Panjṭar chief, who had held them in the light of enemies since their settlement amongst the Sayads of Sittanah, now became very active against them; and, persuading Sayad Amir, the Kotah Mullah, to lend him the influence of his name, soon collected a party, and hunted the band out of his own hills, and killed their leader, Nasîrudin. So active was Fattah Khan's hostility, that he reduced the Mujahidins to a remnant of between seventy and eighty men, who, afraid to trust themselves as heretofore in the villages on the Mahaban, now collected at Sittanah under Mir Aulad Ali as their leader.

Their weakness.

And sufferings.

On the intelligence of their forlorn condition reaching Hindustan, their friends there despatched Moulavi Inayat Ali, from Azîmabad, and Mir Maqsûd Ali, from Bihar, with large supplies of money, and a considerable body of recruits, to their succour. The whole party consisted of about 300 men, and they travelled in separate parties, of five or six together, to Pakli, in Hazarah, which had been fixed on as the rendezvous. Here they were joined by Mir Aulad Ali and his small party; and, after a short rest, commenced levying contributions from the country around. Their plans, however, were soon frustrated, and their party dispersed by a Sikh force under Lieutenant Agnew. Mir Maqsûd Ali was seized and sent a prisoner to Lahour. Inayat Ali, disheartened at this first taste of the life of a Mujahidin, effected his escape, and found his way back to Azîmabad. Many more followed his example; but Aulad

Assistance.

In Pakli.

Their plans.

Frustrated.

Ali, with a small band of trusty adherents, returned to his former friends, the Sayads of Sittanah.

Return to Sittanah.

During the Sikh revolution, and the first years of the annexation of the Panjab by the British, the Mujahidins were an insignificant body, and continued quietly at Sittanah; but Aulad Ali persevered in the original schemes of the founder of the band he was now at the head of, and in due time was strengthened by the receipt of ample funds and numerous accessions to his party from Hindustan. Amongst the new arrivals were Moulavis Wilayat Ali, and Inayat Ali (he who a few years before had deserted from Pakli).

Accessions.

The former superseded Aulad Ali in the leadership of the Mujahidins; and, for the first eight or ten months, was busily occupied in arming and drilling his men as a measure of protection against the tribes amongst whom they lived.

New leaders.

In 1855 Wilayat Ali died of fever, and was succeeded in the leadership of the Mujahidins by Inayat Ali, who moved the head quarters of the band from Sittanah to Mangalthanah, where they fortified themselves. Soon after their settlement in this place, Wilayat Ali's four sons, Moulâna, Abdullah, Mir Hidayatullah, Rahmani, and Mahomed Hassan, quarrelled with Inayat Ali, and separated from his party. In their secession, they were also joined by Moulâna Fayaz Ali and Yâhia Ali; and with them, after a period of wandering about Yusufzai in disguise, they ultimately went down to Hindustan.

Inayat Ali.

Settle at Mangalthanah.

For a couple of years, the colony at Mangalthanah flourished and continued to receive regular supplies of men and money from Hindustan; and, in 1857,

Flourish.

when the Indian mutiny broke out, their leader, Inayat Ali, was very active in stirring up a *jahâd* by means of circular proclamations to the tribes in and about Yusufzai; but he met with but indifferent success.

King of Swat.

At this juncture, also, about May 1857, Sayad Akbar, the king of Swat, died, after a reign of near seven years. He was succeeded by his son, Mir Mubarak Ali Shah, or more commonly Mubarak Shah, but he was dethroned and expelled the country, after only a few weeks reign, by the Swat tribes, who had long been impatient of his father's rule.

His son.

Mubarak Shah returned to his native village, Sittanah, and shortly afterwards joined Inayat Ali's party in the Khodokhail hills.

Schemes.

He had not been many days here before he concocted a plan with Inayat Ali for the surprise and capture of the Murdan fort; but their plans were frustrated by the vigilance of the military and civil officers.

Discovery.

Inayat Ali and his band after this came down to Narinji; and, by means of secret emissaries, sought to stir up the Yusufzais to revolt.

Punishment.

For their conduct in this affair, the Narinji people were punished by a British force from Peshawar, under General Cotton, and Inayat Ali and his party driven up into the hills. From this retreat, on the departure of the British troops, Inayat Ali sent down about a hundred of his men under Moulavi Shariatullah to attack the civil officers' camp at Shaikhjânâ.

Reprisals.

The party made their descent at night; and, surprising the camp, completely plundered and destroyed it; the civil officer, Lieutenant Horne, barely escaping with his life.

Difficulties.

During the mutinies, the Mujahidins were much straitened for money, their hitherto regular supplies having for the time ceased. They continued, however, to find a subsistence in the Mahaban hills, partly on their own resources and partly on the contributions of the tribes around.

New leaders.

At this time Inayat Ali died of fever at Chanai. The leadership was then shared by three men, viz., Moulavi Nasrullah, Shah Ikramullah, and Mir Takki, in preference to Inayat Ali's son, Hafiz Abdul Majid, who was unfitted for the post by a defect in his speech.

Dissensions.

After a season of rivalry and dissension for the undivided authority, Moulavi Nasrullah was elected chief in preference to the others. He now more than ever strove to stir up the Mahomadans of the Peshawar district to rise against the Government, but his schemes were promptly checked.

British troops.

In the spring of 1858, an expedition under General Cotton entered the Mahaban hills; and, dispersing the Hindustanis, destroyed their settlements at Chinglai, Mangalthannah, and Sittanah. The Mujahidins only stood to face the British troops at the hamlet of Shahnurlarai above Sittanah, and here forty of them with their leader, Mullah Ikramullah, were killed.

Destruction of settlements.

After this destruction of their settlements, Moulavi Nasrullah and Mír Takki acted together as joint leaders of the Mujahidins; and, collecting their scattered band, formed a new colony at Malka on the further side of Mahaban. Here they were shortly afterwards joined by Mir

Malka.

Accessions.

Maqsûd Ali, who had returned from a visit to Bihar, and now assumed the title of "*Amir-ul-muhajirin.*" On his way up Maqsûd Ali visited Peshawar, and during a stay there of three months, organized a secret agency for the conveyance of money to his party in the hills, the circulation of proclamations, &c.

Secret agency.

He died, of a painful disease, in the spring of 1862, some six months later than Moulavi Nasrullah, who died on the road to Kabul, whither he had been despatched on a mission to the Amir. After this Moulavi Abdullah, the son of Wilayat Ali, succeeded to the chiefship, but not without a severe struggle, for a strong party had formed in favour of Moulavi Ishak, the son of Mir Maqsûd Ali. The former, however, gained the preference on account of his greater experience and military qualifications, whilst the latter was installed in the next most important post, that of treasurer.

Death of Maqsûd Ali.

Moulavi Abdullah.

These men are at this time the leaders of the Mujahidins, who, according to the best accounts, number between 1200 and 1400 souls. They consist almost entirely of Hindustanis from Bengal (especially Dacca), Oude, the Central and North West Provinces, and the lower Punjab. Their professed object is the re-establishment of Islam throughout India; and, in their present locale, they live strictly according to the *Shariat*. They have adopted a military organization, and are well supplied with arms, including a couple of small cannons. The

Strength of Mujahidins.

Objects.

Organization.

whole band is divided into ten companies, each under a separate leader. They are as follows :—

1. The jamiat of Mian Usmân Sahib, 120 men, twenty percussion muskets, and ten flint-locks.

2. The jamiat of Moulavi Shariatullah, 150 men, thirty percussion muskets, and ten flint-locks and match-locks. This is the chief jamiat.

3. The jamiat of Abdulghafur, 130 men, thirty percussion muskets and twenty match-locks. This is the special gathering of Moulavi Abdullah, and is called the *Sarkari jamiat*. It consists entirely of men from Bengal.

4. The jamiat of Kaim Khan, 130 men, six percussion muskets, and twenty match-locks. This is the oldest gathering, and is called the *Hindi jamiat*. It is composed entirely of Hindustanis.

5. The jamiat of Najaf Khan, 130 men, fifteen percussion muskets, and twenty match-locks. Half are Bengalis and half Hindustanis.

6. The jamiat of Naimudin Sahib, 125 men, mostly Bengalis, six muskets, and thirty match-locks.

7. The jamiat of Munshi Toufirullah, 100 men, ten muskets, and twenty match-locks. This is called the *Nál jamiat*.

8. The jamiat of Munshi Basîrudîn, 100 men, six percussion muskets, and twenty match-locks.

9. The jamiat of Moulavi Ibrahim, 130 men, four percussion muskets, and twenty match-locks.

10. The jamiat of Bahramudin Buhnairi, forty men, no fire-arms. This is called the *Daisí jamiat*, and contains men of Hazarah, Buhnair, and intermediate hills.

All are armed with swords. The superiority of these Mujahidins, as an armed and disciplined body, has enabled them with ease to maintain their position against the tribes amongst whom they have effected a lodgement, whilst their free expenditure of money always secures a party in their interest.

Arms.

The Mujahidins are not really the united and devoted band of warriors for the faith that they are generally supposed to be. They consist of three classes, who are numerically strong in the order here named.

Composition.

1. The *ignorant.*—These are mostly poor artificers or laborers who have been entrapped far away from their homes and connections by false promises and glowing accounts of the blessings and delights of the rule of the Imam Mihndi, who they have been assured has come down to earth, and is collecting his faithful at Mahaban for the Millennium, &c., &c.

Ignorant class.

2. The *crafty.*—These live, without self-exertion, on the means provided by others. They belong mostly to the clerical class, but also number in their ranks outlaws, discontents, and criminals. Their time is spent equally between religious and military exercises.. They are rabid in their abuse of infidels, possess some control over the ignorant, and are the most active in the spread of sedition, &c.

Crafty class.

3. The *religious.*—These have withdrawn from the world and its pleasures, and devote themselves to the strict observance of the religion they believe to be the only true one. They have joined the Mujahidins to escape

Religious class.

from the power or influence of infidels, and to breath an air uncontaminated by their presence. They are thorough fanatics. Their cry is *jahâd*, and they are ready to give their lives for the faith. They are not numerous.

Akhûn of Swat.

In the foregoing account of Sayad Badshah and colony of fanatics, allusion has been made to the Akhûn of Swat. As this personage is a character of very considerable importance, on account of the wide-spread influence he has acquired, and at this time exercises over the bulk of the Mahomadan population of the neighbouring districts, it will be as well here to relate his history briefly.

Parentage.

Abdulghafur, now known as Akhûn Sahib, was born at Jabrai, a small shepherd's hamlet in Bar Swat, about the year 1794. His parents, of whom nothing certain appears to be known, were poor and obscure people, of the Gujar caste; but according to some accounts, of the *Tsapi* caste, who are a branch of the *Mian* fraternity, according to the saying of his disciples and followers. The former would appear to be the correct account; for all admit that Abdulghafur in his youth was employed to tend cattle at graze. His early occupation afforded ample time for meditation; and Abdulghafur was soon noted amongst his own people as a sober, thoughtful lad, with a natural predeliction for a retired and religious life. As a shepherd boy, it is related of him that for years he lived on the milk of a single buffalo, which he always led to pasture tied with a rope to prevent it grazing on the crops of others, rather than drink that of the rest of the herd which grazed on unlawful grounds.

Early life.

At the age of eighteen years, he discovered the world to

Religious predeliction.

be but a wicked one, and resolved to sever himself from it and devote himself to a religious life. Leaving his home, he went to the village of Barangolah, and there became the *Chailah* of a priest, from whom he learned the rudiments of his religion, and the arts of reading and writing. After awhile, according to the custom of the country, he set out as a *Talib-ul-ilm*, or "enquirer after wisdom;" and, in the course of his wanderings, arrived at Gujargarri in Yusufzai. Here he took up his abode in the *jumaat* of Abdul Hakim Akhunzada; and, after a few months stay, again set out on his travels. At Dudair he became the *muríd* or "disciple" of Sahibzada Mahomad Shwâib, at that time the most noted priest in these parts. This man was the disciple of Hafizji Sahib, Umarzai, who in turn was the disciple of Bishaunai Sahib, of Buhnair, a celebrated recluse, who gained his notoriety through the public performance by his *murids* of the four *taríka*, or "modes of religious devotion" he had taught them. These *taríka* were—1. *Nakashbandia*, a perfectly silent and motionless devotion, sitting with the head bowed on the chest, and the eyes fixed on the ground. 2. *Sorawardia*. In which the devotee seated, murmurs, at short intervals and in measured tones, the word *Alla hu*, which is articulated with a suppressed breath, as if produced by a powerful inward struggle for its expression. The devotee also every now and again goes off into a faint from suffocation produced by the word sticking in his throat and preventing respiration. 3. *Kadaria*. In this mode the devotee seated for hours together repeats the following declaration:—"*Ant-ul-Hadi—Ant-*

Wanderings.

Studies.

Nakashbandia.

Sorawardia.

Kadaria.

ul-Hakk—Lais-ul-Hadi—Illahu." "Thou art the guide; Thou art the truth—there is no guide but thee." 4. *Chastia.* In this mode the devotee, at stated times leaps, whirls, and gesticulates himself into a paroxysm of frenzy, repeating "*Allah; Ya-Alla hu,*" and then subsides exhausted and senseless.

Chastia.

Of these four *tarîka,* Abdulgafur adopted the first, or *Nakashbandia*; and, for its undisturbed observance, settled on a lonely spot on the river bank below the village of Baiki, near Hund. Here he built a *zozkhana,* or "camel's thorn hut," at the river's brink; and, shut off from the world, dwelt in it for twelve years. During all this time his diet, it is said, was only *Shamukha,* the seed of a wild grass *(Panicum frumentaceum)* and water. This grain is said to be his chief food at the present time; but the water is replaced by buffalo's milk. At Baiki he soon acquired a notoriety for sanctity, and was flocked to by all sorts of people from the neighbouring country for a prayer or a blessing. Owing, however, to his unfortunate action in the quarrel between Khadi Khan of Hund and Sayad Ahmad, he was forced to leave his hermitage, and for some years wandered about the country unknown and uncared for. At length he settled in a *Ziarat* at Gholaman, in the Khidarzai tappa of Yusufzai, and again soon rose to notoriety as a "Man of God" on account of his superior piety and abstinence, and was, as before, flocked to by eager crowds of worshippers. From Gholaman, he moved over to Salimkhan, at the invitation of the villagers. Here he attached to himself a number of disciples, who spread

Becomes a recluse.

His diet.

Notoriety.

Removal.

Popularity.

his fame far and near through all the country; and, from the miracles he was said to perform, he now got the title of *Buzurg*, in addition to that of *Akhûn*, which he had acquired some years before.

Saintship.

Whilst he was at Salimkhan, in 1835, the Sikhs and Afghans were at war, and the Amir, Dost Mahomad Khan, hearing of his fame, invited him to join his camp, then at the mouth of the Khaibar pass. The Akhûn set out with a considerable gathering of "Ghazis" and "Taliban-ul-ilm," and added to their number on his journey along the foot of the hills; so that when he joined the Amir's camp, he had with him quite a small army of noisy champions for the faith: mostly, however, unarmed.

Joins the Army of Kabul Amir.

His followers.

The Amir's subsequent encounter with the Sikhs proved a decided failure. His army, without waiting the shock of battle, fled back to Kabul in disorder, and the Akhûn, also panic-struck, fled to Bajawar with only a few adherents. These, after a time, also deserted him; and, left alone, he now resumed his early wandering habits, and at length, finding hospitable shelter, settled at Kaldarra, in the Ranizai hills. Here he made many friends, and rapidly regained his former celebrity; and, after a few years' stay, moved up to Saidu, in Swat, where the people gave him a portion of land for his own and his disciples' support. This has been his residence ever since. Soon after settling here, the Akhûn married a woman of the Naikbikhail division of the Akozai clan of

Their flight.

In Ranizai.

At Saidu.

Marries.

Yusufzai, and by her has had two sons. At Saidu, the Akhûn is surrounded by murîds, who live in the village and perform his various commands, attend to and feed the crowds of devotees who daily flock to the "master," and through them circulate wonderful lies.

Miracles.

It is said that the Akhûn daily feeds hundreds of visitors, cures them of all sorts of diseases, and grants their desires in all their multitudinous variety, and all this without the aid of any visible means; for in outward appearance he is very poor, takes no tithes or taxes from the country, and steadily refuses the offerings of the devotees flocking to him from all the adjacent countries. Funds or food and clothing are never wanting to meet the necessities of any number of devotees who may gather at his threshold.

Poverty.

Impostures.

The Akhûn is held in the highest reverence, and believed in as an undoubted *Buzurg*, by the bulk of eastern Afghans. Most wonderful stories are related of his miracles and saintly virtues, which it is idle here to dwell on. They are, however, most firmly believed in by the bulk of the people, despite their absurdly incredulous, and impossible character.

Failings.

It is more wonderful that the people, thus misled, have not yet discovered that their "Buzurg," with all his saintly and miraculous powers, has as yet done nothing to ameliorate their wretched condition, either moral, physical, or social, by a single whit.

Professions and conduct.

The Akhûn professes devotion to the word of God as revealed to Mahomad. He leads a life of devotion, humility, temperance, and charity, and holds aloof from all worldly occupations. Though by no means a man of letters, or learned in theology, he is, nevertheless, consulted in all cases of religious controversy amongst the Sunni Mahomadans of the countries around, and his decision is accepted as final and the law. He also now issues circular edicts regarding religious ceremonies and secular observances. These are acted on and considered as binding as the *Shariat*, which, indeed, they are considered to be by his followers.

Doctrine.

His doctrine is opposed to that of the Mujahidins of Mahaban, whom he has decreed to be *Wahabis* or heretics. The difference, as far as I can understand, exists in the Akhûn's doctrines being tolerant and liberal, whilst those professed by the Mujahidins are intolerant and puritanical.

Conclusion.

Before concluding this chapter, which has already exceeded the limits intended, it only remains to note some of the chief events during the period between the advance of the Sikhs to Peshawar and the arrival of the British as the rulers of the country; and this need occupy but a few lines.

The Sikhs.

As before mentioned, the Sikhs became masters of the Peshawar valley in 1823, by their victory over the united tribes in the battle of Nowshaira. Their tenure of this new conquest, however, though secured by a strong garrison at Peshawar was only characterized by the severity of their rule, the ruinous exactions of their revenue collectors, and the desolating results of their military movements about the country, for their occupation of the valley was far from undisputed or quiet. In 1824, Hari Singh marched through Yusufzai to exact revenue and punish the tribes for their turbulence. A few years later, under Budh Singh, the Sikhs again visited Yusufzai on a similar errand.

The Afghans.

In 1835, Dost Mahomad Khan came down from Kabul to fight the Sikhs. His troops, however, retreated without meeting the enemy, but not before they had plundered the whole country as far as the Indus.

A couple of years later, the Kabul ruler again came down to face the Sikhs. He is more successful than in his previous expedition, kills the Sikh General, Hari Singh, at Jamrûd, pushes on to the Indus, and returns to Kabul through Yusufzai, having squeezed from the unfortunate peasants what little the Sikhs had failed to extract. He and his Durranis departed laden with the curses of the people, who declare them to have been greater tyrants than the Sikhs.

The British.

About this time, Sir Alexander Burnes arrived at Kabul. His mission led to the advance of a British army into these lands in 1838. In 1841 occurred the memorable revolt at Kabul. In the year following came the avenging army under General Pollock. His troops performed their work well, and returned within the British territory only in time to join in the Sikh campaigns that brought us into the Punjab in 1845-46, and ended with the establishment of the British rule through all the country, as far as Peshawar, in 1849.

CHAPTER III.

ANTIQUITIES.

THE country of the Yusufzais, throughout its extent, abounds in the most interesting antiquities; ruins and relics of long-past races, who ruled and dwelt in the strong fortresses and populous cities, the remains and ruined heaps of which alone now exist to tell of the arts, science, and civilization of their original founders. Of these ruins, some of the most extensive and interesting are beyond the British limits, and, consequently, also beyond the reach of examination; but there is still a very large field within the border, the examination of which would well repay the researches of any one versed in archæology. To a description of some of these, the following notice mainly refers.

Abundant in Yusufzai.

Require to be explored.

Tho antiquities in Yusufzai may be classed under two separate chronological heads, as "Ancient Ruins," and "Modern Ruins," which possess also different architectural characters.

Of different classes.

The former class are, without exception, the relics of different bye-gone idolatrous nations, whilst the latter, on the other hand, are of comparatively recent date, and all of Mahomadan origin.

Ancient ruins.

The ancient ruins appear to be mostly of Budhist origin,

Budhist origin.

if not of even more ancient date; for, in the time of Alexander, which was antecedent to the Budhist era, this region was peopled by Indian tribes, who had many strong or extensive fortresses in commanding parts of the highland tracts, the attack and capture of which so greatly added to the Macedonian conqueror's fame. Though the sites of these scenes of his former triumphs are now unknown, there are some still to be recognized as the actual relics of Alexander's achievements.

Alexander's visit.

According to the account given by Curtius, Alexander, on advancing from Kabul towards India, with one division of his army, took the route through the highland tract forming the northern boundary of the Peshawar valley, whilst the other division he sent forward, under Hephæstion and Perdiccas, by the direct route to the Indus. Taxiles, the chief of the country they were to pass through, accompanied this division.

His route.

Between the rivers Choes and Euaspla, says Curtius, Alexander beseiged a city defended by a double wall. On its capture, he left Craterus to complete the reduction of the district, and himself moved on to the country between the Euaspla and the Guræus. In this country, which, without doubt, is the present Bajawar, Alexander's troops fought several severe battles with the warlike and hardy inhabitants, whom they must have thoroughly vanquished to have taken, as Curtius says they did, forty thousand prisoners and two hundred and thirty thousand head of various kinds of cattle. The oxen were of such superior size and activity that Alexander, selecting some of the finest, sent them to Macedonia to improve the breed there.

From this country, Alexander, fording the Guræus, entered

the country between it and the Suastus, the chief city of which was Massaga. This fortified city was captured, but not without very brave and persevering exertions, for its garrison fought with obstinate courage till the death of their leader, when they surrendered and evacuated the citadel. At night they attempted to escape into the hills, but were pursued, overtaken, and put to the sword.

Massaga.

The scene of these occurrences can, I believe, be recognized in the valley of Talash, where are extensive ruins of massive fortifications and other buildings, that are described as covering the surface for some miles along the brow of a steep range of hills. These ruins are still called Gûrî, and the natives have many legendary tales of the *Kafirs* who built and dwelt in them. They are on the south side of the Talash glen, and eight or nine miles from the left bank of the river Guroeus, which there can be no doubt is the modern Panjkora, whilst the Suastus is evidently the Swat stream. The route from Swat to Bajawar from the remotest ages has been through the Talash glen, over the hill pass on its north boundary, and down to the village of Shûkowli, on the bank of the Panjkora river. Here in the winter the stream is forded across to Garrarai; in the hot weather, the passage is effected on rafts of inflated ox-hides.

Sited in the Talash valley.

Route from Swat to Bajawar.

Whilst engaged in the seige of Massaga, Alexander detached a body of troops for the reduction of Bezira and Ora, which have been recognized by Abbott in the modern Baja and Hoond on the Yusufzai plain. The inhabitants of these populous towns fled to their stronghold in the hills, the celebrated rock Aornos. The site of this rock fortress the last authority places on a spur

Ora and Bezira.

Aornos.

of the Mahaban, above the village of Amb. I am assured by natives of the country that there are still existent, on the site above-indicated, the ruins of an extensive rock-built fortress, very difficult of access by reason of the rugged nature of the surface. There is also a popular tradition in the country, derived, I believe, from the "Sikandar Nama," that Alexander actually did cross the Indus by a ford at the foot of the hill alluded to, passing from Amb across to Darband in Hazara. The tradition relates how he gained possession of the hitherto impregnable fortress through the miraculous intervention of a native ascetic he met with on the spot.

Mahaban.

The whole of the Mahaban mountain, as well as the chain of hills generally bounding the Peshawar valley, abound in the ruins of ancient fortresses, and cities of great strength and extent.

Its ruins.

On Mount Mahaban, the largest ruins are those of Mounts Banj, Shakot, and Dakâra; and there are numerous others all along the hill boundary of the Yusufzai plain.

Their origin.

Of these ancient ruins in Yusufzai, all that I have had an opportunity of seeing bear the marks of a Hindu origin in excess of others. Some of them yield Greek coins, as those of Baja in the plain (where I have myself found them) and Barikot and other villages of Swat, but most of them shew signs of a successive ownership by different though allied nations as regards religious constitution.

Coins.

The coins and other antiques found in these ruins, prove the successive existence in this country, and passing away from it, of Greeks, Græco-Bactrians, Indo-Bactrians, Scythians, and Brahmins, previous to the arrival of the Mahomadans with their destroying and devastating principles, the action of which has reduced these former abodes of civilization and prosperity to their present state of ruin and neglect.

Kinds of ruins.

These ruins, the numbers of which have already been alluded to, may, for convenience of description, be divided into six principal classes, each of which will need a few words of separate notice. They are—1. Rock inscriptions; 2. Cave temples; 3. Hermit cells; 4. Idol temples and cities; 5. Topes and monasteries; and, 6. Walled cities and villages.

Rock inscriptions.

I. ROCK INSCRIPTIONS.—Of this class I know of only two instances that have hitherto been met with in the Yusufzai country. One is the celebrated *lât*, at the village of Shabazgarrhi, and the other a fragment of inscribed rock found at Zihdih.

Budhist Lât.

The former is a great mass of rock covered on two sides with well-preserved inscriptions. It lies at the base of a low ridge of hills amongst a heap of lesser rocks and loose boulders. Some thirty or more years ago, this inscription was copied and published in Europe by Mr. Masson. It is supposed to be one of those pillar edicts issued by Asoka, publishing the establishment of the Budhist faith as the State religion about 250 B. C.

Its age.

Detached from the rest of the inscription, and in the upper left corner of the rock as it now lies, are five lines of writing, in a space of about four feet by three feet of the surface.

The writing.

These letters are very clear and distinct, each about three inches long, and free from the black mixture which covers the rest of the rock, and which has evidently been applied for the purpose of taking a copy of the writing. From its detached position, these few lines of writing appear to form a heading setting forth the contents of the inscription which covers the rest of the rock on that surface, an extent of some sixteen feet by eight feet.

Its character.

Beginning at the first line, from left to right, the letters of this detached inscription are as follows :—

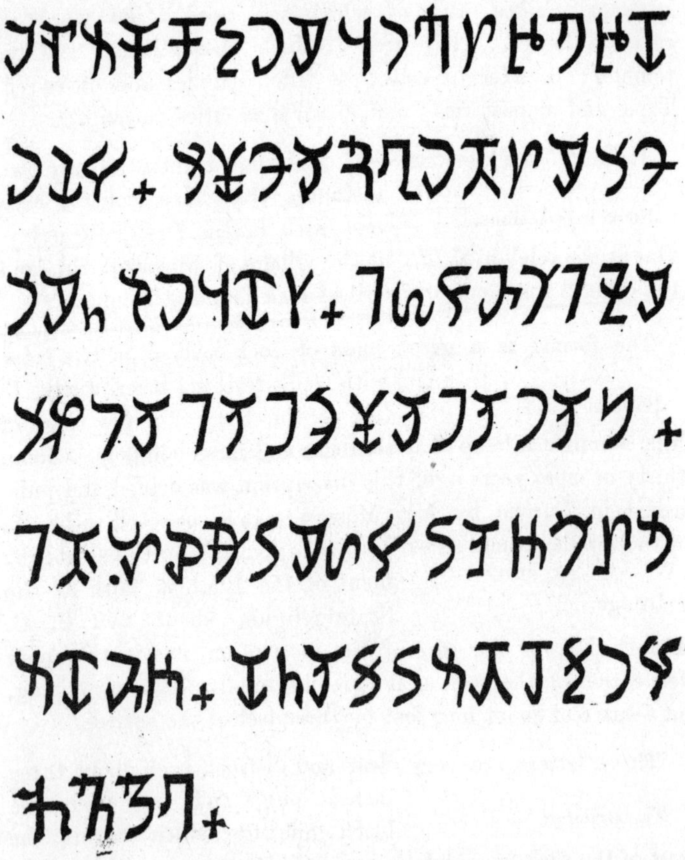

The above is an accurate copy. The small crosses mark the termination of each line.

From the way the letters run, and the present position of the rock, it would appear that this extensive inscription was carved after the rock had fallen down to its present site from the top of the hill. Had the rock been standing upright at the time the letters were carved on it, the writing would read from the base up one face and over its top; but, as the rock now lies, the writing extends along one side or face on to the contiguous smaller surface at the end, which, were the block placed upright, would face upwards to the skies. As the rock now lies, all the writing can be read by any one walking round it; but, on the other hand, if the rock were placed upright, a considerable portion of the writing would be out of sight, and inaccessible.

Position of the rock.

At the foot of the hill, and only a few paces north from the inscribed rock, is a huge upright block of compact amygdaloid trap-rock, which attracts attention by its dimensions and isolation from the rest of the hill. On examination its under surface is found to have been artificially excavated into an irregular dome-shaped cavity, capacious enough to hold four or five men seated. It is supposed to be one of those hermit cells in which the Budhist ascetic loved to pass away his life in naked and solitary contemplation and abstraction.

Curious boulder.

On a detached eminence of rock, about two hundred yards to south-west from this boulder, is a square platform, shaped by great slabs of blue slate, piled above one another, wherever deficiencies in the underlying rock required filling up to complete the level of the surface and the outline of the platform. With this exception, there are now no other remains of walls or buildings discernible, though the irregular position of many of the blocks of slate, and the masses of debris lying around, indicate that the site has at some time past received very rough treatment. From its position, outline, and general resemblance to other more perfect ruins of the kind, this is probably the site of an ancient Budhist monastery or convent.

Other ruins.

In Babar's memoirs of his journey through this district, in the latter half of the sixteenth century, he mentions that whilst encamped at Shahbazgarrhi, some of his troops levelled with the ground a *ziarat,* or sacred shrine, dedicated to the memory of Shabaz *Kalandar,* because it had been built on unhallowed ground, defiled by the previous existence on it of a Pagan temple.

Their history.

According to Akhûn Darwaiza, the ziarat of Shabaz Kalandar was built by the Musalmans only some thirty years or so previous to Babar's visit. It was close to the village of Shahbazgarrhi, which derives its name from the Kalandar who it appears lived and died in it in the odour of the purest sancity. The site and present state of ruin of the platform above-described correspond exactly with the above details.

And origin.

The village itself occupies the extremity of a low spur of bare rocks that project westward on to the plain from the isolated Karamar hill. It is built on the actual ruins of an ancient stone-built town, and the foundations of some of the former houses still exist in tolerable formation in different parts of the modern mud-built village. That this site was in past times occupied by Budhist and Hindu races, is proved by the coins still found in excavating the soil round the old walls.

Adjoining village.

The other instance of rock inscription mentioned as met with in this district, was a small block, some eight feet by three feet. It was discovered a couple of years ago by the Revd. I. Loewenthal, who extricated it from under a dung-heap in the village of Zihdih. The inscription only occupied a portion of the block; this was broken off and subsequently sent to the Peshawar museum. The writing has suffered a good deal; many of the letters are hardly to be traced, and others have become quite obliterated.

Another rock inscription.

They appear to be of the same character as those on the Shahbazgarrhi rock, but are not so clearly, neatly, or regularly carved. The inscription occupies three irregular lines of unequal length.

The writing.

The annexed is a close copy of the letters I was able to trace; those that are untraceable or obliterated, are marked by small dots. The crosses mark the end of each line.

Its copy.

II. CAVE TEMPLES.—Of these there is a splendid instance in the Pajah hill, a high ridge, which, emanating from the Sinawar peak, separates the valley of Sudhum from that of Lunkhwar. The cave is called by the natives the "Kashmir Cavern," (*Kashmir Smûts,*) from a popular notion that it communicates by a subterranean passage with that country. It is situated near the summit of the Sikri ridge of Pajah, and is best approached from the village of Babozai in the Lunkhwar valley, from which it is distant about six miles. Its entrance faces the west, and is high up in the face of a precipitous cliff. The opening is an irregular, natural archway, some fifty feet high and forty feet wide at the base. The approach to the entrance is most difficult and dangerous; it conducts along the side of a perpendicular cliff by a very narrow and steep foot-path. In the gulf below are masses of debris and loose stones, probably the thrown down materials of the former causeway, of which some vestiges remain near the entrance to the cave.

Cave Temples.

Kashmir Cave.

Its approach.

The interior of the cavern is of grand dimensions. For the most part it is a natural excavation; but in many parts the handiwork of man is also plainly discernible.

Its interior.

A few paces within the entrance, and on the right hand, are the remains of strong stone walls, which are traceable in the form of a succession of small square chambers. They extend along the side of the rock for a distance of between fifty and sixty paces.

Stone walls.

On the left hand, and facing these ruined little chambers is a clear level space covered with a layer of pigeons' and bats' dung, from which here and there project the corners of some of the

Level space.

many stone slabs hidden underneath. In the further corner of this space is a masonry tank, about sixteen feet long by ten feet wide; and at the time I saw it, fully ten feet deep. This tank is still in excellent preservation, and its sides shew it to have been built of chiselled and accurately adapted stones, cemented with lime and mortar. The floor was dry and covered with a layer of bats' dung, the depth of which was not ascertained; though, judging from the thickness of these accumulations in other parts of the cave, the layer at the bottom of the tank is probably not less than three feet thick.

Masonry tank.

Between this tank on the left and the debris of walls on the right, and about seventy or eighty paces from the mouth of the cavern, is the commencement of a flight of steps, built of thin slabs of slate cemented with a coarse mortar, and balustraded on either side by a low wall of the same materials. It was not easy to count these steps, owing to the destruction of some and the concealment of others by masses of superjacent debris, met with at frequent intervals. From beginning to end, they are probably not less than 300 in number. The flight follows the course of the cavern, which, for the first half of its extent, proceeds northwards, and then curves round to the east and south-east.

Flight of steps.

From a few paces within the entrance of the cavern up to its curve, all is in pitchy darkness, and full of dangers to one advancing without the aid of torches. Beyond the curve, light is seen in the distant front; and, on arrival at the top of the flight of steps, is seen to pour in through an artificial opening in the roof of an extensive domed chamber, mostly of natural construction, but partly enlarged and shaped by artificial excava-

Darkness.

Light.

This dome is of imposing dimensions, very lofty and spacious. It contains, besides a well-preserved building, some ten feet square, at the top of the flight of steps, a confused and extensive mass of the debris of broken walls, &c., which here and there rise in heaps from below the masses of pigeons' and bats' dung, the accumulation of centuries, and everywhere three or four feet deep. The space enclosing all these ruins is irregularly circular. The opening near the top of the dome, though to appearance small, is in reality of wide dimensions, for bushes grow on its sides, and whole flocks of pigeons whirled in front of it during our visit, in the excitement of fright and curiosity at our unexpected intrusion.

Domed space.

Its contents.

Aperture.

Except towards its end, the flight of steps does not rise much above the surface of the floor of the cave, for the cave itself inclines upwards; but, at the end of the flight, the rise is steep and abrupt, and, perhaps, thirty feet above the floor of the cave, below the small chamber in which it terminates.

Slope of ground.

Near the commencement of this sudden rise, and on the left hand, is a branch cave, which, proceeding towards the north a few paces, suddenly contracts into a low and dark passage. This, after a further progress of a few paces, we found so restricted and narrow as to prevent our passage, though crawling on hands and knees. In this branch cave, with the aid of our torches, we were enabled to trace the remains of walls and a small flight of steps.

Branch cave.

The interior of this cavern is very extensive, and, without doubt, especially at its entrance and upper parts, contains a number of buildings, the configuration and

Extent of cavern.

Hasty visit. *Its consequences.*

contents of which are hidden from view under dense masses of the accumulations already referred to. Our visit was necessarily a hasty one, owing to an anticipated surprise by the tribes beyond the border, on the verge of whose limits the cave is situated. We consequently had not the leisure to search for idols or other remains to prove the correctness or otherwise of our surmises as to the religious character of the place and its Budhist relations. Even had we leisure, it is doubtful whether in our unprepared state we could have investigated much; for the stifling and overpowering effects of the dry pulverulent deposits, now disturbed by the footsteps of our party, quite forbade its further agitation, and we were glad again to get into the fresh air to recover from its nauseating effects.

Ruined city.

On a projecting spur of the hill, directly opposite to and a little way below the level of the cave, are the remains of a compact little city, many of the buildings of which overtop tremendous precipices. In most parts the walls, though roofless, still stand in very good preservation. Indeed, a few small detached chambers still remain roofed with domes of stone, cemented with coarse lime and gravel mortar. But little labour would render the place again habitable; for, in the gorge beneath, are clumps of trees and fresh springs.

The walls. *Sculptures.*

The walls of the various buildings have been built of stone quarried on the spot, and put together apparently without any intervening plaister; the interspaces between the larger stones being filled with accurately adjusted slips of smaller size. From its position, general appearance, and the numerous fragments of idols strewed over the surface, this was probably in former times a priest city. We could trace the outlines of a monastery, but no building like a temple was discernible.

Route.

The approach to this cave from the plain is, by the route we took, a circuitous path. On leaving the plain near Babozai, we travelled up the bed of a rough mountain drain for about a mile and a half; then, turning westward, we climbed up the face of a high perpendicular cliff, at the top of which we came upon an artificial causeway.

Causeway.

This is evidently a portion of the former road from the plain to the cave. Where we came upon it, it runs a level course for nearly half a mile along the side of a precipitous hill, is overhung by menacing crags above, and frowns over yawning chasms below. The road of this causeway is six feet wide everywhere, and leads upwards to a dip between two ledges of hills. Here we left it; and, descending the hollow, tracked along the rocky bed of a now dry mountain torrent overhung and embowered by a variety of trees on either side. This led us up to the dip between the cave and the ruined city, already described.

Springs.

In it are several clumps of trees and springs of water. We did not trace the causeway met about midway of our route either one way or the other; but, judging from similar roads in other localities, it is probable that this one led a more or less level, though winding, course along the brows of the hills intervening between the plain and the cave.

Hermit cells.

Doubts.

III. Hermit Cells.—These are generally met with in the vicinity of other ruins, and not, as one would have expected, in isolated positions far from the noise and bustle of society. This circumstance raises a doubt as to their really being what they are here styled, though no other equally probable supposition offers.

Character.

These supposed hermit cells are irregularly circular and dome-shaped cavities. They are excavated on the under surface of great boulders of rock that lie about the surface of the hills in detached lumps. They are entered by a low uneven opening next the ground, and are generally roomy enough to contain from four to a dozen men seated; but some are only roomy enough to contain one man, allowing him sleeping room.

Examples.

An instance of one of these hermit cells has already been mentioned as existing near the village of Shahbazgarrhi. Others are met with on the outskirts of the ruins of Ranigatt, the ridge of hill between the hamlets of Amankot and Nawigram.

Uses.

Whatever they are, they bear a remarkable resemblance to one another, are evidently artificial formations, and are better suited to the use of the hermit than any other that suggests itself, especially in the absence of anything more palpably the resort and shelter of those ascetics and recluses whom the Budhist religion abstracted in such numbers from the world and the society of their fellow men, to devote their lives to a solitary and silent meditation. The usual Budhist ascetic's cell was a frail bower of the twigs and leaves, or the reeds and grasses nearest at hand in the forests and marshes they generally betook themselves to; but, in populous localities or their vicinity, where facilities existed for a more permanent kind of shelter and place of seclusion, it is not improbable that they were taken advantage of.

Idol temples.

IV. Idol Temples and Cities.—Of these there are a great number in Yusufzai and the neighbouring countries. The principal of those on the plain and bounding hills are at Mount Banj, Ranigatt, Jumâlgarrhi, Takht-i-Bahi and Kharkai, on hills, and Sâhari Bahlol, Bakhshalai, and Dairi Likpani, on the plain.

Banj ruins.

The ruins at Mount Banj are described as very extensive, and situated at the very top of the hill. There are the remains of massive walls and fragments of idols and other sculptures lying about the surface, and the openings of subterranean passages are met with at different spots.

Other ruins.

Character.

The ruins at Ranigatt, Jumâlgarrhi, and Takht-i-Bahi, I have several times visited. In each the architectural character of the buildings is the same. The houses are all built of massive stone walls, and were mostly double-storied, the upper being entered from the outside by a flight of stone steps built up with the wall. The space beneath these steps is generally enclosed in the form of an arched cell. Most of the houses, where detached, consist of only two rooms, one above the other; but, in positions where there is a sufficiency of level surface, they are in the form of quadrangles, with rooms along each side opening into a centralcourtyard.

Arches.

In all the arches are of the same pattern, narrow, high and obtusely pointed, and formed

by the slabs of stone on either side overlapping each other till they meet in the central one, supported by both sides. The annexed diagram illustrates the formation of these arches. Some of them support a very massive superstructure. The idols, coins, carvings, and decorations met with in these ruins are also all of one character, a mixture of Budhist and Hindu remains. With these general remarks as preface, we will now briefly describe each of the ruins separately.

Takht-i-Bahi. These ruins are very extensive, and still in very good preservation. They occupy the crest and northern slope of the Takht-i-Bahi hill, a spur which, projecting westward from the Pajah ridge, traverses the plain for several miles, and separates the valley of Lunkhwar from that of Sudhum. The ruins occupy the western end of this ridge, which is a bare ledge of grey mica and quartz schists, about three hundred feet above the plain, and cover about a mile of surface along a central crest between terminal eminences on the east and west. On these are the boundary buildings of the city, the rest are on the intervening crest, and the ridges sloping down from it to the plain on the north. The hollows between these ridges are the natural drains of the hill.

Takht-i-Bahi.

Site.

The buildings on the eminences flanking the city on the east and west appear to have been positions of observation and defence. For from their elevation they completely overlook the city, and command an extensive view of the country around. They are compact square blocks, with rooms opening inwards on a central court. The walls are now only four or five feet above the surface, but they are very substantial, and everywhere four feet in thickness. Close to these blocks of buildings are two or more deep cellars of masonry, entered by a small opening in the roof, which is a

Form on flanks.

very flat dome. They appear to have served as grain stores. In these buildings we could discover no remains of idols or sculptures.

Crest of hill.

On the crest of the hill, and between the two flanking heights just alluded to, is a succession of detached quadrangles, the massive walls of which are still from six to eight feet high, and about forty feet each way. Along the inner side of each wall, is a series of small compartments, each opening by a doorway into the court-yard in the centre.

Topes.

Close to each of these quadrangles, and only a few paces distant, is a well-defined circular mass of masonry raised about two feet above the surface, and about fourteen feet in diameter. The debris around is rich in fragments of idols, and carved slabs of slate; and beyond these are the indistinct remains of a wall enclosing the circular platform in a square. These circular platforms are probably the ruined and excavated foundations of former *topes*, whilst the adjoining quadrangles were the monasteries of the monks devoted to their care and services.

Plan.

The annexed diagram illustrates their formation:—

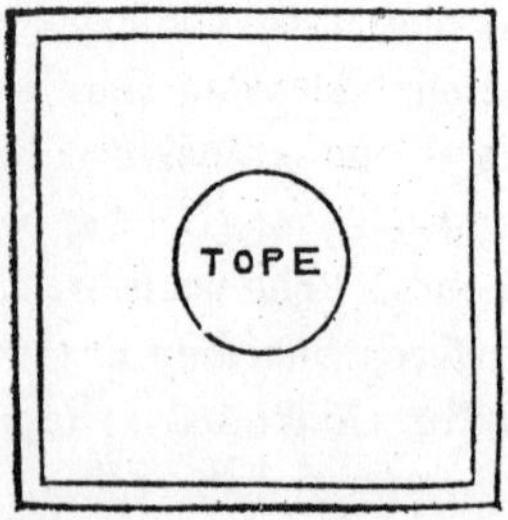

Commanding position.

From their position, these quadrangles (there are five or six of them along the crest of the hill) command an extensive prospect of all the country around. Their ruins in part are still discernible from the plain on the south of the hill; and, in their perfect state, they must have been prominent objects of attraction from a considerable distance around.

Causeway.

The southern slope of the hill on which stand these ruins, is steep and abrupt right down to the plain. In its upper part are some small detached huts of well-made stone walls, and below these is traceable at intervals the line of a causeway that zigzagged to the plain. In some parts it is interrupted by a few steps, and in others has been built up the sides of precipices. In its upper part for a short distance, the causeway is tolerably entire, and forms a road four feet wide and with an easy ascent.

Buildings.

The great mass of the buildings of this ancient city are clumped together on the three ridges that course down to the plain on the north side of the hill, and are also scattered over the upper portion of the intermediate space.

Different kinds.

The ruins on the central ridge are different in character from the rest; we will, therefore, describe them separately after noticing those on either side.

Dwelling-houses.

The majority of the houses on the two side ridges, as well as on the upper part of the central ridge, are two storied. In most the walls are still from ten to thirty feet high, and very strongly and accurately built of stone, apparently quarried on the spot. No mortar seems to have been used to bind them together. They are placed one over another, and the crevices and gaps between are accurately filled with thin chips of the slaty material composing the larger blocks. Over all was applied a thick coating of coarse, gravelly mortar, patches of which still cling to the walls in many parts.

Double storied.

Most of the houses consist of only two small rooms, about ten feet square, and one above the other. Horizontal rows of holes opposite to each other on the inside of the walls mark the sockets in which rested the beams forming the ceiling of the lower and floor of the upper rooms. The latter was always reached by a flight of steps, built into the outer side of one wall, and covering a narrow arched cell, which seems to have served as the residence of a watchman.

Present condition.

In their present condition all the houses are roofless, and not a bit of timber is be found in the whole extent of the ruins. The small size of the rooms in all the houses, leads to the conclusion that timber of large dimensions was then, as it is now, scarce, or entirely absent in the vicinity. The only roofed chambers in these parts of the ruins are the cells beneath the steps conducting to the upper story. They are eight or nine feet long by four wide, and seven high in the centre of the arch. The entrance is by a low doorway, above which in some is a window about eighteen inches by eight, which, like those in the houses, has the inner lower edge bevelled downwards so as to throw the light direct on the floor.

Scattered over the hill.

Some of the houses are clumped close together, but most of them are on detached rocks wherever they offer sufficient level surface.

Scattered amongst the dwelling-houses, but separate from

Curious buildings.

them, are several instances of a curious building, the use of which is not at once very apparent, though they offer equal indications for two distinct suppositions as to their probable use.

Shape.

In their present state, they are massive structures of masonry, some six feet square, about a foot high towards the rise of the hill, and from four to eight feet deep on the side above the slope of the hill. In the centre of the structure, is a circular basin-like cavity, about two feet diameter above, and narrowing downwards to an aperture that communicates by a short passage with an outlet at the base, which gradually widens as it opens on the receding slope of the hill. This outlet bears a striking resemblance to the space under the grating of the fire-trough in a furnace. This is the chief indication that leads to the supposition that these structures may possibly be the remains of fire-altars; for the position of the outlet, its direction and form, all adapt it for the purpose of raking away ashes and admitting a current of air upwards. The most serious objection to this supposition, however, is the fact of there being no signs of even a moderate supply of fuel being obtainable within many miles of the hill, at least in its present condition, and there are no data for the supposition that it was less barren then than it is now.

Uses.

Suppositions.

Supposition.

The other conjecture as to the use of these structures is that they were public privies. Their position amongst the dwelling-houses, and far away from the temples, and their situation on the edges of the natural drainage channels of the hill, besides their admirably adapted structure, favour this idea.

On the lower part of the central spur, the ground rises into a flat eminence before again suddenly dropping in a precipice to the foot of the hill. This space is occupied by the most important and most interesting part of the whole of the ruins. In their fresh state, these buildings must have been an imposing sight. Even now in most parts the walls are lofty and massive. In some places they rise fully fifty feet against the slope of the hill before projecting above the level of the upper surface of the spur.

Central spur.

This pile of buildings, as a whole, consists of two distinct sets, or blocks, separated by a small intervening space of level ground, which was probably a thoroughfare through the buildings.

Buildings.

The upper division is occupied by a very curious idol temple. Its different parts are arranged in a quadrangular form enclosing a space, in the centre of which is an elevated square platform. This platform is now about five feet high and twelve feet square. It is built of large flat stones piled one above the other, and apparently without cement. The sides are decorated with cornices and recesses. In the latter were fixed slabs of slate covered with sculptures in high relief. The top of this platform, which is now excavated and uneven, appears to have been a level surface; for, in the centre of the north side is a much-injured flight of steps leading to the top, which, as already stated, has been destroyed by the excavations of the curious in search of coins and idols.

Upper set.

Description.

Of the latter, a multitude of fragments cover the surface around. Some of these fragments represent portions of human figures, mostly draped and in the erect pos-

Idols.

ture; but the majority by far are fragments of the scenes sculptured on tablets of blue slate, which appear to have once occupied the niches in the sides of the central platform and its enclosing walls. These scenes seem to be representations of various religious and domestic ceremonies, judging from the positions and acts of the many figures represented in them.

Recesses.

Along each side of the quadrangle, and facing one side of the platform in the centre of its court, is a row of semi-cylindrical recesses, each domed at ten feet from the floor. These recesses appear to have formerly contained the gigantic human figures, the fragments of which now strew the surface around. Above each of them is a circular ring of masonry. This is again surmounted by another similar recess to the one below, but of smaller size. Its dome also is surrounded by a ring of masonry. The upper recesses probably held the seated figures of which the fragments mingle with the debris below. In none of the recesses, either large or small, are any figures found "in situ." The whole series are so arranged that the figures placed in them must have faced the platform already described.

Sculptures.

Most of the fragments of sculpture, apart from the scene tablets, appear to have belonged to statues representing the same individual in varied proportions and attitudes; and all are carved in the same style on the same material—a soft, blue micaceous slate of coarse texture. These figures are supposed to be representations of BUDH. Some of them, however, are marked by the Hindu *tika* on the forehead; but in these the features and drapery, &c., are varied.

Their size.

From fragments of the extremities and shoulders, &c., met with in the debris, some of these figures must have stood at least seven feet high. I have also met with fragments of plaister (coarse lime and sand) moulds that must have belonged to statues of a gigantic size. A hand, a foot, and portion of the head, in this composition, were fully four times the natural size; and, to allow for faulty sculpturing, must have belonged to statues not less than, I should think, sixteen feet high. These huge figures probably occupied positions outside the portals of the temple above described, for their fragments are only found outside its limits, on the space between the temple and the buildings next to be described.

Gateway.

From the court of the temple, and towards the north, a flight of six or eight steps in ruins conducts to a passage between high walls. These are now much decayed; but, at the further end, apparently the original entrance gateway, they still rise some twelve feet high. This passage is about twelve paces long by three wide, and on each side of it are the remains of former recesses for the reception of idol figures. Like the temple, this passage bears no traces of ever having been roofed. It conducts from the temple northwards, through the gateway alluded to, on to an open space intervening between it and the pile of buildings on the end of the ridge. This space is of small extent, and is now covered with the debris of fallen walls and broken sculptures, amongst which a few thorny bushes have taken root in beds of sheeps' dung; a deposit which here, as in other parts of these ruins, marks the spots on which the shepherds of the district have been in the habit of penning their sheep.

Open space.

Subterranean chambers.

In different parts of this space are some holes, which, from their unevenness, are evidently the result of decay; for, on examination, they are found to lead into arched subterranean passages, at intervals on each side of which are small apertures communicating with low, dark, and arched cells. We crawled into three of these chambers, and found them all alike, about eight feet square by five feet high, which are also the dimensions in breadth and height of the passages. All are in a tolerable state of preservation. The proper and original entrances to these subterranean passages, of which there are three or four, if not more, under these buildings, are by separate arched openings on the western slope of the spur, some feet below the level of its upper surface. Amongst the heaps of debris covering the surface of this slope, it was impossible to trace any pathway to these entrances.

Their entrances.

Beyond the open space covering these underground cells, is an extensive pile of buildings, consisting of two great quadrangles adjoining each other, and very much alike. Both shew the walls of small chambers along each side, and opening on to a central court. In the debris here, as in the ruins on the other parts of the hill, idols or their fragments are not met with.

Lower set.

These buildings were probably the monasteries in which lived the priests devoted to the idol temple hard by. One can imagine them issuing from their chambers, crossing the intervening space to the gateway of the temple, traversing its passage, and ascending the steps into the courtyard of the temple; here, at the threshold, making their obeisance to the assembly of the gods; and then, assending the platform, walking round its top repeating prayers and obeisances and sacrificing incense or offerings to each individually, and then retiring for meditation to the solemn and dark silence of their subterranean cells.

Monasteries.

These monasteries are built on the very extremity of the hill spur. On three sides the walls rise up the precipitous slopes from far below the level of its upper surface. In some parts, the walls, though only projecting from

Structure.

four to sixteen feet above the surface, are from top to bottom a clear perpendicular drop of fully sixty feet.

Open square.

The western of the two quadrangles here described faces the idol temple. In front of the eastern quadrangle is a square space continuous through a gateway with the space between the temple and the west quadrangle. On its eastern side between lofty walls, on which are extensive patches of mortar plaister and traces of new additions to the original walls, is a gateway leading down by a small flight of steps to a causeway that winds eastward up the side of the hill, and becomes lost in the ruins of the houses there. It was probably the original road of access to the temple for the population of the city above.

Recesses.

On its southern side, and facing the quadrangle, as also on each side of the east and west gateways, are the traces of a series of domed recesses for idols. Most of these are very imperfect below, but above the walls appear fresh, and, more or less, still retain a coating of plaister. On these walls there are no decorations whatever.

Extent of ruins.

The entire ruins of Takhti Bahi, exclusive of the temple, contain between 180 and 200 houses.

Reservoirs.

On the ridge of the hill between the eastern and western limits of the city are two artificial reservoirs for water. One of these, on the crest itself, is about eight feet square and built of masonry. Its cavity is nearly completely filled up with debris. The other is a few yards below the crest of the hill, on its northern face and western end of the city. It is about fourteen feet square and twenty feet deep, and is excavated out of the solid rock. The floor is covered with a layer of soil, on which a couple of fig trees have taken root, and now struggle out their tops through the opening above. From the appearances of the site, it is probable this reservoir was excavated over a natural spring. Besides these there is another reservoir at the foot of the hill where it joins the plain on the north, and under the centre of the city. This is the outlet of a natural spring artificially enlarged. It still contains water, but in very small quantity; hardly a couple of gallons well up at its mouth in the month of February. In the hot weather, I believe, it is perfectly dry. Such a reservoir is in the colloquial called *Bahai*; hence the name of the hill and its ruins.

Tradition.

A curious tradition is current amongst the people of the country in connection with this *Bahai*, to the effect that it communicates with the Indus by some underground channel, and that its waters are similarly affected with those of the "father of rivers." That is to say, when the Indus is clear and calm, so is the Bahai; when the Indus becomes flooded, and flows a stream of turbulent muddy waters, the Bahai is agitated by a whirlpool, and overflows its brim. It is even added that large timbers are sometimes found whirling in its eddy, and are thrown out on the plain! Except a fig tree, and a few thorny bushes around its opening, there is nothing in the appearance of the place to indicate any constant or great supply of water. Except these reservoirs (there may be others in the ruins besides those noticed), there appears to have been no other source of water-supply for the population of the city above described; nor, as far as is known, are there any signs of perennial springs having at former periods existed on other parts of the hill—the present utterly bare aspect of which appears to have been its original condition,—for there are no symptoms of any soil fit for the support of vegetation, except at its base.

Water supply.

Who the founders and first inhabitants of this city were is not clear, though the probabilities are in favor of the Budhists. A large proportion of the sculptures are Budhist. Those of Hindu origin, marked with the *tika*, are probably, like the additions and alterations in the walls near the temple, of subsequent date. According to the Hindus in this country, these ruins were formerly the residence of Raja Bharât and the Pândû kings. Hindu relics in abundance are met with in the ruins, such as small copper coins, with a rampant lion on one side and an elephant, superscribed with Sanscrit letters on the other; also small agate and larger slate beads of the Hindu rosary, or *mala*, are found in great numbers, as well as fragments of different kinds of red pottery.

Founders.

Hindu account.

This city is said by the traditions of the people to have been sacked and burned by Mahmud, of Ghazni, and since then abandoned as a habitation by man.

Destruction.

II. THE JAMALGARRHI RUINS.—These very much resemble those of Takhti Bahi, though neither so extensive nor grand, nor possessing so fine a temple. They occupy the crest of a bare ridge of rock some 200 feet above the plain, and directly opposite the village after which they are named. The hill belongs to the same ridge as Takhti Bahai, and possesses exactly the same physical characters. The ruins also are for the most part similar to those on Takhti Bahai, and need not, therefore, be here described.

Jamalgarrhi ruins.

About the centre of the ruins, and in proximity to a large quadrangular wall in ruins, is the base of a well-defined tope enclosed within a square of low walls, in the sides of which are niches for sculpture tablets, fragments

Tope.

of which and idols lie about the surface. This spot was excavated in 1852 by Colonel Lumsden, who found some very fine sculptures in a broken state. The heads of Budh were superiorly carved out of blue slate; and, from their size, must have belonged to statues at least eight feet high. The same coins and heads, &c., are found here as in the ruins of Takhti Bahi; and, like that hill, too, this ridge has no signs of former vegetation, or perennial springs; but at the foot of the hill, where it joins the plain, and in the bed of a natural water-course, is a deep, wide, and substantial masonry reservoir, still in good preservation, and always containing water throughout the year.

Sahri Bahlol.

III. THE SAHRI BAHLOL RUINS.—These are situated on the open plain, about a couple of miles south of the Takhti Bahi hill. They consist of a great mound encircled at 100 or 150 yards, or more, by a ring of low detached tumuli.

City.

The central mound is an artificial heap of earth some sixty feet high in the centre. Its surface is covered with a dense mass of loose stones and the debris of decayed walls. All are enclosed within an oblong wall of defence and fortification, with a gateway in each face. On the west face I cleared away the debris from part of this enclosing wall. It rises straight up from the level of the plain, and is built with surprising neatness and accuracy of slabs of the mica schist of the neighbouring Takhti Bahi hill.

Quadrangles.

The buildings on this mound are arranged in quadrangles with small chambers opening from each side on to a central courtyard, on one side of which is an entrance gateway. There are no signs of any idol temple or other religious edifice amongst this mass of ruins, nor are idols or sculptures found in their debris.

Everywhere the rooms are square and of small size, and

Chambers.

lead to the supposition that they were formerly domed, and not roofed with beams.

Granaries.

In different parts of these ruins, we came across masonry structures which we supposed to have been wells. I cleared one of these of the rubbish with which it was filled, and at eighteen feet down exposed a slate pavement. This was removed, and the excavation carried down to forty-five feet below the surface. Down to the slate floor, or pavement, the sides of the well, which is eight feet in diameter, are of masonry in very good preservation. Below the flooring there was no masonry, but the earth was compact and hard, and intermixed with it were fragments of red pottery and stone. Directly underneath the pavement was found a small idol representing Budh in a sitting posture. It is evident these structures were not meant for wells, and the deeper excavation proves the mound to have been of artificial formation. Some Hindus, on examining these structures, recognized them as grain stores, and assured me that similar buildings are very common in the cities of India under the name of *Khdon*. From the close packing of the houses, this city appears to have been densely peopled in the days of its prosperity.

Tumuli.

The ring of tumuli, mentioned as encircling this city, appear to have been the sites of a series of idol temples. On each the surface is strewed with fragments of red pottery, idols, and other sculptures; but the traces of former walls and edifices, if they exist, are hidden under the surface. Outside the line of these tumuli, and on the east of the city, is a splendid masonry well, dry at bottom, but eighteen feet diameter and upwards of eighty

Well.

feet deep. There are several such wells near the ruins of ancient cities in various parts of the plain.

Monastery and tope.

Quite detached from this city, and about 800 yards to its south, is a tope and monastery, both enclosed within a boundary wall of oblong shape, the outline of which is just traceable on the ground. I have excavated the whole of these ruins, and with the following results:—

The tope.

The tope is a bluntly conical tumulus, thirty-four feet high, and with a flat circular surface above, about sixteen feet in diameter. The base all round is completely enveloped in a dense layer of rubbish and loose stones, amongst which are found fragments of idols.

Exploration.

In examining this structure, the debris was removed on the east side, and a cutting on the level with the plain carried right through the whole substance of the tumulus to its centre. The mass throughout was composed of great slabs of the slaty rock of the adjacent hills, placed one above the other in intervening layers of clay and lime. Amongst these stones, as on the surface debris, were many masses of petrifactions. They are coarse, friable deposits of sulphate and carbonate of lime on bundles of twigs, whisps of straw, and small branches of some tree with a pithy centre. These petrifactions are so abundant, that amongst the other and so different stones, they at once attract attention and give rise to various surmises as to their origin; for, if naturally formed on the spot they are now found on, they indicate a very different previous condition of the place as regards wood and water, unless it be granted that they are the result of rain water percolating through the substance of the tope during many centuries. But of this having been the case there is no evidence, for the structure of the tope in its interior is firm and compact, and required hard work with the pick-axe to disintegrate it. The appearance of the spot is more in favor of its having been formerly very marshy ; for there are still stagnant pools in the vicinity, and the surface level is low. The dwellings on this spot also are all raised some feet above the level of the plain, on solid platforms contained within walls of masonry.

Form.

The outline of the tope is circular at the base, where are two ill-defined bands, one above the other, and three feet each in depth and width. Above these the top appears to have been a thick circular column surmounted by a domed mass, which, like the whole of the building, is of solid masonry.

Grave.

In the centre of this tope, and on a level with the ground, an oblong cavity lying north and south was dug into. Its sides were formed of loose stones partly fallen in and covering a quantity of ashes, fine dust that gave out a musty odour of the grave, and small bits of charcoal. On turning over these contents, a very strong sepulchral smell was noticed, and presently discovered to proceed from a quantity of human and other bones, all more or less broken up and crumbling.

Its contents.

From the corners of the cavity a few live toads hopped out ; and an idol, twenty inches high, was also found. It represents a man in the standing position, and is better carved than the generality of figures met with, from which it also differs in many points. The hair was long, wavy, and, in curly ringlets, hung over the shoulders. A double necklace of beads hung in front of the chest, and the body is enveloped in loose folds of drapery, like a sheet, wrapped round the loins and thrown over the shoulders. Both hands and feet were broken off, and the fragments were not discovered. The bones were recognized as portions of a human skeleton, mixed up with the rib bones of the cow or horse, the leg, wing and breast bones of various birds, of which the skulls of the common fowl, kite, sand-grouse, and owl were recognized; there were besides, the skulls and bones of the common rat and an animal of the same species, though much larger in size. All these remains are now in the Peshawur museum.

Skeleton.

About three feet above the grave just described, and imbedded in a hard layer of clay, was found a second human skeleton; it lay full length, with the head to the south and feet to the north. In the process of extraction the bones crumbled to powder; but the right hand and right knee, some left ribs and the left foot, some of the lower bones of the spine, and portions of the hip bones, were recognized "in situ." From this grave to the top of the centre of the tope is a height of thirty-four feet.

Court-yard.

The tope thus explored stands in the centre of a court-yard, about 120 feet each way. Along each wall are the remains of a series of chambers; those at each corner are larger and project outwards. The walls of this enclosure are still between one and three feet high.

Monastery.

Contiguous with the southern wall is a square mound, some twelve feet high, and covered with weeds and thorny bushes. On excavating it a wall was soon come upon; and, following the course of this, a complete quadrangle, with chambers all round, was in time exposed to view. These rooms all open on to a central court-yard, raised about eight feet above the plain. Outside each corner of the quadrangle is a circular platform continuous with the walls of the quadrangle.

This building was probably the monastery or *vihara* of the monks attached to the service of the adjoining tope. Several curious reliques were found in its different chambers. In a small arched recess in the wall of one room was found a small urn of red pottery, full of cinerised human bones; in others were found agate and slate beads, fragments of red pottery, as bowls, water vessels, lamps, and figures moulded of the same material, as bullocks, horse and rider, &c.; also a metal nose or earring, a wristlet, pieces of iron spits, and a little bell like those used by Hindus in their devotions. Besides these was found a very remarkable plate of copper. It consists of a circular wreath of olive (?) leaves surrounding a Maltese cross. In each compartment thus formed is a circular disc of copper; at the base of the wreath is a projecting band, slit transversely, as if for the passage of a ribbon, by which the whole was suspended.

Reliques.

In an apartment on the north face, was found an idol figure, nearly eight feet high, and carved out of a single slab of blue slate. It stood on a granite pedestal, placed on the ground six feet below the level of the other rooms. On this pedestal, and at each side of the feet, which were destroyed, we found, exactly as they had been left, a common *chiragh;* one of them was blackened at the tip by the wick that had burnt out at the socket. The idol is supposed to represent one of the Pândû kings. The hair is frizzled and gathered into a top-knot; the ears are elongated and pierced for ornaments; the *tika* is above the root of the nose, the tip of which has been knocked off; the right arm beyond the elbow is missing. This limb it appears had been joined on to the rest of the figure in the flexed position, for there are a number of holes in the folds of drapery above and below on this side, for the reception of the binding pegs. The left hand hangs by the knee, on which rests the weight of the body.

Large idol.

The whole figure is enveloped in a sheet thrown over the shoulders and brought across the chest. The folds of this drapery are very cleverly done; for, whilst every crease and fold is accurately carved, the contour of the body it covers is distinctly perceptible. This idol, and all the other reliques, I sent to the Peshawar museum.

Carving.

THE NAWIGRAM RUINS.—These occupy the top of a low ridge of granite close above the hamlet after which they are named. They are very extensive, and differ from those already described only in material, not in general plan or architecture. There are the same pointed arches and underground passages, the same sort of doors and windows, and the same sort of quadrilaterals with chambers, &c. The statuary and sculptures also represent the same figures and scenes, in the same material, a soft, blue slate, of coarse texture; but the general aspect of these ruins, is very different from that of the others. The various structures are built of accurately fitted and carefully chiselled blocks of clean, light-coloured granite, evidently quarried on the spot. The neatness and accuracy of the architecture is wonderful. The generality of the blocks of granite measure three feet, by two by one foot. The scenery on the top of this ridge, in the midst of its ruin and desolation, is most wild and picturesque. Huge rocks rear up amongst rugged walls and heaps of chiselled stone that cover the surface in most appropriate disorder; whilst scattered clumps of trees and shrubs, forming dark retreats and hiding places, add to the charms of the scene. Our visit to the Nawigram ruins, which are also called those of Ranigatt, from a prominent boulder rising up from their midst, was hasty and incomplete. We did not see the northern end of the ruins at all, but were told that amongst them was a large tumulus encircled by build-

Nawigram ruins.

Character.

Scenery.

ings, in the debris of which were mixed fragments of sculptures and idols. These ruins are also called Bagram, as well as by the names above mentioned.

Boulders.

Amongst the ruins we examined, we noticed several boulders of rock, the under surfaces of which had been carved out into domed cavities capable of sheltering from two to a dozen men. They are now used as the cooking and sleeping places of shepherds, who graze their flocks on the rich pastures of this hill.

Kharkai ruins.

The Kharkai ruins. These I have not seen; but, from all accounts, they appear to be like those of Takhti Bahi, in every respect, as to position, material, plan, architecture, sculptures, &c.

Topes and monasteries.

V. Topes and Monasteries.—Several of these have been already described in the notice of the Takhti Bahi and other ruins. That discovered and examined near Sahri Bahlol is the most perfect example in the Yuzufzai plain. Natives of the district describe a very perfect tope of stone and mortar, built on the slope of a hill near Gâligai, in Swat. It is commonly known as the Shingardar Gumbaz, or tope, or dome. Its top is described as flat and supporting a second but smaller dome, now in ruins. In the vicinity are the remains of walls and buildings. I can hear of no idols having been found there.

In Swat.

Walled cities & villages.

VI. Walled Cities and Villages.—Of these, there are most abundant remains all over the district.

Of the walled cities, the most perfect and well-defined is that already described as Sahri Bahlol, the city of Bahlol.

There are the ruins of a great city on the plain, three miles north of Katlang. In parts the plough has worked its way over great patches of the crumbled houses; but the scattered clumps of walls still standing are sufficiently high to attract the attention from a considerable distance. On the western border of these ruins is a splendid masonry well, dry at ninety feet depth, in good preservation, and the counterpart of the one at Sahri Bahlol.

Examples.

Similar to these ruins are others near Bakshalai, Baja, Maini, Topi, Hund, Zihdih, &c., &c. In each the general features are much the same as those described in Sahri Bahlol, though they are in a much more ruined condition.

Villages.

Of the ancient villages, I believe each of the 200 or more bare mounds of earth that attract the attention of the traveller through any part of the district, to be the actual site and remains. Many of them are at the present day covered with the huts of the modern population.

Heaps of ruins.

All these mounds are of the same character, and are often more extensive than the modern villages built upon them. The surface soil on and about them is thickly strewed with fragments of red pottery. Below the surface, the soil is loose, and contains bones, human and other, pieces

Their contents.

of red pottery, Hindu beads, glass bracelets, ashes, charcoal, a few idols and coins, mostly Hindu. In some parts, at four or five feet below the surface, are found massive stone walls. Many of these mounds have been dug into by the natives for these large stones, as there is no other source of supply on the plain. In the search for these are dug up Budhist and Hindu idols, and a variety of coins, including Greek, Bactrian, Scythian, Hindu, and Mahomadan;

the last named, however, only in mounds now occupied by modern villages.

Scarcity of stone.

The general paucity of stone buildings in the mounds is easily accounted for by the absence of the material from the spot, and the difficulty of conveying it in sufficient quantity from the hills. In some parts the blocks of stone are of great size, and their transport from the hills must have been very difficult, unless effected by means of wheeled carriages, for many of the mounds are in an alluvial plain at least fifteen miles from the hills. This circumstance will also account for the utter obliteration of the mass of the former buildings; for, like the modern villages, they must have been built of mud. The traces of stone walls, above alluded to, were probably parts of the village temples. Near the foot of the hills these mounds almost entirely consist of piles of stone, covering the foundations of walls and chambers.

Investigation a necessity.

The above feeble description of the various ancient ruins in the plain of Yusufzai cannot convey a just idea of their numbers and importance. A systematic investigation of them would most assuredly yield a rich store of curious ancient relics, and would add much interesting and valuable information to our present scanty store, as regards the ancient condition of this country and its successive peoples.

Accidental discoveries.

As it is, through accidental disturbance of their debris, either by new settlers on the ruins, or by the scrapings of the plough, or by the excavations of searchers for treasure, a mass of coins, sculptures, pieces of pottery, &c., have been collected, and are now scattered about amongst individuals of the population.

The coins especially are met with in great numbers and of

Coins. varied stamps, and bear testimony to the habitation of this district by at least four distinct and successive nationalities in ancient times, previous to the arrival of the present Mahomadan population. The most ancient coins are apparently purely Greek; most are of copper, some of silver, and a few of gold.

The earliest.

Greek coins. The earliest I have met with is a square copper coin of Appollodotus, about 110 B. C. The others most frequently met with are of Menander and Diomedes. They are circular discs; on one side is the impress of a helmeted or bare head, and on the other a war-horse mounted and caparisoned, or a religious bull, or some other emblem or device not intelligible. The inscription on one side is in pure Greek letters; on the other, in the Pali or Indian (old) character.

Bactrian coins. Next to the Greek coins are those of the Bactrian sovereigns, or rulers of principalities. These are apparently of two kinds, representing different historical epochs.

Two kinds. One set bears the impress of a helmeted or bare European head on one side, and a mounted or naked horse on the other, and are mostly without any writing at all; the other set has no impression of heads

Description. at all, but on one side is a full-figured and humped bull, and on the other either a leopard, lion, or elephant; and the last is sometimes bestrode by a rider. On one side is a Greek inscription "*Of the great King of Kings,*" and on the other an unintelligible Indian one. Most of these coins

Budhist emblems. are marked with a star, a trident, or other Budhist emblem. They are not so numerous as those next to be mentioned; and all I have met with have been of copper and circular.

The next class of coins are those of the Scythian conquerors; they are very common. One side bears the impress of a human figure; the features, attitudes, and clothing vary in different coins; and, in all the persons represented, appear to be acting some religious or other ceremony. The other side bears the impression of a humped bull. On both sides there are inscriptions in a mixed character of Greek and Pali letters. A great variety of unintelligible emblems are marked on these coins. On some of them the name Kanerkes is legible in Greek letters; on others, Azes. A very common coin of this class has on one side a full-figured man, dressed in the sheepskin coat, hat, and boots, as at this day worn by some Tartar tribes. The individual thus clothed, however, wears an ample beard; and, standing erect, is pointing with the right hand to a flaming altar, by the side of which is a trident; in or near the left hand is a mace, or club. Most of the coins of this class that I have met with in this district bear the marks of the action of fire, and all are of copper and circular.

Scythian coins.

Description.

Common example.

The next class of coins are purely Hindu; they are thin discs of copper and silver. The former are stamped on one side with the figure of an elephant. Above its back is an inscription in old Sanskrit letters; on the other side is a rampant lion. The silver coins are stamped on one side with a horse caparisoned and mounted, the rider holds a bannered lance in his hand; on the other side is a humped bull, crouched, but saddled; above is a Sanskrit inscription. These coins are extremely common in the ruins near Baja, Topi, and Maini. Only a few days ago, upwards of eight hundred of these silver coins were turned up by the plough in a field near Baja.

Hindu coins.

Description.

The next class of coins are those of the Mahomadan rulers. Except those of recent date, they are almost illegible, though evidently of different sovereigns or dynasties. The oldest, both of silver and copper, bear Arabic inscriptions on both sides. On one it is apparently the *Kalima*, or Mahomedan, creed. The study and collection of these coins is most interesting and important, for they illustrate, by their several peculiar symbols and characters, the various successive dynastic revolutions that this country has undergone in remote times. Though most imperfectly described above, the series is continued down, link by link, to recent times. This country, indeed, offers a most interesting field for research to any one with the leisure and ability to unravel its hidden history as spoken by these coins.

Mahomadan coins.

Description.

Collection and study.

At present the ground is too little known, and, therefore, unsafe for one to hazard an opinion in any way decided as to the origin of the numerous ruins of which I have attempted a description in these pages; but, judging from the coins, and the dates we get from them, it appears certain that during the ascendency of the later Greek sovereigns, the Bactrians, and the Scythians, Budhism was the sole religion of the people then successively inhabiting this country. In corroboration, there is the *lat* at Shahbazgarrhi, supposed to date from 250 B. C. Whether the idol temples were antecedent, cotemporaneous, or subsequent to this date, is not clear; but, from the Greek stamp of the sculptures and statuary, the evidence is in favor of their being at least cotemporaneous, if not antecedent; for the signs adduced in support of the idea that they are of subsequent date, are themselves later additions to pre-existing forms.

Want of information.

Deductions.

Fa Hian, the Chinese pilgrim, who visited this country in 402 A. D., (on the authority of Mm. Remusat, Klaproth, and Landresse, in their translation of the French edition of the "Foe Koue ki,") mentions by name Swat as *Su ho to*, Mahaban as *Ma ha fa na*, Mangalthanna as *Mang ki li*, the Indus as *Sind theou*, &c., and describes Budhism as most flourishing in all this region. The hills and valleys were covered with topes, temples, and monasteries, and spots rendered sacred by the visitations of Foe, whilst the country swarmed with priests devoted to their worship and service. A couple of centuries later came Houan Thsang. He found the decay noticed in some districts by Fa Hian to have greatly extended. The glory of Foe had indeed departed; for the Hindus were firmly footed in the country, and continued to flourish till the commencement of the eleventh century, when they were utterly destroyed and supplanted by the Mahomedans, as we now find them.

Fa Hian.

Houan Thsang.

The buildings erected by the first comers of this new race of conquerors constitute the "modern ruins" of the district. As might be expected, considering the circumstances, these are neither many nor of note, for the Mahomedans came not to settle the country. Their sole aim and object was the extirpation of idolatry from the face of the earth, and the plunder and massacre of its professors.

Modern ruins.

I know of but one set of masonry ruins in this district that belong to the Mahomedan era. These are the ruins of a mosque, fort, well, and tomb, built of red bricks, at Kapurdagarrhi. In themselves the buildings are insignificant, but they attract attention as being almost the only brick ruins, or buildings, in the whole district; for all

Examples.

the modern villages are, without exception, a mere collection of mud huts.

Insignificant.

At Nowshaira and Zaromaini, there are the ruins of some red brick buildings, also of this class, but they are not extensive or attractive. The tablet found in the Kapurdagarrhi ruins has already been referred to in the previous chapter; the other Mahomadan ruins, as far as I know, are not worthy of notice.

Ziarats.

Their numerous ziarats and tombs have no architecture nor historical interest. On the contrary, their histories are stupid fictions; and the devotees at these shrines, though they wont admit it, are, nevertheless, aware of the

Their sham.

sham; but they like the deception, for it suits their purposes and tastes.

CHAPTER IV.

INHABITANTS.

Conquest.

Custom.

The tract of country now called Yusufzai was conquered and colonized some four centuries ago by the Yusufzai tribe of Afghans. It takes its name after the tribe, according to a custom amongst the Afghans of naming a country after the tribe possessing it. This rule applies also to the tracts inhabited by the several clans of a tribe. Thus, different districts of Yusufzai, the limits of which have been detailed in a previous chapter, and the local divisions of which are given in the map accompanying this report, are frequently named after the tribe at the time holding it. Thus, the Dir country and northern Swat are commonly styled Malizai, southern Swat and the northern border of the Yusufzai plain are similarly known as Baizai, &c., &c.; and these main divisions are again sub-divided into smaller districts named after the division of the clan holding it. As in Malizai are the districts of Sultan, Paindah, Nasrudinkhail, Naikbikhail, &c.

Examples.

Other tribes.

Though the Yusufzais hold the country named after them and their numerous clans and divisions, they are not the only, nor even the most numerous, race inhabiting the country in its varied extent and surface.

Amongst them are found a few small colonies of other Afghan tribes; but the bulk of the population is made up of scattered families or small societies of several different races, foreign to, and distinct from, the Afghan.

Origin.

Of these the origin is mostly obscure, though they are generally supposed to be the descendants of stragglers or remnants of the northern invaders, whose armies are known to have passed through this region in former times.

Exceptions.

The Hindki and Hindu tribes are excepted from this mixed population. The former are immigrants from the east in comparatively recent times, and the latter are the representatives of the original possessors of the country in the remotest times. Another supposition is, that both tribes are of the same origin, with this difference now, that the former are converts to Mahomadanism, whilst the latter still adhere to their ancient religion and customs.

Mixed population.

Of the mixed population above alluded to, each race will be described separately hereafter. In this place, however, it may be noted that they now differ but slightly, either in religion, manners, or language, from the Afghans amongst whom they dwell, and from whom they are not readily distinguished by the stranger.

Differ from the Afghans.

They do, nevertheless, differ from the Afghans in some notable and important points. The chief of these are hereditary right in the soil, occupations, and I may add domestic habits and physiognomy. None of these races, as a rule, have any possession in the soil. They are all more or less vassals of the dominant Afghans, and compose the industrial population by whom are performed the cultivation of the soil, the tending of cattle, and the various industrial arts and trades.

Description.

These conditions have become materially altered in that portion of the country now under British rule; but they still hold good in the independent territories held by the Afghans in Yusufzai. A description of the polity and customs, embracing these points, of the Yusufzais, will form the subject of the next chapter. In this it is proposed to notice separately each of the different races composing the general population, detailing such points in their history, character, and habits, as are observable by the resident amongst them, or obtainable from the records of their historians, or the traditions cherished by their "grey-beards."

Dominant race.

As being the dominant race we will commence with the Yusufzai Afghans.

Yusufzais.

This tribe, like the rest of the Afghans, call themselves *Bani Israil*, or "Children of Israel." Their traditions tell them that they came to this country from the territory of Ghwara Margha, in Khorassan. This tract, I have ascertained (whilst on a journey through that country) to be on the south of the river Tarnak, between its source at the Mukur hill and its passage under the fortress of Kilati Ghilzai, in Afghanistan; and, as will be seen presently, this locality agrees well with the following account of the former settlements of the Yusufzais, as recorded in Akhûn Darwaiza's "Tazkira."

Descent.

After relating the descent of the Afghans from "Yâkûb," surnamed "Israil," and recounting some of the chief passages in their ancient history, derived, as he tells us, from oral accounts of their old men (and which in the main correspond with the history of the Israelites, as brought down to us in the Scriptures), the Akhûn goes on to say that they ultimately settled in the limits of Kandahar, and did not spread from this extensive territory till the time of Sultan Mahmud Ghazi, with whose army numbers of the Afghans went to Hind; and, settling there, gradually became lost amongst the pagans. Of the Afghans accompanying Mahmud's invasion of India, every man took his wife, family, and chattels with him; for it was the custom of the Afghans, on invading a country, to take their families and property with them, so that "on getting the victory they at once settle in the newly acquired country, and subdue its people, killing some, banishing others, and making vassals of the rest." The Afghans, with Mahmud's army, entered Hind by the Multan route, and few ever returned to their former country. The rest of the Afghans continued to inhabit the Kandahar territory. From amongst these, according to the traditions of their "grey-beards," sprung the present tribe of Yusufzai. Their history is in this wise:—

Early settlements.

Emigrate to Hind.

Via Multan.

Shairiûn.

In former times, an Afghan, named Shairiûn, dwelt in the Kandahar country. He left two sons, named Kand and Zamand.

Kand.

Of these, Kand also left two sons, named Ghorai and Khakhai.

Ghorai.

Ghorai left four sons, viz., 1. Doulatyar, from whom are sprung the tribes of Mahmand and Dudazai; 2. Khalil; 3. Zirân; and, 4. Chamkani.

His sons.

These four brothers one day quarrelled over the division of a slaughtered ram, Chamkani, by some oversight, not having received his share of the broth after the division of the flesh. He and his family in consequence separated from their brethren and settled on the Sufaid Koh. To this day his descendents have not mixed with those of his brethren. Even the few families who have since rejoined the Ghoraikhail, receive no share in the land or its produce.

Chamkani.

At this day the Chamkanis are settled in the Sufaid Koh and hills of Kafiristan. Their food is millet, and their clothing sack-cloth. Their women are bare-headed and bare-footed, and wear at most but a scanty rag about their waists. They, moreover, go to the woods for fuel and grass, and tend the cattle at graze, as do the women of the Khattak tribe.

Their religion.

In his time, says the Akhûn, the Chamkanis, as well as all the other Afghan tribes in Sufaid Koh, had become thorough infidels. All of them had accepted the heresy of the *Pir Tarik* (whose history has been given in a previous chapter), and had abolished from amongst themselves the observance of prayers, alms, and fasts. Learning and the wise, they reckoned enemies; the difference between "lawful" and "unlawful," they ignored; the kuran and the holy traditions of the prophet, they treated with contempt, trod under foot, and burned; priests and true believers generally, they hunted and murdered in the hope of a future reward! "God preserve us from such infidelity," piously exclaims the Akhûn.

Location.

The Ghoraikhail, with the exception above-noted, are now located in the northern parts of the Peshawar district and the adjoining hills.

Khakhai had three sons, viz., 1. Mundai; 2. Mukh; and, 3. Turk. The two first were by the same wife, named Marjân; the third was by a second wife named Basso, who was Marjân's sister. The offspring of Turk are called Turkilanri. They were followers of the *Pir Tarik*, and are absolutely without religion. They are located in the country to the north of Bajáwar.

Khákhai.

Mukh had a daughter named Kaki. She married one of her father's shepherds, named Ziraki. Their descendants are the Kakiani, or Gigiani tribe, which also includes the few direct descendants of Mukh. The Gigianis are located in the hill country on the south and east of Bajawar.

Mukh.

Mundai left two sons, named Umar and Yusuf. Of these, Umar emigrated to Hindustan and there married a foreign woman, by whom he had a son named Mandanr. During the son's infancy, Umar died, and his brother Yusuf, according to Afghan custom, went down to fetch the widow up to his own home. After many objections on the part of the widow, Yusuf ultimately succeeded in taking her away to his pastoral home, and afterwards had five sons, viz., 1. Uria; 2. Isa; 3. Musa; 4. Mali; and 5. Ako. From these sons and Mandanr are descended the present Yusufzai tribe, as will be described hereafter. Meanwhile, let us see what the Afghans say regarding their settlement in their present locality.

Mundai.

On their arrival in the Kandahar territory, the Afghans divided the country amongst their several tribes by lot, as was their custom from the remotest times. In this distribution the brother tribes of Kand and Zamand became separated by the tribe of Tarîn, whose lot fell on the land between theirs.

At Kandahar.

The Khakhai clan of the Kand tribe were placed nearest to the Tarîns, and shared with them the Argistan canal which formed the boundary line between their respective lands. This water-course proved the source of constant feuds between the two tribes between whose lands it flowed. Ultimately the Khakhais, who, from their hemmed in position, could get no assistance from their brethren of the Zamand tribe, nor from the Ghoraikhail clan of the Kand tribe, were overpowered and driven from their lands by the Tarîns, who were assisted by the rest of their clans composing the great Ghilzai tribe.

Location.

The Khakhais at first sought refuge with the Ghoraikhails, and were granted a strip of poor land at the foot of the hills for their subsistence; but they were after a time ejected from these by the Ghoraikhails, who themselves were reduced to a difficulty for the subsistence of their cattle, owing to a serious inundation of their lands on the plain. This misfortune was produced by excessive and unusual summer rains having completely washed away all the pasture from the face of the country. The Ghoraikhails were, therefore, forced to resume the lands they had in more prosperous days given away to the Khakhais.

Quarrels.

On being again cast adrift, the Khakhais emigrated to the Karonaiki lands; but, owing to their numerical weakness and general poverty, they were unable to maintain a position against the hostility of the neighbouring tribes. They, therefore, moved on; and, after a period of wandering, settled in the hill country near Kabul.

Wanderings.

During their wanderings, the Khakhais were joined by the Hatmankhails, their brothers in misfortune; for they, too, were wanderers in search of a new settlement,

Reinforcements.

having been driven out of their lands, in the Tâk and Gomal districts, by more powerful tribes. These two tribes have ever since moved together, and assisted each other; but, being Afghans, they are eternally at strife, and have not yet learned to appreciate each other. Whilst settled in the Kabul territory, the Khakhais were joined by the Mahmandzais, a clan of the Zamand tribe, but long separated from their brethren on account of feuds, and now wanderers in search of new settlements, having, like the others, been ejected from their own lands by more powerful neighbours.

Settle in Kabul.

These three tribes continued to dwell in the Kabul territory in close proximity to each other for many years, and became very rich, for their flocks and herds flourished on the fat pastures of the country. Their numbers also increased day by day; for their women, having no griefs and anxieties now, as in the days of their poverty and weakness, became most prolific. In short, these tribes in the course of years increased very greatly in numbers, strength, and wealth, more especially that of Khakhai, as represented by its clans of Yusuf and Mandanr.

Increase.

Rebel.

The tribes thus improved and strengthened, soon became aware of their power, and commenced to commit irregularities. Armed bands of them used to plunder the roads through their settlements; and, attacking their neighbours, used to carry off their cattle and plunder their homes. The Khakhais especially were distinguished for their lawlessness and insubordination, for they frequently carried their raids up to the very gates of Kabul.

Punishment.

To check these irregularities, Mirza Kuli Bég, the Governor of Kabul, summoned their chiefs to his court to render an account of the acts of their clansmen;

but his messengers were treated with disrespect, and turned away with indecent threats. On this the Mirza marched an army against them; many he slew, others he sold into slavery, and the rest he plundered, and drove into the recesses of the hills.

Shaikhs.

When driven into the hills and glens forming the entrances to Kabul, the Khakhais had amongst them three noted Shaikhs. Amongst the Afghans, says Akhûn Darwaiza, the *Shaikh* is a holy man, who has the power of performing miracles, looking into futurity, and predicting events by means of converse with the genii. They are thoroughly believed in by the Afghans, and invariably consulted in matters of difficulty or importance. They are, in truth, but blasphemous infidels; nevertheless the Afghans hold them in the highest esteem, and readily sacrifice life, honor, and wealth in their service, considering them as lords in matters both spiritual and temporal. This is exactly the character of the Yusufzais of the present day.

Their names.

The three Shaikhs, above alluded to, were two brothers, named Mada and Mado, sons of a woman of the Isazai tribe, and Shaikh Usmân of the Malizai tribe. In their banishment to the hills, the Yusufzais, by common consent, flocked to the brothers, Mada and Mado, and enquired what was to be the future of the tribe, whether good or bad, and also upbraided them for not having in due time warned the tribes, so that they might have avoided the losses and hardships that had so lately overtaken them. The brother Shaikhs told them to go and kill their rival, Shaikh Usmân, first, and that they would then say what was written in the fate of the tribe. The assembly accordingly seized Shaikh Usmân to kill him. The Shaikh told them he was well aware of their intentions, but could not resist, as it

Their acts.

was fated that he should fall into their hands. He promised, however, that, if they set him free, he would at once inform them of what was to happen. They released him, and he told them that a desperate fight was impending between themselves and Mirza Kuli Bég, and that they would come off victorious; but that the leader of their footmen would lose his life. To this the brothers Mada and Mado assented, but added that the leader of the footmen who would lose his life was one of themselves; and so it proved on the day of battle.

Prophecy.

Thus assured of the future, the Yusufzais grew bold; and, issuing from the hills, made frequent raids on the country around. Troops were sent against them on several occasions, but they were always defeated. At length Mirza Kuli Bég, finding them quite inaccessible in their mountain retreats, changed his tactics and adopted a kind and conciliating policy towards them. He summoned their chiefs to his court, received them with every mark of respect, presented them with fine clothes and rich gifts and fed them sumptuously, and bid them consider his court as their own home.

Raids.

Expeditions.

Change of policy.

Now the Afghans, observes Akhûn Darwaiza, are a sensual race, and easily entrapped by an appeal to their cupidity and avarice. Their mullahs, shaikhs, pirs, and paishwas have all gained their authority and pre-eminence amongst them simply by feeding and clothing their masses for a time gratuitously; the character of the individual, whether good or bad, is not considered. Be he heretic or infidel, so that he once establish a notoriety for charity and

Afghan character.

Priest-ridden.

piety, is of no consequence; the people blindly follow and act up to his sayings. It was by such simple devices that the tribes were brought under the control and bondage of their priests. For the same reason the Mirza's liberal policy proved a complete success. The Afghans, indeed, flocked to his court in such numbers, were so uncouth in their manners and independent in their bearing, that they became quite an inconvenience, and it became necessary to restrain them.

Massacre.

On one occasion, when a large number of them were collected about the court, a man of the Chaghurzai tribe proposed the assassination of the Mirza. But the act was unanimously forbidden by the others, as they were at the time the Mirza's guests. One of the Gigiani tribe reported the circumstance to the Mirza, who forthwith had all the Afghans about his court seized, and massacred, over two hundred of them, as a warning to the rest of the tribes and as a punishment to the Yusufzais in particular, for it was their clansmen that suffered. Only two of their number were pardoned, viz., Malik Sultan Shah, and his youthful nephew, Ahmad. The latter afterwards rose to eminence in his tribe as a military leader; and, before his death, had settled the Yusufzais in all the limits of Bajawar, Swat, and Buhnair.

Malik Ahmad.

Weakness.

The Yusufzais were rendered so helpless by this slaughter of their best men, that they were easily driven from their hill retreats by more powerful tribes, and for a time roamed about the glens and defiles of Nangnahar at the northern base of the Sufaid Koh. Here they were at constant strife with the Tarkilanris who dwelt in the adjoining country of Lughman, but finally overcame them in a decisive battle at Hissarak. In this

Battle of Hissarak.

fight the Yusufzais were assisted by the Mahmandzais, who for their services claimed most of the country, and turned the Yusufzais over to the Gigianis, who were then settled in Bâsawal. But after a time the Yusufzais, not being able to hold their own against the Gigianis, retraced their steps and settled on the borders of Nangnahar, amongst the Dilazaks, a tribe of Afghans who had for many years occupied all the country about Peshawar and the Indus.

Dilazaks.

Amongst the Dilazak tribe the Yusufzais dwelt peaceably and were granted a strip of land near the hills for their support. In the course of time their numbers having increased the Yusufzais were hard pushed for space and demanded a larger share of the land. The chiefs of the two tribes met in conclave at Sufaid Sang, or Spîn Kanrai (the *white rock* in Persian and Pukhtu respectively), to discuss the matter. In the course of conference the chiefs quarrelled and fell to fighting. Many Yusufzais were killed, and their clans were forced ultimately to retire to the shelter of the hills of Tahtarra and Shalmân. From these, after a time, they descended into the Peshawar valley; and, unhindered, occupied the tracts at the foot of the hills. Here they increased in numbers by the arrival of others of their tribe coming to join them through the Khaibar pass, and ultimately seized the Barr Bara stream for the irrigation of their new lands. The Shalmani Dilazaks, to whom this stream belonged, collected their clans to recover the stream and eject the Yusufzais.

Congress.

Its result.

Aggression.

Their efforts proved unavailing; and the Yusufzais, being joined by others from beyond the Khaibar, shortly seized the Doaba, and thence spread into Hashtnaggar,

Advance.

or 'Ashnaghar. In this last district they fought a bloody battle with the Shalmanis, and slew their chief, named Jalo. The rest of the tribe fled to Swat, and settled in the lower part of the valley as far as Alladand.

Anecdote.

In connection with this fight, Akhûn Darwaiza relates that he heard from the mouth of one Dalo Chaghurzai, who declared that he was present at the execution of the Shalman chief, Jalo, that when his head was cut off, so full of *boza*, or "beer," was his stomach, that as much beer flowed from the wound as did blood!

It is doubtful who these Dilazaks were. The Afghans, though acknowledging them as Pathans, assign them an Indian origin. They were probably a race of Rajput descent, and quite distinct from the Afghans.

'Ashnaghar.

The occupation of 'Ashnaghar by the Yusufzais, was by no means a quiet one. They suffered constantly from the attacks of the Dilazaks, who, occupying the rest of the plain up to the hills of Swat and Buhnair, daily plundered their cattle whilst at graze on the *mairah*, and murdered stray members of their tribe caught on its wastes.

Combination of tribes.

Unaided, the Yusufzais were too weak to cope with the Dilazaks of the plain. Their chief, Malik Ahmad, therefore proposed that they should invite the co-operation of the whole of the Khakhai clans, for the country was a tempting one, and large enough for all; but, owing to private feuds, the Gigianis and Tarkilanris would not join the Yusufzais, who then formed a combination amongst themselves and the Ghoraikhails, and also secured the assistance of the Mahmandzais on condition of giving them 'Ashnaghar as the price of their services; whilst the Ghoraikhails were to have Doaba as their reward.

The united or combined tribes then advanced. The Yusufzais, under the guidance of Malik Ahmad, marched from 'Ashnaghar, twenty miles, and encamped on the Gadar stream, close to the village of the same name, without meeting any opposition ; but next day the army of the Dilazaks advanced from their chief town, Langarkot (the present Kapurdagarrhi), about six miles distant, and attacked the Yusufzais. As soon as the opposed forces met, a tremendous fight ensued. The Hatmankhails (who were with the Mahmandzais) and the Yusufzais distinguished themselves, and did great execution. The Hatmankhails are described as having fought in a novel manner. Their archers came into the battle with fifty shields, made of untanned ox-hides sewn together, and termed *karwat ;* each was carried by a couple of men, and afforded protection to half a dozen men, who, from behind its shelter, poured in volley after volley of arrows against the enemy with perfect safety to themselves.

Their advance.

Battle.

Mode of fighting.

The Yusufzais did not wait to see the victory won by this means ; but, throwing aside their bows, and drawing their swords, pressed forward for a hand to hand conflict with the harrassed and disconcerted Dilazaks. They were led by Ali, a noted swordsman of the Ismailzai clan, who, leaping across the Gadar rivulet, singled out the foremost of the Dilazaks, and slew him on the spot.

Swordsmen.

The rest of the Yusufzais and their allies at once poured across the stream ; and, after a short, sharp, and decisive contest, drove the Dilazaks off the field, and pursued them as far as Jalbai Jalsai, a distance of twenty-five

Dilazaks routed.

miles, and from this they forced them across the Indus to Hazarah.

Their flight and fate.

The rest of the Dilazaks abandoned their homesteads, and followed their brethren across the Indus, and with them in turn seized a number of villages in Hazarah, whilst their own homes were being burnt and plundered by the Yusufzais. Of the Dilazaks, who could not effect their escape, numbers were butchered, their women and children were kept, or sold as slaves, and the rest subdued to vassalage.

Invade Swat.

After the Yusufzais had been some time in possession of their new conquest, they determined on invading Swat, of which country they heard the most favorable reports. For this purpose Malik Ahmad and Shaikh Mali collected a force; and, with the women, cattle, and flocks, &c., marched towards the Shakot pass and encamped at its entrance; for the Swatis, learning of their approach, had occupied the force in strength and guarded it night and day. Whilst delayed here, it was discovered that the Malakand pass was left quite unguarded. The Yusufzai leaders, therefore, decided on taking it by surprise, and thus entering Swat. At night their old men and women collected at the entrance of the pass, and with the beating of drums, war songs, and derisive yells at the enemy on the heights above, kept their attention fixed in anticipation of an immediate attack. Meanwhile the young men and warriors, under the guidance of their leaders, set out for the Malakand pass, the passage of which they effected by day-light without opposition. The Swatis presently seeing their villages in flames, were seized with a

Shakot pass.

Stratagem.

Its success.

panic, and fled in all directions into the hills. The Yusufzai slew all that fell into their hands; and, bringing the rest of their people through the Shahkot pass, encamped on the banks of the Swat river.

Subdue Swat.

They at first only subdued a small portion of the south-west end of the valley; but, as they daily got stronger, they enlarged their limits by the seizure of adjacent villages, till, at the end of twelve years, they were spread throughout the Swat valley and its boundary hills, and the country between them and the Indus on one side and Bajawar on the other. The last great fight of the Yusufzais was in the Talash valley, and their victory here established the supremacy of the Yusufzais in all the country between Nawaghai on the west and Tanawal on the east.

Last battle.

After this the tribes enjoyed a season of peace, ease, and plenty; and, for the first time became enquirers after the true faith and devoted to religion.

Peace.

In an evil hour, however, they allowed themselves to be deceived and led astray by heretics, and chose in place of the pure doctrines of the true faith (says the Akhûn Darwaiza), the blasphemies and deceptions of ignorant and scheming adventurers. But they were soon visited by the punishment their sins deserved; for their whole tribe was overwhelmed with a succession of misfortunes and calamities that well nigh left the country empty of them.

Heresy.

During the reign of the Emperor Akbar, they were continually harrassed and driven from the plains into the hills, where they were glad to shelter themselves in caves. At this time they were so reduced by successive wars, pestilence, and famine, that they had not the men to cultivate

Its fruits.

their lands. In these hard times, mothers sold their children, and husbands their wives, for a mouthful of food. It is even said that some wretches were forced to eat the flesh of those who had died from starvation, in order to escape the same fate.

Repentance.

Their remnant, after a turning away from their sins, were taken under the protection of Zain Khan Kokà, of Kabul, who, having thus severely chastised them, finally reinstated them in their original lands.

Prosperity.

They once again enjoyed a season of peace and plenty, and rapidly increased in wealth and numbers, and now for the first time paid revenue to Government. Its amount, according to Akhûn Darwaiza, was rupees 1,000 cash for the whole district, and five *takka* of Hindustan, (about equal to two annas of British currency) per plough, and six *takka*, per house.

Division of the country.

At this period, probably, for the better collection of Government revenue, the Yusufzais, under the direction of their chief priest, Shaik Mali, divided the country, both hill and plain, by lot, amongst their several clans and their sub-divisions, as a perpetual and hereditary possession. This distribution of the country holds good to the present day throughout the country. Such is Akhûn Darwaiza's account of the Yusufzais, though here greatly condensed. Since his day they are in no way changed as regards character and location.

Distribution.

In Shaik Mali's distribution of the country held by the Yusufzais, he allotted the plain country and the Mahaban hill to the Mandanr tribe, and all the rest to the Yusuf tribe.

Mundai's sons.

As formerly mentioned, Mundai, the son of Khakhai, left two sons named Umar and Yusuf.

Umar.

Umar left one son, named Mandanr, and died during his infancy. Mandanr left seven sons, viz., 1. Usman, 2. Utman, both by an Afghan woman; 3. Mani, 4. Malik, 5. Khidar, 6. Ako, and 7. Mamo, all by a slave girl. The last five are collectively styled Razar. And the tribes sprung from Mandanr's sons are collectively styled Mandar, Mandan, or Mandanr, and, of course, include the Razar division.

Yusuf.

Yusuf left five sons, viz.; 1. Uria; 2. Isa; 3. Musa; 4. Mali, and 5. Aka. The tribes sprung from these are collectively styled Yusuf. And Mandanr and Yusuf together are styled Yusufzai; for, as has been stated, Mandanr became the step-son of Yusuf on his father's death.

Yusufzai.

Let us now notice each of these two great divisions of the Yusufzais separately.

Mandaur.

Mandanr, at the time of Shaik Mali's distribution, was settled in the plain country, which after them was formerly called *Mulk-i-Mandanr*, though now it is more generally known as the Yusufzai *samah* or plain. Mandanr had seven sons, and each of these, by the clans they gave their names to, has a separate share or district, termed *tappa*, and named after the clan whose possession or *daftar* it may happen to be.

Districts.

Each *tappa* is sub-divided according to the divisions of the clan possessing it, and these are further sub-divided according to the sub-divisions of each division composing the clan, and which are termed Khail; and these are yet further sub-divided according to the families composing the Khail. This will be more particularly explained in the next chapter; here we will confine ourselves to the divisions of the tribe and their respective limits.

Location.

The Mandanr clan, consisting of seven principal divisions, is altogether located in the south-west portion of the Yusufzai country, and possesses most of the plain country, or Mulk-i-Mandanr, the Mahaban mountain and its slopes, and portion of the Chamla valley. Of these separate tracts, only the plain is within the British boundary, and it is divided into seven chief *tappas*, corresponding with the divisions of Mandanr, for in Shaik Mali's distribution, each tribe had a portion in the plain as well as in the hills, and the residents on these separate tracts used to exchange lands with each other at fixed intervals, so that the land should be equally enjoyed by all. Since the establishment of the British rule this custom has become obsolete and the tribes in the plain have lost their possessions in the hills, and gained instead the plain lands of those who at the time of annexation were in the hills; it has been the same *vice versa* with the hill tribes.

Tribes.

Location.

Of the Mandanr seven divisions, Usmânzai and Utmânzai are the largest; the other five are small and scattered, and are collectively called Razar. These divisions are at this time all located in the plain, or Mulk-i-Mandanr, the limits of which are the Pajah hill and its Takhti Bah-i spur on the north, the Indus and Kabul rivers on the south, the Mahaban mountain, Garru, and Alishair hills on the east, and the Hissarah Kandah ravine on the west. In former times the Mandanr clan could turn out 20,000 matchlock-men, mostly from the Usmân and Utmân tappas.

Usmânzai.

The Usmân tribe, or the Usmânzai, consist of two main divisions named Kamalzai and Amazai. Each of these again consists of two divisions, viz. Kamalzai consists of Misharanzai and Kisharanzai, whose chief towns are Toru and Hoti respectively. Amazai consists of Doulatzai and Ismailzai, whose chief towns are Chargholai and Kapurda-garrhi respectively. About one-half of the Amazai tribe are settled on the north eastern slopes of the Mahaban, beyond the British border, where they have given their name to the country. They still intermarry and communicate with their brethren under British rule; but, in matters of internal government, are quite distinct from them. They have a tribal chief of their own, who resides in their capital town, Charorai, and, in matters affecting the politics of the tribe in connection with their neighbours or others, they side with the Bonairwals, the authority of whose chiefs they acknowledge. They are all highlanders, are rich in cattle, buffäloes especially, and cultivate every available space of ground with wheat and Indian corn. They can turn out about 2,000 matchlock-men.

Divisions.

Location.

Politics.

Wealth.

Strength.

The Utmân tribe or Utmânzai, consists of four divisions, viz. Alazai, Kamazai, Akazai, and Saddahzai. The three first are beyond the British border, and occupy the southern spurs from Mahaban on the right bank of the Indus. A very considerable portion of their original lands, about two-thirds, are now occupied by a foreign tribe, who were in former times invited over from across the Indus as military mercenaries, and in reward for their services were granted the lands they now hold, on the western and southern slopes of the Mahaban. They are called Gaddûn, and are a branch of the Kakar or Gakkar tribe.

Utmânzai.

Gaddûns.

They consist of two principal divisions, viz. Salar and Mansûr, whose chief towns are Gandaf and Bîsak, respectively. They can muster about three thousand matchlock-men, but are not considered a fighting tribe, as they contain amongst them a large number of Indian settlers. The three Utmânzai tribes sharing the hills with them are supposed to be much better soldiers, but they are numerically weak, and cannot muster more than about twelve hundred matchlock-men. The Saddahzai division of the Utmânzais consists of five sub-divisions, viz., 1. Abakhail, 2. Umarkhail, 3. Mirahmadkhail, 4. Bihzâdkhail, and 5. Khodokhail. The four first of these are all within the British border, and occupy the south-eastern corner of the plain. Their chief towns are Hund, Swabai, Marghoz, and Kilabat, respectively. The Khodokhails are beyond the British border, and occupy the western slopes of Mahaban between the Gaddûns on one side and the Chamla valley on the other. Their chief town is now Chingli. The former one, Panjtar, was destroyed in 1858 by the British troops under General Cotton. The Khodokhails have two villages within the British border, viz., Baja and Bamkhail. The Khodokhails can muster about fifteen hundred or eighteen hundred matchlock-men.

Saddahzai.

Razar, which comprizes the other five divisions of Mandanr, consists of five *tappas*, viz. 1. Akokhail, 2. Malikzai, 3. Khidarzai, 4. Mamozai, 5. Manizai. These five are all within the British limits, and are located between the Amâzais and Utmânzais. Their chief towns are Ismaila, Yar Husain, Shiwa, Nowikila, and Adina, respectively.

Razar.

These are the tribes composing the Mandanr clan. They are reckoned at about 40,000 souls, and with foreigners settled amongst them, about 120,000 or 140,000 souls, including the tribes on Ma-

Mandanr population.

Strength.

haban. They can muster, it is reckoned, between 25,000 and 30,000 armed men, the majority with matchlocks. From eight to ten thousand are allotted to the hill tribes, and from seventeen to twenty thousand to the tribes on the plain. The calculation is not far out.

Yusuf.

The Yusuf clan are for the most part altogether beyond the British limits. Their divisions are in this wise. Yusuf had five sons, viz., 1. Uria; 2. Isa; 3. Musa; 4. Mali; and 5. Ako.

Uria.

Uria was surnamed Badi, on account of his pride and quarrelsome disposition, and the name stuck to his descendants, who were styed Badikhail. They are now extinct; and the tradition in reference thereto is to this effect. It is the custom amongst the Afghans to divide the paternal inheritance amongst the sons when they arrive at manhood; a portion being reserved for the parents for their support in old age. When, therefore, the sons of Yusuf divided their father's property amongst themselves, the mother asked for her share to be a separate one. The other sons remained silent, but Uria rebuked her with an indecent speech and gesture. The mother thereupon invoked a curse upon his head, and prayed that his progeny might never exceed thirteen souls. The Badikhails never did exceed that number; and, till the time of their becoming extinct, dwelt in poverty amongst the Chaghurzais.

His fate.

Isa.

Isa had eleven sons. Nine of them were killed whilst yet young men, with their father, in an affray with the Mughals. The survivors were named Hassan and Yâkûb. A posthumous son was born, named Aka. Their representatives in the present day are the Hassanzai, Akazai, and Maddakhail tribes. All of them are settled close to each other on the spurs of the Mahaban and Dumah mountains on the right bank of the Indus, and next to the Chaghurzais, with whom they ally themselves in matters of tribal policy. Each of these tribes has also extensive settlements on the left bank of the Indus in the hills of Agror, a district of the Hazarah country. The Hassanzais are the most numerous and powerful. The tribes settled in the hill country on the right bank of the Indus can produce from a thousand to twelve hundred matchlock-men. They are described as hardy and brave mountaineers.

His tribes.

Musa had one son named Ilias. From him is sprung the Iliaszai tribe, now consisting of five divisions, viz., 1. Salarzai; 2. Gadaîzai; 3. Makhozai; 4. Ashaizai; and, 5. Panjpai. The Salarzai and Gadaîzai are located in Buhnair on the southern slopes of the Ilam and Dosirra mountains. The Makhozai occupy the eastern slopes of Dosirra, beyond the Gadaîzais, with whom they communicate by means of the Nawighâkhi pass. The Ashaizais are located on the plain of Buhnair under the isolated Jafir Koh. The Panjpais are located on the adjoining plain, on the right bank of the Barhandu river. Collectively, the Iliaszai tribe are reckoned at about eleven thousand souls, and can muster about two thousand matchlock-men. Their chief towns are, of the Salarzais, Jowar; of the Gadaîzais, Padsha; of the Makhozais, Shukaoli; of the Ashaizais, Turasak; of the Panjpais, Bagra.

Musa.

His tribes.

Mali left four sons, viz., (1) Doulat, and (2) Chaghur, by one wife, named Watti; and (3) Aba, and (4) Isa, by a second wife, named Nuri. In the present day the tribes sprung from these are collectively termed Malizai

Mali.

(they must not be confounded with the tribe of the same name located in Dir), which consists of three main divisions, viz., 1. Doulatzai; 2. Chaghurzai; and, 3. Nurizai, which includes the descendants of Aba and Isa together. The Doulatzais are located on each bank of the Barhandu river or stream, between Shalbanda and Bajkatta, and also occupy the Top-darrah glen and the bounding hills. They consist of three divisions, named Mandizai, Barkazai, and Ismailzai, whose chief towns are Shalbanda, Kalpani, and Bajkatta respectively. The Chaghurzais are located on the Dumah mountain, and its western and eastern slopes. Their chief town is Tiraj. They are thorough mountaineers, hardy and brave above all the neighbouring tribes. Their chief wealth is in cows, buffaloes, and goats. The Nurizais are located in the south-west corner of the Buhnair plain, and in the adjoining Chamla valley. Their chief town is Raigha. The Chamla valley, though under the control of the Buhnair tribes, is for the most part occupied by a mixture of Yusufzais, priests, and traders. Each of the Mandanr tribes has its representatives in this valley in the villages of Kogah, Surah, and Kuria. Collectively the Malizais are estimated at sixteen thousand souls, and can muster between three and a half and four thousand matchlock-men.

His tribes.

Ako left six sons, viz., (1) Khwazo, (2) Aba, (3) Bazid, and (4) Sharak, by one wife, named Zohar; and (5) Alam, and (6) Utmân, by a second wife, named Rani. The four first are now comprized in the two great divisions of Khwazozai and Bâizai, and the two last in the great division of Ranizai, or, as it is often spelt, Ranrizai. With the exception of a few of the Bâizai tribe, all these tribes are located beyond the British border. Collectively, they are reckoned at ninety-six thousand

Ako.

His tribes.

souls, and have besides a numerous foreign population settled amongst them. Each division requires a separate paragraph.

Khwazozais.

Their limits.

The Khwazozais occupy all the country north of the Swat river as far as Dir, and the mountains separating it from Kashkar; the eastern limit is formed by the Kohistan separating Malizai or the Panjkora country from Yassan; and the western boundary is formed by a line drawn from Talash through Tor-i-tigga, Ayasairai, and Janbatai to the Kistoji Kamoji mountain. For reference, see the map accompanying this report. The tribe occupying this extensive tract, consists of five divisions, viz.,

Divisions.

1. Adinzai; 2. Shamozai; 3. Naikbikhail; 4. Shamizai, or Sabujuna; and, 5. Malizai. The four first are all located in the Swat valley on the right bank of the river, and in the glens between the southern spurs of the Larram and Munjai mountains. Their respective limits are marked on the map accompanying this report. But it must be borne in mind that the lands thus limited, though the *daftar* or hereditary possession of the tribes after whom they are named, are at successive fixed intervals occupied by other tribes, owing to the Afghan custom, before alluded to, of periodically changing lands between the divisions of one tribe.

Afghan customs.

In Swat.

Of the four tribes located in Swat, the Naikbikhails and Shamizais have each two sub-divisions. Those of the Naikbikhails are Abakhail and Ashikhail; and those of the Shamizais are Sibbat and Junah, the combination of which gives Sabujuna, the name by which they are generally known.

Malizai.

The remaining division of the Khwazozais, the Malizai tribe, occupy all the rest of the country north of the Larram and Munjai mountains, and give their name to the tract of country as far as Dir, which is all designated Malizai. This tribe consists of three great divisions, viz., Sultankhail, Paindakhail, and Nasrudinkhail. The Sultankhail are located in the Tormung and Karoh *darras*, or valleys, and can muster three thousand matchlock-men. The Paindakhail occupy the valleys of Oshairai and Nihag, and can also muster three thousand matchlock-men. The Nasrudinkhail are located in the Jâfar *darra,* and on the banks of the Panjkora river from Khal to the Kamrani hill, and can muster about two thousand matchlock-men. All three divisions of the Malizais acknowledge the rule of Ghazan Khan, of Dir.

Their limits.

The Bâizais also occupy a scattered extent of country. They extend from the Lunkhwar valley, in the British limits, through Swat on the left bank of its river, and along the northern slopes of the Ilam and Dosirra mountains, into the highlands of Ghorband and throughout the valleys draining from these to the Indus. The tribe consists of seven main divisions, viz., 1. Babozai; 2. Maturizai; 3. Baratkhail; 4 Abakhail; 5. Musakhail; 6. Azizkhail, or Azikhail; and, 7. Zangikhail, or Jinkikhail. The Babozais are partly settled in the Lunkhwar valley, within the British limits; but the main portion of the tribe are settled in Swat and the narrow glens of Puran and Chakaisar on the right bank of the Indus. The Maturizais, Baratkhails, Abakhails, and Musakhails, are all settled next each other in the Swat valley, along the left bank of the river, and in the adjacent slopes of Mounts Morah, Ilam, and Dosirra. The Azikhails and Zangikhails also have settlements

Bâizai.

Their limits.

Divisions.

Location.

X

in Swat; but the bulk of both tribes divide the districts of Chakaisar, Kana, and Ghorband, between them. Collectively, the divisions of the Bâizai clan are reckoned at thirty-eight thousand souls, and can muster about six thousand matchlock-men. They are weaker than the Khwazozais, who are reckoned at forty-five thousand souls and twelve thousand matchlock-men, of whom four thousand are in the tribes located in Swat, on the right bank of the river.

Strength.

The Ranizais are all beyond the British border. They occupy both slopes of the Totai hills from Hazarnao to Malakand, and the western end of the Swat valley on both sides the river, and including the southern slopes of Barangolah hill. They are reckoned at thirteen thousand souls, and can muster about three thousand matchlock-men.

Ranizai.

Limits.

Strength.

This completes the tribes of Yusufzai, and the tracts held by them; but there are also some other tribes of Afghans settled within the Yusufzai limits, who need a brief notice. These are the Khattak, Mahmandzai Hatmankhail, and Talash tribes.

Other Afghans.

The Khattaks are an extensive colony, who, in former times, left their tribe on the south side of the Kabul river, and acquired land in the plain of Yusufzai in return for military service rendered to the Yufuszais. They occupy all the southern angle of the Yusufzai plain between the "Sari-mairah" and the junction of the Kabul and Indus rivers. They also have a small colony in the Lunkhwar valley. Their numbers in Yusufzai are reckoned at about fourteen thousand souls; and they formerly could muster about three thousand matchlocks.

Khattak.

The Mahmandzais, whose history has been related, occupy the 'Ashnaghar, or Hashtnaggar, district. They were settled in this tract towards the close of Akbar's long reign. They have always remained distinct from the Yusufzais until recent times, on account of sectarian differences in matters of religion; and, moreover, being nearer to the city of Peshawar, they have always been, more or less, subject to its successive Governors; whilst the Yuzufzais on the adjoining plain managed, by the aid of their mountain retreats, to maintain, more or less, of an independence. The district was for a long time held as a hereditary jagîr by the 'Alikhail Khans, till Yar Mahomad Khan Barakzai, became ruler of Peshawar; and he farmed it himself, in common with the rest of the Peshawar district. His rule lasted sixteen or seventeen years, and was succeeded by that of the Sikhs in 1832. During their stay they squeezed as much as they could out of the country; and, in 1845, made the district over to Sayad Mahomad Khan, the son of Sardar Pír Mahomad Khan; and he held it till the British annexed the country in 1850. The population of Hashtnaggar is a very mixed one, and is reckoned in all at about five and twenty thousand souls, and can muster about five thousand matchlock men.

Mahmandzai.

Their history.

Population.

Strength.

The Hatmankhails occupy the hills on both sides the Swat river from Kohi Mor to Khanora, and their boundary meets that of Hashtnaggar at the base of Sapraisar hill. The Hatmankhails are a hardy and brave tribe of mountain brigands. They are reckoned to number between eighteen and twenty thousand souls, and can muster about five thousand matchlock men.

Hatmankhail.

Strength.

The Talash valley contains a mixture of all the surrounding tribes, including Tarkilanris from Bajawar. The valley is held in common by the tribes, as the main road from Swat to the countries on the north-west lies through it. The population is reckoned at about six thousand souls, and can muster two thousand matchlocks. The valley is under the control of two local chiefs who acknowledge the supremacy of Ghazan Khan, of Dir.

Talash.

By the preceding details of the Yusufzai tribes and their matchlock-men, the aggregate total of the population amounts to 246,000 souls, taking the Mandanr clan at 140,000, and the Yusuf clan and other Afghan tribes, as above detailed, at 106,000. Their matchlock-men, by the same calculation, are in the aggregate 73,200, taking the Mandanr clan at 30,000 men, and the Yusuf clan and other Afghan tribes at 43,200.

Population of Yusufzais.

Strength of Yusufzais.

According to the native reckoning, the Yusufzai population altogether, in round numbers, is taken at 900,000. This is undoubtedly an exaggeration, and probably 400,000 is nearer the truth; for, in the calculation above made, a large number of foreign settlers amongst the Afghans have been excluded; throughout the country their aggregate is probably not far short of 150,000 souls, as will be noticed presently. The calculation for the matchlock-men does not produce a very high figure when it is considered that almost every adult male of the population is an armed man, and that the generality of the matchlocks used sell amongst the tribes at from four to ten rupees a piece; swords sell at from five to fifty or a hundred rupees a piece, according to quality and finish.

Settlers.

The mixed population above referred to, is com-

Mixed tribes.

posed of Gujars, Awâns, Kashmiris, Hindkis, Mullahs, Slaves, and Hindus.

Gujars. **Occupation.** **Position.** **Taxes.** **Note.**

Of these, the Gujars demand the first notice. They are of the Jat or Rajput race, are Musalmans, and are divided into clans and khails, like the Afghans. They are a very numerous race, and form the entire population of many villages. They have no hereditary possession in the land beyond the British limits, but are merely the vassals of the Afghans. They follow no mechanical trades or handicrafts, but are entirely devoted to the rearing of cattle and the cultivation of the soil, which they hold in lease from the Afghan owners, on fixed terms that vary in different localities. Generally they are these—to keep the land *âbád;* to pay a land tax, either in cash or kind, to the Khan of the district at the collection of each harvest (the amount varies from Rs. 3 to Rs. 10 per plough); and to arm for military service at the call of the Khan or chief of the *tappa* they live in. Besides these, they provide the Khan, or Malik, under whose protection they live, with certain supplies for the use of his *hujra,* such as ghi, barley, fodder, bedding, &c. They also pay the Khan, or Malik, a tax on the occasion of a marriage amongst themselves; it is termed *Bakrai,* and the sum varies from Rs. 4 to Rs. 40, or more. They also are forced to provide *baigár* labor when required. The above terms also apply equally to all the other settlers in this country, except the Mullahs and Hindus. In fact, the Afghans, as the possessors of the country, are the only untaxed part of the population, excepting only the

Mullahs, who, as will be mentioned presently, manage to tax the Afghans, after a fashion, in common with the rest of the population of the country.

Designation.

All the foreign tribes thus settled amongst the Afghans and taxed, are termed Hamsaya, or Fakir, the Mullah and Hindu classes alone excepted. As a class, the Gujars are a fine, healthy, and athletic race, and in many points resemble the Afghans amongst whom they dwell.

Origin.

They are supposed to be the descendants of the possessors of the country previous to the arrival of the Afghans.

Numbers.

In numbers they equal about the whole of the rest of the population not Afghan, and may be roughly estimated at 75,000 souls. As a rule, they are comfortably, if not richly off, according to their own standard of comparison, and maintain more independence than the other settlers.

Hindkis.

The Awâns, Kashmiris, and other Hindkis, together number about 19,000 souls. The Awâns may be taken at 3,000; they are only found in the Yusufzai plain. The Kashmiris may be taken at 6,000, and the Hindkis at 10,000, in round numbers. These tribes conjointly comprise the mechanics, artificers, and petty traders. They live in separate societies, according to their occupations, and only intermarry amongst themselves, as *Jolah* with *Jolah*, *Chamâr* with *Chamâr*, and so on. In Yusufzai they have the following trade guilds, or societies, viz :—

Occupations.

Bâghwân.—Gardeners, fruiterers, &c.

Charikâr.—Ploughmen, cultivators.

Chamâr.—Tanners, curriers, or workers in leather.

Darzi.—Tailors, embroiderers, &c.

Dúm.—Musicians, ballad-singers, and pimps, called also *Mírási*, or "Prince of Sinners."

Gadba.—Shepherds and cattle graziers. They are also called *Rawánri.*

Gholam.—Slaves—Masc. *Mrai ;* Fem. *Windza.*

Jolah.—Weavers, rope-makers, &c.

Kullâl.—Potters and brick-makers.

Loár.—Ironsmiths, called also *Taudi Kârigar.*

Musalli.—Sweepers, grave-diggers, &c., also called *Shahkhail.*

Nandáp.—Cotton dressers and cleaners.

Nangraiz.—Dyers, also called *Dobi.*

Nái.—Barbers, dentists, cuppers, &c.

Pansâri.—Druggists, perfumers, &c.

Parácha.—Carriers, pedlars, also called *Tattar.*

Taili.—Oil and soap-makers.

Tarkanr.—Carpenters, called also *Sari Karigar.*

Zargar.—Gold and silver-smiths, jewellers.

Vassals

All the above classes, excepting the *Gholams*, are, by the Afghans called by the generic term *Hamsaya* and *Fakir*, which mean "dependent," and "vassal," respectively. Though naturalized by many generations of habitation in the country, they have no possession in the soil in the tracts beyond the British border, and for the most part within the British limits as well. They rent their houses, and generally a patch of land as well, from the Afghan owners ; for, as a rule, none of these classes can live entirely by their trades, the demand for their services being too small to yield a return sufficient for the support of a family ; their dealings also are as much (in the state they are now) by barter as by cash exchanges.

The Gholam, or slave class, are very numerous, more

Slaves.

especially beyond the British border, within which they are not now bought and sold. They are the descendants of former captives of war, or purchases from the hill tracts north of Kabul. They perform the household, farm, or agricultural labours for their masters, and are in return fed, clothed, and sheltered; and, as a rule, are much more comfortably off than many of the independent mechanic class. The men are termed *Mrai,* and are valued as faithful servants and body guards. They are said to be true and brave in the defence of their masters. The women are termed *Windza.* They perform the household duties in the women's departments, grind the corn, &c. They often serve as the concubines of their master, and sometimes rise to favour, are set free, and then legally married to their former master. Most of the Khans and Maliks still possess their hereditary slaves, and some of them own over a hundred of both sexes. They are, however, now fast diminishing by desertions and the prohibition of new purchases within British limits.

Priesthood.

The Mullah class is a very numerous and important one, and numbers in all about 34,000 souls. It consists of two great divisions, viz. the *Astânadâr* and the *Mullah* classes.

Astânadâr.

The *Astânadâr* are, as the name implies, "place possessors;" those whose ancestors in remote or recent times acquired the title of *Zburg*, or *Buzurg*, or "Saint," by a notoriety for superior holiness and piety and the performance of miracles during life, and who after death left memorials of the same either in the shape of mosques, shrines, or other sacred spots, or merely traditionary accounts of their sanctity. In the present day, the descendants, by virtue of the sanctity of their ancient *Zburg,* and the present benefits dispensed at his *astan, ziarat,* or "shrine," as well as by the unanimous accord of the people, enjoy, besides a superior and uncontested character for sanctity and righteousness, many secular and religious privileges. Any Mussulman may become the founder of a race of Astânadârs provided he have the qualifications of a Zburg, and be acknowledged as such during life. With the Afghans, there are four different classes of the Astânadâr, viz. 1. Sayad; 2. Pîr; 3. Mian; and, 4. Sahibzada.

Sayad.

The Sayad class are all of Arab extraction, and believed to be the direct descendants of the Khalifa 'Ali, the son-in-law of Mahomad. Their origin being from so holy a source, they are, of course, esteemed as uncommonly holy personages. Their bold, obtrusive, and continual publication of their sacred character and descent draws from the ignorant a reverential and aweful respect, and at the same time gives them great influence over the mass of the population they dwell amongst. They use this to their own advantage, and manage to get from the Afghans considerable tracts of land in gift as a perpetual and hereditary possession, besides the usual alms-offerings. The Astânadârs of this class are very numerous, and in some localities constitute entire village communities. In these they live peaceably and undisturbed as agriculturists, and enjoy the respect and good-will of their duped neighbours. The Sayad is always addressed by the title of Shâh.

Pîr.

THE PIR CLASS.—The Pîrs are the descendants of Afghans or Pukhtuns, whose ancestors somehow became recognized *Zburgs* during life, or got the title after death through the cunning and exertions of interested parties. In the latter case, they are certainly fictitious characters; and, in the former, not a few must have been false "seers" indeed, if they in any way bore the character of their descendants of the present day. The memory of these *Zburgs*, whether fictitious or real, and whether of Pîrs or the other Astânadârs, is perpetuated by holy shrines that mark the supposed or real sites of some of their holy deeds or miracles, or they mark the place of their death or burial. Sometimes these spots are authentic, but most frequently they are discovered to religious devotees and bigots by angels! Whatever their origin, they are all held sacred, and each possesses its own peculiar virtues and qualities for benefiting both man and brute. Some shrines cure fever; others opthalmia, and so on. Some have the power of rendering women and cattle of the same gender prolific; others vouchsafe the desires of intriguing lovers. Some protect their devotees from evil eye and a host of calamities; others ensure riches and worldly prosperity; and so on, *ad libitum.* Such shrines are named *ziarat,* and are named after the saint whose memory they perpetuate. Some saints dispense a multitude of blessings at their respective shrines; they are consequently greater favourites than others less distinguished, and are worshipped at many ziarats dedicated to them in different parts of the country. From the great multitude of these *ziarats*—for every village has two or three, or more, of them—the righteous in the good old days must have filled the land with the abundance of their numbers; and, with the Yusufzais, these must, indeed, be degenerate times; for, even angels' visits are, now a-days, few and far between, and the man of God seldom has his sleep disturbed by the ghostly visits, laments, and threats of injured and unremembered saints of former days. Such is the case at least within the British limits. As descendants of holy Pukhtuns, the Pîrs exact many exclusive and hereditary rights and privileges from their own people. Their hereditary share in the soil, the *daftar,* is rent free; their tribes are exempt from labor and taxes of every kind; and, in common with the rest of the "priest order," they receive a share of the produce of the fields and flocks. They claim the pre-eminence amongst their own religious orders, and the precedence amongst their own people, with its concomitants of respect and deference, where-ever they move amongst them. The Pîr takes the front rank, and leads the congregation in their prayers. He is addressed as *Badshah* whenever spoken to ; and, on joining an assembly, is welcomed by the rising of the congregation, who remain standing till the Pîr is seated. Besides these, the Pîr has the entrée to the women's apartments, a portion of the Afghan's house most jealously closed to all others of whatever creed or caste. Most Pîrs are believed to possess some secret power or charm, termed *uhda* or *huda*, either inherited or newly acquired, by virtue of which they can by a prayer, a glance, a touch, the application of spittle, a charm, or the repetition of some gibberish incantation, cure all sorts of diseases, grant wishes, avert evils, &c., &c. As one would be naturally inclined to suspect, they have gained all this power by a clever play on the superstition and ignorance of their brethren, amongst whom cunning, deceit, and extortion, as long as cloaked by religion, or what is so styled, may be carried to any extent. Besides the many privileges they enjoy, the Pîrs, like the rest of the "priest order," to whom also most of the foregone remarks equally apply, derive a very considerable income from their dupes amongst the general population. For their services, except when exercised with unnecessary ostentation towards the very poor, are by no means gratuitous. On the contrary, the amount of fee for the smallest service, either in cash or kind, or both combined, is more in proportion to the assumed sanctity of the Pîr than to the means of his dupe. All Pîrs are comfortably off, if not rich. Their social position and privileges are hereditary, and quite independent of individual merit; for many can neither read nor write, and are equally ignorant of the religion they profess. Many of them are bad characters, and some of them are notorious highwaymen and burglars. In all his acts, the Pîr, as well as the rest of the Astânadârs, proves the truth of the Persian proverb *Mal i muft dil bai rahm.*

THE MIAN CLASS.—In descent, hereditary privileges, and qualities of sanctity, the Mians much resemble the Pîrs. Their ancestors, however, were not Afghans, but *Hamsayahs*, or "vassals," dwelling amongst them. They enjoy much the same privileges and powers as the Pîrs, though in a less degree, but are debarred from entering the women's apartments. They hold extensive tracts of land in perpetual gift and hereditary in their families. Such lands are termed *sairai*, and are not bestowed by one individual, but equally by each individual of the tribe amongst whom they dwell. This will be explained in the next chapter. Like the Pîrs, the Mians (in either case not each individual, but only favoured ones) possess individual and special powers of *uhda* against pestilence, famine, floods, and other calamities. They also profess to discover thieves, liars, adulterers, murderers, &c., by means of incantation and ordeals. In worldly wealth and comfort, they rival the Pîrs, but are more numerous; and, in some localities, form entire village communities.

Mian.

THE SAHIBZADA CLASS.—Resembling the Pîrs and Mians in most points, the Sahibzadas rank after them, because their ancestors are supposed to have been a cut below their cotemporary saints. They are not so numerous as the other classes, but are more wealthy. The Swat Sahib, or Akhûn, represents a *zburg* whose descendents will be styled Sahibzada.

Sahibzada.

The *Mullah* class, or "priest order," differs from the Astânadâr in being the active portion of the clergy. Abandoning the world for a religious life, they devote their energies to the study and teaching of the doctrines of Islam. The Astânadârs may or may not be devoted to a religious life, though, if they are, they rise in the estimation of their fellows. But the great majority, however, content with their happy lot, lead a comfortable and worldly life;

Clergy.

those who do devote their lives to religion become classed with the community now under notice. The Mullah fraternity comprises four divisions, collectively styled *Mullayân*. They are, 1. Imâm; 2. Mullah; 3. Shaikh; and, 4. Talib-ul-ilm.

Imâm.

The Imâm is simply the leader of the congregation belonging to a mosque, or *jumâat*, as it is here called. He is also the head official attached to the mosque, takes the front place in the prayers, and occasionally reads and expounds the Kuran to the congregation. Every mosque has its own Imâm, or Paishwa, as he is sometimes called. The office and title are both hereditary.

Mullah.

The Mullah is an ordinary priest. There are generally several attached to each mosque. They call the *azân*, and perform the prayers and other duties of the Imâm in his absence. They are mostly occupied in teaching the Talib-ul-ilm the Kuran, the forms of prayer, and the doctrines of Islam, and the village children how to repeat their "belief" and say their prayers. They often succeed to the office of Imâmât. The title and occupation is mostly hereditary.

Shaikh.

The Shaikh is one who, relinquishing worldly pleasures, becomes the disciple, or *murîd*, of some *zburg* or saint. Neither the title nor occupation is hereditary.

Talib.

The Talib-ul-ilm, or "Seeker of Wisdom," is the name applied to a mixed class of vagrants and idlers, who, under the pretence of devoting themselves to religion, wander from country to country; and, on the whole, lead an agreeable and easy life. The Taliban-ul-ilm wherever they go find shelter in the mosques, and can always get a sufficiency of food for the mere asking. As a rule, they are very ignorant and remarkably bigoted. Some of them, however, are very observant travellers, and pick up very useful information regarding the countries and peoples they visit.

Means of support.

All these divisions of the Mullah community are supported by the produce of rent-free lands attached to the mosques on which they quarter themselves. They also receive periodical presents of clothes and daily supplies of food from the people of the *kandi*, or quarter in which their mosques are situated.

Hindus.

The Hindus, if not the aboriginals, are settlers in the country from the remotest times. They are generally called Khattri, and are reckoned at about twenty-two thousand in number. They are found in almost every village throughout the country, in perfectly distinct little societies of from a couple to fifty or more families. Though dwelling in the heart of a bigoted Mahomadan population, they retain most of their religious rites and national characteristics undisturbed. As being the means by which all the money and business transactions of the general population are carried on, they enjoy the protection of the Afghans, and are on the whole a very flourishing class. From individuals they at times suffer much oppression, but in the end they contrive to secure an equivalent; for the entire trade of the country, internal and external, is in their hands. The Hindus are a very important section of the general community. They are entirely devoted to trade and business pursuits, and under no circumstances bear arms.

CHAPTER V.

GOVERNMENT AND CUSTOMS.

The Yusufzais in their own country are altogether an agricultural people, and live entirely on the produce of their fields and flocks. In former times, previous to their emigration eastward into their present limits, they were shepherd tribes, more or less nomadic, and used to a hardy, open-air life, the charms of which were continual changes of scene and adventure as they roamed from country to country in search of fresh pastures for their cattle and flocks. The erratic life they thus led often brought them into contact with hostile tribes, who contested the country with them, whilst quarrels amongst themselves as to the extent of their respective grazing grounds, early inured them to the use of arms, and produced an inherent taste for a military life.

Agriculturalists.

Former life.

Its effects.

Like other barbarous peoples similarly situated, their nation was composed of a number of tribes, or great clans, each of which was split up into a multitude of lesser tribes made up of numerous small societies of mem-

Social composition.

bers of the same family. Though collectively bound to each other by the relationship of a common descent, the tribes individually formed distinct communities, governed by separate tribal chiefs or patriarchs. Amongst themselves these several tribes had rival interests, that, continually producing feuds and jealousies, kept them estranged from, or opposed to, each other; but, in their relations with foreigners, putting aside their individual feuds and jealousies, the tribes all coalesced, and, for the time being, acted in unison under the guidance of the elders of their patriarchs or tribal chiefs.

Relationship.

Rivalry.

When not threatened by a foreign enemy, the great tribal divisions formed distinct and rival communities, each possessing its own tract of the country, holding it by force of arms, and vigilantly guarding it against encroachment by the neighbouring tribes.

Coalitions.

The progress of the Yusufzais from the west to their present quarters has been described in the preceding chapter. Since their arrival in these parts they have been a fixed population, wholly devoted to the culture of the soil and the tending of their cattle.

Settled life.

Their several tribes have been described in the previous chapter. Here it may be noted that each consists of a number of families who form separate but concordant societies, and who, in matters that affect the interests of all alike, confederate under the elders of the senior family.

Family confederacies.

The larger divisions of the tribe are termed *koum,* or

"race," and bear the adjunct *zai* after the proper name of each, as *Yusufzai,* "the sons of Joseph," *Iliaszai,* "the sons of Elias," *Musazai,* "the sons of Moses," *Isazai,* "the sons of Jesus," &c. The lesser divisions are termed *khail,* or "clan," with the proper name of each prefixed, as, for example, *Akokhail,* "the clan of Ako," *Maddakhail;* "the clan of Madda," *Musakhail,* "the clan of Moses," and so on. Each *zai* and *khail* has its own representative chief. As many of them are generally associated together to form one tribe, the chief of the most powerful clan is recognized as the head of the tribe they collectively form.

Distinguishing terms.

Examples.

Each great division of the Yusufzai tribe has its own separate tract of country; and each of these is, in the first place, portioned out between the primary divisions of the several tribes holding them, and after whom they are generally named, though, perhaps, possessing another designation as well. Thus the Yusufzai plain is named Mandanr, the Lunkhwar valley Bâizai, the Sudhum valley Doulatzai, &c.

Tribal settlements.

Each of these tribal portions of the country is next divided into districts, or *tappa,* for each of the secondary divisions of the tribe. As, for example, Razar into the tappa of Malikzai, Manizai, Ismailzai, &c.

Their divisions.

Each *tappa* is in turn divided into lots termed *daftar* or "registered hereditary possession," as the Kamalzai tappa, into the Mishranzai *daftar,* and Kishranzai *daftar.*

Tappa.

Again, the *daftar* is divided into family lots termed *brakha,*

Daftar.

or "portion;" and these finally are divided into plots termed *patti*, for each of the several households, who are termed *brakha-khor*, whilst their individual share or *patti* is termed, according to the division, a *draiama, shpagama*, or *dolasama brakha*, or a "third," "sixth," or "twelfth portion."

Object.

By this arrangement, the Yusufzais are located in the country by societies lineally connected, and each family has its own possession in the soil, which is hereditary in the male descent.

Illustration.

Original allotment.

To illustrate the division of the land, we will take those of one clan as a sample of the rest. At the time of the settlement and division of the Yusufzai country by Shaikh Mali, the lands apportioned to the Kamalzai were divided into 400 equal lots for cultivation only, leaving the greater portion of their territory as pasture land for the cattle of the whole tribe in common. Of these 400 shares, 200 were allotted to the Mishranzai, or "elder branch," who settled at Toru, and the other 200 shares were allotted to the Kishranzai, or "younger branch" who settled at Hoti. The latter shares were subsequently divided into two equal portions of 100 lots each; one for Hoti, and the other for Mardan. These last were then distributed as follows: twelve lots were set aside as *sairai*, or "free gift" lands, for the support of various orders of the priesthood. The remaining eighty-eight lots were distributed amongst the Pukhtun community. Thus sixteen lots were given to the Mândûri tribe, whose ancestors came to the country as the military mercenaries of the Yusufzais, and the

Its sub-division.

Disposal.

other seventy-two lots were divided equally between the three divisions of the Kishranzai family settling at Mardan, each receiving twenty-four lots as its share. Thus, one went to the Khankhail, the second to the Rustamkhail, and the third to the Badakhankhail. Each of these shares was then treated as an integral portion, and divided into equal lots corresponding in number with the families composing the *khail* to whose lot it fell. The number of these lots, and consequently their extent, varies in each *khail* share; but all the families of one *khail* share equally with each other. Thus, of the three Kishranzai divisions, above-mentioned, the Khankhail at this time happens to be represented by only one family, which consequently owns as its share the whole of the original twenty-four lots undivided. But the Rustamkhail consists of a number of families in two divisions, viz., the Bahadurkhail and Bamokhail. Each of these owns a portion equal to twelve shares, or half of the twenty-four originally allotted to the Rustamkhail which they compose. The Bahadurkhail and Bamokhail shares are then divided into equal lots, corresponding in number with the families composing the khails respectively; and these family portions in turn are divided equally amongst the several brothers composing it, and finally by them amongst their children. When, owing to the increase of population or other cause and the consequent sub-division of the soil, each man's portion becomes insufficient for his support, then the village chief, in concert with the village *jirgah*, or "assembly of representatives," takes in a portion of the village grazing grounds that may be fit for cultivation, and, as in the first instance, divides it into 100 equal lots, or whatever the number may be into which the lands of the particular village were originally divided, for the

Distribution.

Further sub-division.

New allotments.

Sub-division.

number is a varying one in each different tribe. The Kishranzai number is 100, and the new land, thus lotted off, is distributed in the same manner as the first lots. Thus, in the case of Mardan, twelve lots are assigned as *sairai*, sixteen lots for the Mândûris, and the remaining seventy-two lots equally between the three divisions of the Kishranzai, at Mardan, and, by these amongst their respective sub-divisions and families, as above described.

Distribution.

The division of the land is arranged in the following manner. The *jirgah*, under the direction of the khan, or, in his absence, the chief malik, proceed to the ground to be divided and measure it off by means of a rope, which varies in length from fifty to a hundred or more feet. This rope is termed *purrai*, and the process of measuring, "casting the *purrai*," whilst the land measured off is termed a *wand*; it is generally of a square or oblong shape. The land thus measured off is then divided into equal lots for distribution amongst the khails to share in it. Thus, in the case of Mardan, the *wand*, after allotting the *sairai* and Mândûri shares, is divided into three equal parts, one for the Khankhail, one for the Rustamkhail, and the other for the Badakhankhail, whose respective maliks and elders then divide them amongst their respective divisions and families. The *sairai*, or "church lands," which sometimes, though rarely, are resumed by the original owners, are generally marked off by a line drawn parallel to one side of a *wand*, and across the other divisions, so that each share contributes an equal portion towards the "church lands;" as is shewn in the annexed diagram representing a *wand*, and its primary divisions.

Method.

Example.

PLAN.

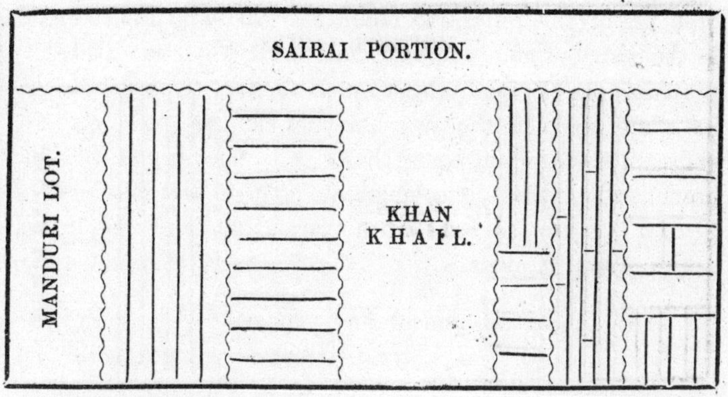

RUSTAM KHAIL. BADAKHAN KHAIL

BAHADUR KHAIL. BAMO KHAIL.

Explanation.

The marginal straight lines in the above plan mark the limits of the *wand*, and the waved lines its primary divisions, and their distribution to the khail divisions. Thus, in the case of Mardan, after marking off the Sairai and Mândûri portions, the remainder is divided into three equal lots for the Khankhail, Rustamkhail, and Badakhankhail, respectively. Each of these is sub-divided according to the divisions of each khail, as the Rustamkhail lot into two equal parts, one for the Bahadurkhail, the other for the Bamokhail, and these are divided into equal lots for their respective families, as above shewn. In the above plan, the Badakhankhail share is arranged to illustrate the ultimate division of the land. It is first divided into three equal shares for each of three divisions of the khail. One of these is halved for the two branches of one of these khail divisions. One of the branches is supposed to have four, and the other five, families. The next *khail* share is supposed to be divided between five families, and three of these shares are divided for the branches of three several families, viz. one between three, another between four, and the third between two branches of the respective families to whose lot the share fell in the distribution. Similarly, the third khail is divided, in the first place, equally between six families. One sub-divides its share between the two branches supposed to compose it, and another into four equal shares, one for each of the four branches supposed to compose it. These divisions are yet further sub-divided between the various males of each branch of the several families.

Casting lots.

After the measurement and primary division of a *wand*, its distribution is regulated by lot, or, as it is termed, "casting," the *pucha* or *hisk*. It is thus managed. The representative of each of the khails to share in the distribution selects a private mark (a piece of wood, or a rag, a grain of maize, or pellet of sheep's dung, or a stone, or any substance near at hand), which, in the presence of all, he hands over to the "grey beard" appointed to cast the lot, declaring it to be his token. The "grey beard" having collected all the tokens and seen them severally recognized, gathers them together in the skirt of his frock, and then walks round the *wand*, followed by the assembly; and, as he passes them, throws out on each of the plots marked off the first token that comes into his hand. The several plots then become the possession of the khails severally represented by the tokens thrown out on them.

Subsequent divisions.

Each plot is then successively divided and allotted in a similar manner to the divisions of the khails and their several respective families. In the ultimate divisions, the portions of land are often of very small extent, and are frequently styled *pucha*, after the process above described.

In thus dividing the land for cultivation, the *wands* are

Detached lots.

in detached plots all round the village, roads, water-courses, and wastes intervening, Each *wand* is known by a separate name, just like a farmer's fields at home, mostly expressive of some quality of the soil, or position, &c., as *irai wand, shigai wand,* "the ash field," "the sand field," &c. The division of the land, it will thus be seen, gives each section or tribe, or clan, a fixed possession in the soil. The land itself is termed *daftar*, or "register," but its amount in each case is termed *brakhah*, or "share," which, in individual shares, is specified by prefixing the extent of sub-division as *dirshama brakhah, attama brakhah,* or "thirtieth share," "eighth share," &c., as the case may be. It will also be observed that each individual's *daftar* is not in one unbroken plot, but scattered according to lot in the different *wands*. This is necessary, so that each shall share alike, as far as possible, in the good and bad land. Very often, and beyond the British border always, in one tribe where the several khails possess lands of varying quality, the lot of some having fallen on good and that of others on inferior land, it is customary to exchange places at fixed periods of five, ten, or more years. The land always remains the *daftar* of the original owners, but is mapped out afresh for distribution amongst the new owners, who all share equally with those of their own tribal divisions, without reference to rank. In these exchanges between the tribes, only the houses are left standing, and often these are deprived of their timbers. The effects of this custom are ruinous to the land, for no man cares to spend his labour and money on improvements which for years will become the property of others. The system of division of the land is equally a bar to its improvement, whilst it is besides a fruitful source of feuds and bloodshed; for, in the smaller divisions, the several mem-

Individual portions.

Exchanges.

Their effects.

bers sharing it, rather than divide the field, agree to divide the produce, and this is never effected without quarrels that frequently produce tribal feuds and the loss of many lives.

New settlements.

Where the majority of a village community have enough land for their support by cultivation, they do not take in portions of the pasture lands, nor can individuals at their will cultivate on such tracts. Individuals who cannot support themselves on their own lands by reason of its small extent, either lease it to others, and themselves seek a livelihood by foreign military service, or else, where several are in the same predicament, they found small hamlets within the limits of their own tribal lands.

Bânda.

Such hamlets are termed *bânda*, and they often increase to the size of important villages. They are not the property of the people founding and inhabiting them, but belong to the tribe in common, each khail and its several families receiving its own share of the land, which they can cultivate themselves or let to others, generally for a certain proportion of the produce, either a third or fourth of the crop. The tribal chief is also chief of all *bândas* that may be founded within the limits of the tribal lands.

Whose property.

Inhabitants.

The founders and inhabitants of *bândas* are generally *Gujars* or *Hamsayas*, and they rent the land from the Pukhtun owners on the terms above stated. As a rule, there are few Pukhtun families settled in the *bândas*, though all the tribe in whose lands they are have their respective portions in it. The only exception is where the *bândas* inhabited by Mians, or Sayads, or other religious orders, become their hereditary possession by common consent of the tribes, who thus forego all claim to a share in the lands thus disposed of. The *bândas* of these religious orders are always flourishing little settlements, for they pay no taxes, and are never oppressed by the rest of the population. In some respects they resemble the "cities of the priests" of the ancient Israelites, and some of them become noted as sanctuaries for the refuge of criminals fleeing from justice. The spread of *bándas* in the plain of Yusufzai is a sign of the prosperity of the country under British rule.

Cities of the priests.

The division and distribution of the lands forming the site of a village are made in the same manner as those for cultivation. A share in each forms a man's *daftar* or "*register*," and the owner is termed *daftari*. The division of a village corresponding with the primary division of a *wand*, or the *brakhah* of a khail in the fields, is termed *kandi*, which may be divided into other *kandis*, according to the divisions of the khail. Each kandi is a collection of separate tenements of the individual families forming a khail or clan section. Each tenement is termed *kandar*, and consists of the house termed *kor*, and the court-yard termed *gholai;* these shelter the family as well as their dependants and cattle. Each *kandi* has its own *malik* or chief, whose authority is confined to it. His duties are to maintain order, settle disputes amongst the householders of his *kandi*, to collect the revenue, and see to the fair distribution of the crops, &c. Each malik is subordinate to the chief or *khan* of the tribe; to him he makes his reports, and from him he receives his orders.

Village system.

Each *kandi* has its own church or *jumâat*, its own assembly-room, or *hujrah*; and, in villages beyond the border, its own tower of defence, or *burj*.

Kandi.

The *jumâat* is under the care of an establishment of priests *(Mullah)*, who are subordinate to a leader styled *Imâm*. They are supported by rent-free lands

Jumâat.

attached to the mosque, and receive besides daily supplies of food from the residents of their kandi. Their duties are to lead the congregation in their prayers, instruct the people in the doctrines and observances of Islam, to teach the young their belief and prayers, to perform marriage, circumcision, and burial services when required, to fix the times of the appointed feasts and fasts, &c., &c. On each occasion of the marriage and other services, they receive presents of money, cattle, food, or clothes, &c., according to the means of the donor.

Hujrah.

The *hujrah* is a public room with court-yard and stables attached. In most instances it is the property of the malik of the kandi, who is expected to feed and shelter all visitors and travellers; beds, bedding, and forage are provided by the *fakirs* or *hamsayahs* in rotation. In the *hujrah*, the malik meets the residents of the kandi for the discussion and settlement of their public business. Here also the residents and visitors assemble to smoke, gossip, learn the news of the day, and discuss politics. It is also the sleeping place of all the bachelors of the *kandi*; for, as it is customary with the Afghans, no friend, nor traveller, nor relative, a bachelor at manhood, is allowed to sleep in the house. This custom is possibly owing to the construction of the houses, which provide no privacy for the women.

Burj.

The *burj*, or "watch tower," now only exists in villages beyond the border. It is always attached to the house of the malik, and is in constant use as a place of refuge and observation in case of feuds between the different khails of a village community, as well as against enemies outside. In villages where a khan resides, there is, besides the *burj* of each *kandi*, a fort or *garrai*, which encloses the whole of the khan's *kandi*.

From the foregone particulars, it will be observed that

Individual patrimonies.

each family of the Yusufzais has its own patrimony in tenements and lands; that they live in village communities according to tribal or clan descent, and in these again in smaller societies of the families of the clan sections. These are governed by their own maliks, who in turn are subordinate to the tribal chief, or khan.

Chiefs.

Both these offices are hereditary, except in the case of manifest incapacity from mental imbecility or physical deformity, or from some objectionable quality of temper or general conduct; but there is nothing to prevent a man of courage and ability raising himself to the position of either.

Their power.

The independent powers of these chiefs—for the terms merely represent different degrees of rank of the same kind—are very restricted indeed. In matters affecting the welfare or interests of the tribe or clan, they cannot act in opposition to the wishes of the general community.

The jirgah.

These are ascertained through the maliks by *jirgah*, or council, of the "elders" of each clan, and its sectional khails, separately first, and collectively afterwards. Each clan is a separate democracy. Their members are guided in their views by the grey beards or elders, the patriarchs of the different families, who, in concert with the malik, decide all matters relating to their own society. This is the regular course; but, in actual practice, the Yusufzais generally take the law into their own hands, and, on the principle that "might is right," generally act much as they please.

Disputes.

Disputes between members of the same clan are sometimes settled by their friends, the injured party receiving an equivalent for the injury suffered, but very seldom without the assistance of the elders and the malik; and

How settled.

Pukhtunwali.

they in their decisions are guided by the usages of Pukhtunwali, a code framed on the principles of equity and retaliation. Thus A kills B's plough bullock; the matter is referred to the *jirgah;* they decide that B shall kill one of A's plough bullocks; he does so, and all parties are satisfied. Or A kills B's *charaikar,* or bondsman. B must be provided with another by A and the matter ends. But if A kills B, then B's relatives demand the life of A; and, if the *jirgah* succeed in handing him over to B's next of kin for revenge, the matter ends in A's death; otherwise, if A escapes, and one of his family is not sacrificed, a feud breaks out till the injured party is revenged. Between members of the same clan, such disputes seldom lead to extremes; but where members of different clans are the principals, their respective clan divisions take up the quarrel as a personal one, and a settlement is seldom effected; for reprisals are made on both sides, and ultimately leads to a lasting estrangement or feud between the tribes; for, barbarians as they are, they are most sensitive to any insult or slur on their honor and independence.

Examples.

Feuds.

Each tribe under its own chief is an independent commonwealth, and collectively each is the other's rival if not enemy. The families composing each never render more than an allegiance to their khan in whose defence they arm and take the field. Previous to the British annexation of a portion of their country they never paid revenue regularly to any government.

Tribal system.

Independence.

When undisturbed from without, the several tribes are always opposed to each other; feuds, estrangements and affrays are of constant occurrence; the public

Turbulence.

Anarchy.

Confederation.

roads and private property are alike unsafe. The men although wearing arms as regularly as others do clothes, seldom or never move beyond the limits of their own lands except disguised as beggars or priests. Everywhere family is arrayed against family, and tribe against tribe, in fact one way and another every man's hand is against his neighbour. Feuds are settled and truces patched up but they break out afresh on the smallest provocation. Such is the ordinary condition of Yusufzai beyond the border. But when danger threatens from without, all family feuds and clan jealousies are at once forgotten and all unite to repel the common enemy.

Former state of Yusufzai plain.

Present condition.

Safety.

Previous to the British occupation of the Yusufzai plain, so rife were these feuds and disorders that men ploughed their fields with a rifle slung over the shoulder or a sword suspended at the waist, and watched the growth of their crops with armed pickets night and day. Similarly their cattle never went out to graze except they were protected by armed footmen or mounted guards. Happily all this is now altered, and the change is appreciated by the mass of the people. The cultivator now casts his seed on ground far away from his village and is troubled by no anxieties for the safety of the crop. Children now lead out the cattle to graze and amuse themselves at play on the mounds formerly held as pickets. Men and women follow the tracks across the dreary and desert *mairah* wastes unhindered and undisturbed, and in their visits from village to village daily perform journeys their grand-parents never dreamed of. The tales of heroism and deeds of bloodshed, of which almost any mound and hollow in the country is the site, are now fast becoming traditions, and are only heard of from actors amongst the old men, who in their village homes delight the youth untutored in the use of arms with thrilling recitations of the manly deeds of their fathers.

No regular government.

From the foregone description it will be observed that the Yusufzais have no regular form of government. Every man is pretty much his own master. Their khans and maliks only exercise authority on and extract revenue from the mixed population, who besides paying a third or fourth of the produce of the land they cultivate to the owner, render certain fees and taxes to the chief of the tribe or clan they are settled with. These have already been detailed with the services exacted from them. From Musalmans, not Pukhtuns nor priests, the chief sources of revenue to the khans are the *bakrai* or "marriage tax," and the *lwugi tawân* or "hearth tax." The Hindus only pay the *juzia* or "poll tax." These are the recognized taxes, but in practice many other tyranical exactions are made on frivolous pretences by chiefs who have the courage and power to do so.

Taxes.

Note.

Such are the main features of the government of the Yusufzais, let us now notice their customs and character.

Character.

Of the latter some idea will have been conveyed by the foregone remarks; here it may be added that owing to the pastoral and agricultural life they lead, the Yusufzais are for the most part very illiterate; even their priests or educated class are as a body lamentably ignorant, though in the midst of the surrounding darkness they are shining lights.

Like the rest of the Afghan nation generally, the Yusufzais view themselves as a peculiar and favored people. The most notable traits in their character are unbounded superstition, pride, cupidity and a most revengeful spirit.

Special traits.

Their superstition is incredulous and has no limits. Miracles, charms and omens are believed in as a matter of course. An inordinate reverence for saints and the religious classes generally is universal, and their absurdly impossible and contradictory dicta are received and acted on with eager credulity. The *ziarat* or "sacred shrine" is habitually resorted to by all classes and both sexes. At these the devotees confess their sins, and implore forgiveness, unburden their hearts of all manner of secret desires, and beseech favours, all in the full belief of a sure hearing and answer. The wayfarer never passes one without checking his steps to render obeisance or invoke a blessing. The people pride themselves on these outward signs of a holy life, and boast of their love and reverence for their "pure prophet" and his "blessed religion," and congratulate themselves on their resigned obedience to his commands as conveyed to them through their holy men and priests. In all this they act sincerely from the heart, for they certainly do cherish and pamper a very numerous priesthood at considerable self-denial.

Superstition.

Withal this, however, and as might be expected in a religion that, without appealing to the loftier and purer qualities of the heart, merely binds its followers to the observance of outward forms and ceremonies, they never allow their religion or its ordinances to stand in the way of their desires when these run counter to them. In their religious tenets they are *sunni* Mahomadans and distinguish themselves as *chârîârîs.* In common with other

Effects of religious training.

Tenets.

Observances. Musalmans they hold the observance of prayer, alms, fasts, and pilgrimage to be the binding and fundamental duties of their religion. To omit any of these is considered a great sin, and if persevered in exposes the offender to excommunication as an infidel. The observance of prayer especially, with the appointed ceremonies and at the fixed periods, is deemed the most important duty, and is less neglected than any of the others. The prayers consist of two parts, termed *fard* and *sunnat*. The former must always be repeated, the latter may be omitted in case of pressing hurry. Before any prayer can be repeated the ablution by *aodas*, or in the absence of water the purification by *taiammum* must be performed; the place of prayer as well as the body and clothes of the person must be *pak* or "pure." A multitude of trifles are always conspiring to render either impure or *palît*. The religious man is consequently always on the look out and dodging about to avoid contact with imaginary impurities. The fixed prayers are *shr* at day-light, *mâzpakhîn* at noon, *mâzdigar* afternoon, *mâzkhâm* at sunset, and *mâzkhotan* at evening.

Prayer.

Kinds.

Purifications.

Appointed times.

The distribution of alms is very generally observed by all classes according to their means. The priesthood, widows, orphans, maimed, blind, aged, &c., are the recipients. They are of two kinds, termed *zakât* and *khairât*. The former are appointed by the kuran, the latter are according to the inclination of the donor. Alms are sometimes given in money, but more generally they are gifts from the produce of

Alms.

Kinds.

Tithes.

the fields or flocks, &c. None of the Yusufzais pay the *ushr*, or tithe for the support of the church, though its exaction has frequently been attempted. Their objection is that by so doing they would acknowledge themselves the subjects of a sovereign, whereas it is the glory of most of the tribe to boast of the independence they maintain.

Fasts.

The fast is the Mahomadan *Ramazân*. It is very strictly kept from sunrise to sunset every day throughout the month, and is considered a meritorious penance, ensuring abundant future reward. Only travellers and invalids are allowed to eat during the fast; children are classed with the latter. Keeping the fast is termed *rozha*, and not keeping it *kozha*. Those who cannot keep the fast, in whole or part, during the month of Ramazan, must make up the difference afterwards before the arrival of the next Ramazan.

Pilgrimage.

This is termed *haj*, when made to the proper place, Mecca. Those who cannot go themselves, or send a substitute —and with few exceptions they comprise the whole tribe—content themselves with periodical visits to the sacred shrines in their own limits. This is termed "doing the ziarat." Friday is the favourite day, and is, therefore, named "*ziarat day*." On this day whole villages turn out for the pilgrimage round their own ziarats. Sometimes pilgrims go the round of the noted shrines in the country. Hassan Abdul, Pir Baba in Buhnair, and the Kakakhail in Khattak hills are the chief favorites in this country.

Pride.

The pride of the Afghans is a marked feature of their national character. It is also a prominent one of the Yusufzais. They eternally boast of their descent, their prowess in arms, and their independence, and cap all by "Am I not a Pukhtun?" They despise all other races; and, even amongst themselves, each man considers himself equal to, if not better than, his neighbour. Hence most of the bickerings and jealousies so rife in every every family throughout the tribe. In their bearing towards strangers of rank, they are manly and plain spoken, but towards the weak and low, they are abusive and tyrannical. They enjoy a character for lavish, or at least liberal, hospitality. This they do deserve, but not to the extent they boast of; for what passes for hospitality is, in most cases, a mere customary interchange of services or favors. Owing to the disturbed and barbarous state of their society, and the absence of public places of accommodation for travellers, such as sarais, it is the custom of the several tribes to lodge and feed each other when travelling. Thus guests and strangers are fed and sheltered free of all charge in the village *hujrahs*, but both the accommodation and fare are of the simplest and least expensive kind. Strangers or foreigners generally receive neither food nor shelter, but beg the former from house to house, and find the latter in the mosques. In out of the way and unfrequented localities, where the population is sparse and poor, there is a shew of greater hospitality and welcome; but it is not genuine, and as often as not, if the guest be worth it, he is robbed or murdered by his late host as soon as beyond the protecting limits of the village boundary, if not convoyed by *badraga* of superior strength. This *badraga* is merely an armed body of men who, for a consideration, agree to convoy travellers through their own limits. Any Mussulmân may act as *badraga*, but only the one supplied by the chief of the district is safe; any others are liable to be attacked by rivals or

Its fruits.

Hospitality.

Over-estimated.

Badraga.

enemies. The convoy can only defend within their own limits; beyond these men of the next district take their place. Every tribe and their divisions have their own separate and distinct limits, within which they are quite independent of each other. A man of one district who drives off to his own home the cattle from a neighboring district is only reached by the injured tribe making reprisals on the offenders. Thus, for example, if a man drives off a buffalo from the Salarzai district to his own home, in the Gadaizai district, both in Buhnair, he is safe until the owner of the stolen animal succeeds in tracing it. He cannot make the thief restore it, or punish him for the theft, but retaliates by seizing the first Salarzai man, or any of their cattle, that he may lay hands on. The matter then becomes a dispute between the two tribes, and is generally settled by each party restoring the other's property. The cattle first carried off is termed *dúrâ* or *dúrâ dopa*, and the reprisal made is termed *bota barampta*. Where a man of one tribe owes a man of another tribe money or other property, and refuses to make payment, then the creditor seizes and keeps the first man, or any property, belonging to his debtor's tribe until the debt be paid. Sometimes the tribes meet in *jirgah* for the settlement of these disputes; but generally individuals are allowed to settle their own disputes amongst themselves. The consequence is the anarchy and disorder that characterize the life of the Yusufzais. The most remarkable illustration of the pride of the Yusufzais is their exaggerated notion of their own honor, *Nang i Pukhtâna* as it is termed, any slight or insult to which is instantly resented. The existence of such sentiments amongst them is very strange, for they glory in being robbers, admit that they are avaricious, and

Reprisals.

Example.

Results.

Nang i Pukhtâna.

cannot deny the character they have acquired for faithlessness. The distinctive laws of *Nang i Pukhtâna* are very numerous, both as regards their dealings with their own race and with strangers. The chief are *Nanawatai, Badal,* and *Mailmastai.*

Nanawatai.

By *Nanawatai,* or "the entering in," the Pukhtun is expected, at the sacrifice of his own life and property, if necessary, to shelter and protect any one who in extremity may flee to his threshold and seek an asylum under his roof. This applies even to the protector's own enemies, and by some tribes the asylum is extended to all living creatures, man or brute, or fowl; but the protection is only vouchsafed within the limits of the threshold or premises. Beyond these the host himself may be the first to injure the late protégé.

Badal.

Badal, or retaliation, must be exacted for every and the slightest personal injury or insult, or for damage to property. Where the avenger takes the life of his victim in retaliation for the murder of one of his relatives, it is termed *Kisâs.*

Mailmastai.

The laws of *mailmastai* bind the Pukhtun to feed and shelter any traveller arriving at, his house and demanding them.

Strict observance.

To omit or disregard any of these observances exposes the Pukhtun to the ridicule and scorn of his associates, and more especially as regards the *badal* and *kisâs.* These are never forgotten, and whilst aptly illustrating the revengeful spirit of the people shew the means by which it is kept up. It is a common thing for injuries received by one generation to be revenged by their representatives of the next, or even by those two or three generations further removed.

Children in their infancy are impressed with this necessity as the object of their lives.

Character assigned by foreigners.

According to their neighbours, the Yusufzais are said to be naturally very avaricious and grasping, selfish, and merciless, strangers to affection and without gratitude. They have all these faults, but the condemnation is too sweeping and severe. Though not always sincere, in their manners the Yusufzais observe many outward forms of courtesy towards each other and strangers that one would not expect in a people living the disturbed and violent life they do. The salutation *as salâm alaikum*, and the reply *wa alaikum salâm*, are always interchanged. Not to return the salam is always considered wrong, and not unfrequently is taken as a personal slight, and avenged accordingly. Friends meeting after a long absence embrace, and in fervent phrases enquire of each others' welfare, never stopping to give a due reply in the midst of their counter gabblings of *jor yai, kha jor yai, khushal yai, takra, taza kha takra yai, rog yai*, &c. Strangers passing each other on the high roads exchange courtesies as each plods on his way, and *starai ma sha*, or "be not fatigued," (which corresponds with the *mandana bashi* of the Persians) is answered by *loai sha*, "be great," or *ma khwaraiga* "be not poor." The visitor entering a village or its *hujrah* is greeted with *har kala rasha*, "always welcome," and replies, *naiki darsha*, "good betide you," or *har kala osa*, "may you always abide." There is no term exactly corresponding with our "thank you," but under similar conditions the usual phrases are *khudâia di obakha* "God pardon you," or *khudâai di loai ka* "God prosper you," or *khudâai di osâta* "God preserve you." Friends parting commit each other to the care of God with the sentence *da khudâai pa âmân*, "to the protection of God" and its reply *khudaâi dar sara naiki oka* "God act well with you." Of the necessity of such a commission there is

Courtesies.

no doubt, and in this country the traveller invariably conceals his route and time of departure. Thus, if going direct from Murdan to Peshawar by night he gives out that he leaves for Nowshaira in the morning.

Position of the woman.

Jealousy.

One other point connected with the character of the Yusufzais requires mention before proceeding to a description of their domestic habits, social customs and amusements. It is the estimation in which they hold their women. They are most suspicious and jealous of them. It is quite enough for a man to see his wife speaking to a stranger to arouse his passion. He at once suspects her fidelity, and straightway maltreats or murders her. The women are never allowed in public to associate with the men, though amongst themselves they enjoy a certain amount of liberty.

Its effects.

The abuse or slander of a man's female relations is only to be wiped out in the blood of the slanderer and not unfrequently the slandered one, whether the calumny be deserved or not, is murdered to begin with. The Yusufzais though so jealous of them treat their women with no respect or confidence, but look on them as so much property in which their honor is invested, and to be watched and punished accordingly.

Elopements.

Nevertheless elopements, termed *matiza*, are one of the most fruitful cause of feuds.

Domestic habits.

In their domestic habits the Yusufzais are very simple.

Dwellings.

Their dwellings are mean mud and lath cabins, full of vermin and foul air, and surrounded by cesspools and heaps of every kind of filth.

Diet.

In their diet they are frugal and often abstemious, very few are intemperate. Their food is plain and wholesome, and almost entirely the produce of their cattle and lands. Milk in its various forms, the common cereals, vegetables, and meats, together with pot-herbs and edible fruits that grow wild, constitute the diet of the mass of the people. Sugar, and in some parts wild honey, is much used, but spirits are quite unknown. Tea is very little used and only by the rich, but coffee is not even known by name. Tobacco, for chewing, smoking and snuffing is in too general use. Opium also is used to some extent, and so are the different preparations of Indian hemp, but mostly in the plain country and only amongst the abandoned and debauched, who are pointed at as disreputable characters and a disgrace to their names.

Personal habits.

In their persons the Yusufzais are singularly indifferent to cleanliness. Their ablutions seldom extend beyond the *aodas* or *wúzú* appointed as the necessary purification before prayers. Many wear clothes steeped in indigo to hide the dirt. The ordinary dress consists of a loose frock, or *kamíz*, and wide trowsers, or *partog*, with a *patka* to wind round the head. All are of coarse cotton cloth of home manufacture, and are frequently worn, without a change, till in tatters. The dress of the chiefs and well-to-do is of the same kind, but of better material, of English manufacture. The dress of the women only differs from that of the men in the substitution of the *oranai*, or chequered sheet, for the patka. This sheet is of the same material and pattern for the whole tribe.

Dress.

Field sports.

Other occupations.

The Yusufzais, like most Afghan tribes, have a natural fondness for field sports, such as hawking, hunting with dogs, and shooting. Frequently they combine with these pleasures the more exciting business of highway robbery, cattle-lifting, and burglary. With many, these are the ordinary means of livelihood; otherwise the population is more or less wholly devoted to the care of their flocks and fields. Many take military service under the neighbouring governments, but none ever engage in the industrial or mechanical trades, and few have the capacity to manage the business of a merchant. All such are the special occupations of different classes of the vassal population, as already mentioned. The workmanship is always of the most simple and coarse kind, such as is suited to the wants of a poor agricultural people.

Industrial pursuits.

At home the Yusufzais are of a lively and merry disposition, and are very fond of music and poetry; to enjoy these they have frequent social gatherings at their village *hujrahs*. The poetry possesses some merit, and is worthy of attention from us by way of encouragement. Their music, too, though noisy, and the result of vigorous performance, is not without its own peculiar merits, to judge from its exciting effects on a Yusufzai audience. In all cases the professional musicians belong to a distinct class, termed *Dum* and *Mirasi*. Their instruments are the *nagára* or drum, the *surnai*, or flageolet, and the *rabab*, or violin. The last is often accompanied vocally. The *mirasis* are improvisatores and actors. Their recitations are of an epic character, generally some departed warrior of the tribe being the hero; but love songs and burlesques are also common subjects. Some of the last named are clever and witty, and do not spare the British officials who have become noted in the country. Often, however, both the recitation and acting are of quite a different character. The obscenity and beastliness of these equally with the others draw loud plaudits from the audi-

Disposition.

Amusements of the men.

Music.

Plays.

ence. In their social gatherings and amusements, the men are never joined by their women. These have their own separate gatherings, where they sing and dance to the music of the *Dums* in an adjoining court. The women, however, except on the regular festival days, to be mentioned further on, have few gatherings for amusement or recreation. They are mostly occupied with their several household duties, but find time also to visit each other from house to house, gossip, talk scandal, and do other quarrelling. With rare exceptions, they are entirely uneducated, and are described as coarse and obscene in their conversation. In public they are silent, and always veil themselves before strangers. They are said to possess a martial spirit, and often urge their men to many a deed of blood to gratify their own private piques, or to resent some imagined or real slur on their honour. Their daily occupations are the usual domestic duties of the household, such as fetching water, preparing butter, grinding corn, cooking, spinning cotton, &c. Often the wealthier classes engage in the lighter of these duties by way of occupation, but more frequently they are better employed with their dress, jewellery, and personal adornments, such as plaiting the hair, dyeing the hands and feet with *nakriza*, or "hinna," and painting the eyelids with *rânja*, or "surma." The women are even more superstitious and religiously disposed than the men, and their credulity it seems increases with the absurdity of what is offered for their belief. They are very fond of visiting the *ziarats* and the graves of departed relatives. On Fridays, it is a common sight to find the village graveyards and ziarat enclosures crowded with troops of women, old and young. Some in silence move about between the graves,

Amusements of the women.

Their spirit.

Occupations.

Toilette.

Superstitions.

strewing them with flowers, or pebbles, or bits of pottery. Others sit down and indulge their grief for a lost dear one in loud sobs and wailings of the deepest sorrow, and for hours together call to the dead in the most affectionate terms mingled with loving rebukes for deserting his own to the cares and toils of a weary life. Mourning for the dead appears to be the special duty of the women. When a death occurs in a family, the women of the *kandi*, or quarter, and others in the neighbourhood, repair to the house, and gathering round the corpse, which is for the purpose laid out on a bed in the court, perform the *vír*, or *wuzar*, the lamentation. It is a very mournful and impressive sight. The women, some twenty or thirty, if the deceased were a man of position, stand round the corpse and weep in concert, and in an accustomed manner and tone. They are led by the senior matron, who, advancing a step or two in front of the rest, slaps her face with both hands, and amidst loud sobs, exclaims in sharp, shrill, and hurried breaths, *hai! hai! hûai!* "alas! alas! woe, alas!" and at the last syllable stamps one foot on the ground. The rest repeat in chorus after the leader, and continue the same exclamations and gestures with increasing vehemence and gesticulations for half an hour or more, by which time their faces are swelled from repeated slapping (at least those of the near relatives); the eyes are bloodshot and sore from the unusual drain of tears, the hair hangs in wild dishevelled locks, and the actors are more or less exhausted by the performance. The sound of the *wuzar*, or *vír*, can be heard at a considerable distance. Often the weepers divide into two parties, who repeat the *vír* in rapid succession, but in different keys; the one party commencing at the cadence of the other's exclamation.

Mourning.

Ceremonies.

Description.

At the conclusion of the lamentation, the women retire.

Burial rites.

The body is then washed in the prescribed manner by one of the Shahkhail class, who for his labour gets his day's food and the clothes on the body. After the washing, the corpse is swathed in burial clothes—a winding sheet, in two pieces of coarse cotton cloth. One piece is wrapped all round the body, and the other is spread over its back and front from head to foot. The two great toes are fastened together with a string. In this state, placed on a bed and covered with a sheet, the corpse is carried off to the burial ground, where round the grave are collected the priest of the quarter in which deceased resided, his relatives, friends, and a crowd of beggars and idlers. Women form no part of the assembly. On depositing the corpse near the grave, the assembly rise and stand in rows to its east and facing the west. The priest then advances a few paces and performs the prayers appointed for the burial of the dead in an audible and solemn voice, and is followed by the congregation repeating after him. At the conclusion of the prayers, the body is lowered into the grave,

The grave.

which lies north and south, and is next laid in the *lahad* with the face inclined to the west. The *lahad* is a small sepulchre on the west side of the grave, or *kabar*, and a little below the level of its floor. It is roomy enough to allow the corpse to sit up when summoned by the angels *Nakir* and *Munkir* to render account of his life and deeds. After the body has been deposited in it, the *lahad* is shut off from the *kabar* by large flat bricks placed upright against its opening, as represented in the annexed section. The *kabar* is then

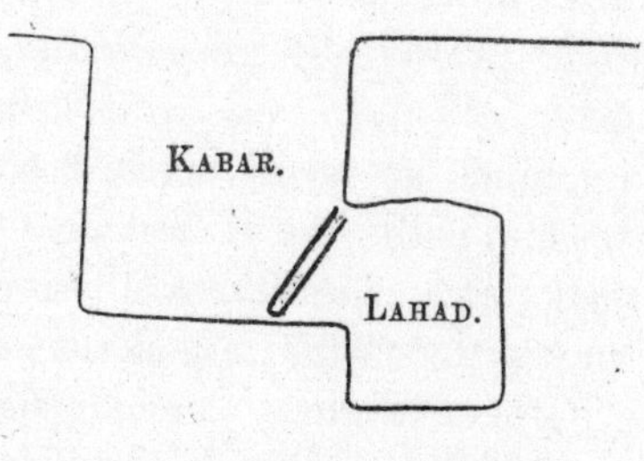

filled up with earth, none of which reaches the corpse itself. Before lowering the corpse into the grave, the deceased's relatives disburse the *izkât*, consisting of money and sugar, to the priests and beggars around. The ceremony of burying the dead is termed *janâza*. At its conclusion the assembly disperses; but deceased's friends repair to his late home, and for three successive days perform the required mourning. During these the women repeat the *vîr* or *wuzar*, friends drop in to repeat the *fatihah*, here called *lâs niwah*, from the custom of holding the hands together in repeating "the condolence for the dead," and the priests and poor are fed. On the fourth day the women visit the grave in a body. This concludes the mourning ceremony for all, except the members of deceased's family, who continue to receive the condolatory visits of their friends, and themselves visit the grave, at least every Friday, till the fortieth day, on which they give a feast that concludes the ceremony for them also. Amongst the Yusufzais, although they are accustomed to violent deaths and murders, the death of a member, especially if a male, is always the source of sincere mourning and grief, and is a calamity generally very much dreaded. The people have all sorts of superstitious terrors of the mysteries beyond the grave; and, believing in good and bad omens, observe some curious customs to avert the dreaded calamity. On the filling up of the grave, it is believed that the angel Gabriel blows a terrible blast on the trumpet for the raising of the dead, who, waking from his death-sleep, finds an angel perched on each shoulder. The one taxes him with his evil deeds, reveals his hidden thoughts and secrets, and notes them all down in a book. The other recounts the meritorious deeds of his life, notes the prayers and other religious ceremonials that have been properly observed, and the fact of his having died in the true faith.

Charity.

Condolence.

After death mysteries.

The two records are then balanced against each other; and, according to the result, the soul is welcomed to paradise, admitted to purgatory, or despatched to hell. Amongst the numerous superstitious rites observed by the Yusufzais for the aversion of impending death, or in atonement for the soul thereafter, two are worthy of special note as being also Israelitish observances. In the one, resembling the "Passover," a healthy animal of the herds or flocks is sacrificed, and distributed to the priests, who sprinkle the blood upon the lintel and door-posts of the house to be protected. In the other, resembling the "scape-goat," a similar animal is conducted round the house or village, formally loaded with the sins of the people, and then driven off beyond the limits to become the property of any body who may seize it. Always in the case of sickness, the afflicted, according to his means, feeds the priests and poor, and sacrifices sheep and oxen as sin-offerings. This is also done after the commitment and repentance of any great sin; and similarly thank-offerings are made on recovering from illness or escaping from any other impending calamity. All such offerings are generically termed *kurbâni*, or "sacrificial."

Dread of death.

Sacrifices.

Passover.

Scape-goat.

Sin-offering.

Thank-offering.

In their marriage contracts, the pride of the Yusufzais is again strongly marked. The rites and ties are for the most part binding according to the Mahomadan code. But in this there is much variation in the different

Marriage.

divisions of the tribe. The majority are content with one wife at a time, many marry two, and the chiefs and wealthy take the full number of four, besides as many concubines as they can afford to keep. Frequently children are betrothed by their parents to maintain clan relationship or friendly alliances. Sometimes, as in out-of-the-way places, where the population lead a more simple and less restrained life, the contract is made by mutual desire of parties well acquainted with each other. Generally, however, the selection is made without previous acquaintance through the means of members of the *Dum* class, who are termed *raibar*, or *dallál*, i. e. "go between," or "agent." This class, both men and women, are the repository of the family secrets of the whole tribe; and, in their special calling, they play off the negociating parties upon each other, according as they are paid. They are very circumspect, however; and, for their own safety, keep their secrets to themselves. As soon as the parents of a girl have accepted the proposals of a candidate for their daughter's person, he visits the father in company with the *dallál*, and takes with him presents for the parents and the object of his desires. If approved of, he is invited to visit again, when the amount of dowry is agreed to. If in possession of the requisite means, the marriage day is fixed; if not, he is acknowledged as the betrother, and a period fixed for him to collect the dowry. As soon as the terms are agreed to, the father and the wooer drink "eau sucré" out of the same vessel, as a token that the compact is binding, and as a proof of good faith. After this ceremony the engagement is published, the friends of either party congratulate each other, and the hopeful benedict makes frequent or few visits, according to circumstances, with

Betrothals.

Match-makers.

Terms.

Ratification.

Antecedents and consequents.

presents for his affianced, though he never sees her. The engagement is termed *kozhdan*, the dowry *mâhar*, the youth *zalmai*, or *chandghol*, the maid *paighla*, or *chandghâla*, the ceremony *nikah* the feast *wâdah*, the procession *janj*, the bride *nâwai*, the bridegroom *sakhtan*, the mother *mairman*, the father *mâirah*, the infant *mâshûm*, the girl *jînai*, and the boy *halak*.

The *janj* consists of the friends of both parties. On the appointed day the bridegroom sets out with his friends, male and female, to the house of his bride; they go along in a divided procession, the men by themselves and the women by themselves, with music, singing, and firing of matchlocks, &c. This party is termed *janjiân* ; at the house of the bride they are welcomed by her party of friends, termed *manjian*. The two parties coalesce, and the men and women in separate associations pass the day and night in feasting, music, and gossip. During the night the bride and bridegroom are made man and wife by the priest, who, in the presence of witnesses, asks each party if they accept each other on the conditions he at the time names in detail. This repeated three times, and affirmative replies being received from each on all three occasions, the priest, naming

Nikah.

both parties, declares them man and wife, and asks a blessing on their union. This is the *nikah*. Next morning the bridegroom takes his bride to his own home, and is conducted thither by his own *janjiân* with the usual demonstrations of happiness. The *manjian* remain at the bride's house to comfort the parents. At his own house the bridegroom keeps the guests three days and nights occupied in feasting, music, &c., then, dismissing them, unveils his bride, and sees her for the first time. All the expenses of the marriage are borne by the bridegroom. Both parties receive presents from each of their friends; but it is an understood agreement that they in turn will make presents of the same value to each of them when a similar festival occurs in their respective families.

Failing to do this, and to return jewels borrowed for the occasion, is a fruitful source of feuds. The marriage expenses are very heavy. The lowest sum is fifty rupees, the average is about two hundred rupees for the common people. The rich require as many thousand rupees and more to get married respectably. Marriages are never performed during the Ramazan, or between it and the *loai akhtar* or *id-i-kurban*, because the first is a period of fasting, and the second the time for making pilgrimages.

Expenses.

Forbidden times.

The proper place of pilgrimage is Mecca; but, as few are able to undertake so great a journey, the mass of the people go the rounds of the ziarats in their own vicinity. There are three principal places of pilgrimage here, and each has its own fixed annual festival. These are the *Jandah* at Peshawar, *Kaka Sahib* in the Khattak country, and *Pir Baba* in Buhnair. The first two festivals are termed *maila*, and last three or four days each. Immense crowds of holiday folk assemble at these shrines, at appointed times, once a year; before the Ramazan at Peshawar for the *Jandah maila*, and after the Ramazan for the *Kaka Sahib maila*. Numbers of Hindus and petty traders attend at these festivals, and in temporary booths open out shops for the sale of a vast variety of merchandise. Bands of musicians, actors, &c., move about the crowd, delighting the women and children with their obscene jests and disreputable performances. The men are amused by wrestlers, conjurors, &c., vie with each other in equestrian exercises, *naiza bazi*, trials of strength, and other athletic sports. Gamesters and prostitutes also are present, and reap rich harvests from their victims. In these

Pilgrimage.

Jandah.

Kaka Sahib.

Pilgrim crowds.

festivals enemies often meet and settle their disputes with their swords. Previous to the British rule, these assemblages were always very unruly and disorderly crowds, and much blood was split. Now, however, they are better conducted, but still four or five deaths from violence always occur.

Pîr Baba.

At the Pîr Baba ziarat there is no *maila* owing to the unsettled state of the country. It is a sober place of pilgrimage. In the spring, however, parties of both Mahomadans and Hindus collecting there set out for the ziarat of *Jogiano Sar* on the summit of the Tortaba spur of the Ilam mountain. Here they encamp for three days, and in separate parties enjoy a season of recreation, described as a mixture of religious devotion and debauchery. The people going to this festival (which is termed by the Hindus *Ramtakht)* collect a sum of four or five hundred rupees for the chief of the district before he ensures their safety. Frequently, when the country is actively disturbed, the festival is altogether passed over.

Birth.

Amongst the Yusufzais, the occasion of the birth of a male child is one of great rejoicing and feasting amongst the friends of the happy mother, who does not, however, partake in them till the forty days of her purification be accomplished; for, during this period she is kept strictly secluded, ministered to by female friends, and made to observe the most absurdly superstitious rites before the final ablution that restores her once more to society. The birth of a female child is in no way noticed, except as a misfortune.

Circumcision.

About the eighth year, often much earlier, the boy is admitted into the fold of the Mahomadan church by the outward sign of circumcision. The ceremony involves some days of music, feasting, and rejoicing. After the final dinner, it is customary for the guests to contribute money, according to their means, for the expenses of the entertainment. The general result is profitable to the host if a man of rank; but it is otherwise with the poor. After circumcision, the young Yusufzai is taught his creed and the ordinary forms of prayer, and is instructed in the principal tenets and observances of the Mahomadan religion; and this, with but few exceptions, is all the education he receives. At twelve or fourteen years of age, he joins his father in out-door work, either tending the flock or working in the fields. From this time, also, he is obliged to sleep away from the rest of the family, and either spends the night in the *hujrah*, of his *kandi* with the rest of the bachelors, or, if the season allows of it, sleeps at his father's *khirman*, or threshing-floor, or his *harat* or irrigation well. At twenty years of age, or thereabouts, he receives a portion of his father's land as his share of the patrimony, and seeks a wife if about to settle at home; otherwise he leaves his home and seeks a livelihood by military service in foreign countries. In the decline of life, he returns to his home, resumes his share in the land, and spends the rest of his days, if old, in idle ease, under the shade of his own fig tree, and seeks to make amends for the sins of his youth by a punctual performance of the stated prayers and extra devotions at the mosque of his forefathers. His last wishes are to be buried in the family grave in his own village cemetery. The Yusufzais are very particular on this point, and it is considered a point of honor to convey the bones or bodies of relatives dying in foreign lands, or distant places, to the village graveyard. If already buried in another place, the relatives travel down, however far it may be, and, exhuming the body, carry up the bones for interment in their own village burial ground.

Education.

Occupation.

Patrimony.

Decline.

Death and burial.

The life led by those who live and die at home has been described in the preceding pages.

Resumé.

In brief words, they are occupied in the culture of the soil and the rearing of cattle; and vary the monotony of their daily pursuits by family feuds and tribal fights and reprisals, or by the exciting ventures of cattle-lifting, highway robbery, or plundering raids into the lands of their neighbours.

Alarm drum.

In every village the alarm drum is always ready to warn the tribes of approaching danger. Its unmistakable roll warns the women and children to keep within doors, and calls the men together to defend their rights and honor. The drum is an effectual and speedy means, especially at night, of warning the tribes scattered over an extensive country of the approach of danger from without. The first village alarmed at once sounds the well-known roll, only used on such occasions, from the top of the highest house. The warning is at once repeated by the next village, and then by the next to it, and so on, till in a few minutes the whole country is aroused and on the alert. In each the chiefs are surrounded by the men all armed and ready for action,

Its effects.

guards are posted at the entrances to the village, pickets are thrown out to defend the approaches, and spies are sent off for information. Meanwhile messengers pass quickly between the nearest villages, and in a few hours the intelligence is spread all over the country; the tribes are all at once armed and hasten with their support wherever assistance is required, or stay at home to defend their own loved hearths.

Such are the Yusufzais in their government and customs.

Recent changes.

These conditions have in a measure become changed for the better in that portion of the tribe under the British rule. To outward appearance, the turbulent, restless, and savage Yusufzai of but a few years ago is now a peaceful, well-behaved, and industrious agriculturalist—a remarkable contrast to his still savage and faithless brother in the hills, beyond the influence of British rule. Than this fact there is not needed stronger proof of the blessings conferred by a strong, just, and merciful Government, under which life and property are secure, the fruits of industry reaped by the labourer, and liberty of speech and action, so far as not seditious or criminal, unhindered; whilst a justice, such as was before unknown to them, is now available with equal facility to all, of whatever tribe, creed, or rank.

Improvements.

That these blessings are appreciated by the people, is made apparent by the improvement of their condition during late years, and the influx of settlers from beyond the border; indeed, they themselves, though owning many discontented characters, admit the blessings of their present condition as compared with their former state of life. The villager now never troubles himself with anxieties as to the safety of his cattle or crops, and is not always on the watch for an enemy in every corner. The alarm drum now is never heard, and the youth are untutored in the use of arms. Owing to their long enjoyment of peace and ease, and their confidence in the strength of the Government, many have sold their arms to tribes beyond the border. Despite all these advantages, the mass of the people would gladly revert to their former state of barbarism and anarchy, for they have not yet learned to like their beneficient rulers, though they cannot deny being satisfied with the results of their government.

Appreciation.

Preference for anarchy.

In a description such as this, where brevity is necessary, it is difficult fully to illustrate the benefits the Yusufzais have reaped under the British Government

Benefits already reaped.

during the past fourteen years, and I will not attempt it. That great improvements have been effected is indubitable; that the people are happy, protected, and rapidly getting rich, is equally so; and that serious crimes, though still very prevalent, are greatly on the decrease, is a fact. But there is no doubt, also, that much remains to be done. Canals for irrigation and district roads are much wanted, as are bridges on the roads already laid out. The sanitary improvement of villages and rules for their regular conservancy are urgent necessities; and, with the necessary authority, could be, without difficulty, carried out. The planting of trees, construction of sarais and wells, also demand attention. For the want of some of these, nearly half the plain is an uncultivated waste.

Benefits that may be reaped.

The time for initiating these improvements has now arrived. Of the certainty of this, every day's converse with people gives proof.

Favorable time.

CHAPTER VI.

CLIMATE AND PRODUCTIONS.

Varied. THE climate of the Yusufzai country is as varied as its surface.

Of the plain. In the south-western, or plain portion, it in the main resembles that of the Panjab generally; but the summer rains are much less persistent, and, I believe, less abundant also; whilst the frosts of winter are more prolonged and also more severe.

Rain-fall. The quantity of rain collected during the year 1863—and it was all that fell at Murdan—amounted to 27·52 inches. Of this the most part, or 16·79 inches, fell during the two months of July and August. The rains of this year, however, cannot be taken as the standard for the Yusufzai plain, because the season was an exceptional one, the rains being very much heavier than usual, and producing destructive floods in several parts of the district. The rain-fall at Murdan during the preceding year better represents the usual yearly quantity. The registered fall at Murdan for both years is shewn in the subjoined table :—

Months.	1862. Date.	Rain.	Total.	1863. Date.	Rain.	Total.
January,	13	·2		18	·25	
	16	·04		23	·72	
	17	·2		29	1·	
	18	·4	·84	30	1·55	3·52
February,	11	·02		1	·25	
	12	·1		7	·12	
	13	·23				
	21	·120	·470			·37
March,	8	·6		10	·04	
	9	·01		11	1·8	
	14	·5		12	·05	
	15	1·2		13	·15	
	16	·65				
	19	·02				
	24	·29				
	25	1·33	4·60			2·04
April,	2	·52		15	·15	
	5	2·1				
	7	·14				
	13	·2				
	18	·22	3·18			·15
May,	13	·05		24	·02	
	24	·02		27	·08	
	25	·1				
	26	·7				
	28	·1	·97			·10
June,	13	·03		23	·4	
	16	·1	·13	30	·5	·9
July,	1	·22		3	·25	
	2	·2		7	·3	
	8	·1		9	40	
	21	·95		10	3·1	
				11	2·8	
				20	1·	
				22	·15	
			1·47	26	·3	
				31	2·3	10·63
August,	6	·02		2	·28	
	11	·1		3	·92	
	18	·9		4	·53	
	26	·05		5	·11	
	27	·4		12	·78	
				14	·19	
				16	·1	
				18	1·25	
			1·47	19	2·	6·16

Months.	1862.			1863.		
	Date.	Rain.	Total.	Date.	Rain.	Total.
September, ...	7	·8		12	·1	
" ...	8	1·2	2·	20	·25	·35
October, ...	4	·4	·4			
November, ...	17	·02				
" ...	22	·1				
" ...	25	1·1				
" ...	26	·5	1·72			
December, ...				16	·1	
" ...				18	·25	
" ...				25	1·20	
" ...				27	1·50	
" ...				29	·25	3·30
	Rainy Days.	Rain. Inches.	Total. Rain.	Rainy Days.	Rain. Inches.	Total. Rain.
	44	17·250	17·250	39	27·52	27·52

Temperature.

I have no regularly kept record of the variations of the thermometer for any complete year; but the observations that have been recorded give the range from 22°F. at sunrise in January of 1862 to 135°F. in the sun's rays, and 98°F. in the shade, at 2 P. M. in August of the same year. From November to the end of April, the average temperature at mid-day is about 54°F. out of doors, and about 63°F. in doors. From May to the end of October the average temperature is about 103°F. out of doors, and about 91°F. in doors at mid-day.

Sudden changes.

During the rainy months of July and August, when thunder-storms prevail, there is frequently a sudden change of the temperature of from 20°F. to 25°F. in the course of the twenty-four hours.

The prevailing winds are westerly and north-westerly

Winds. from November to April, and easterly and south-easterly from May to October.

Clouds. From November to April are more or less cloudy months; and in the two last sudden and violent hail and thunder-storms occur. From May to October the atmosphere is more or less completely obscured by a dense haze, except during the brief intervals when cleared for a few days by dust, hail, or thunder-storms.

Storms. Throughout this period thunder-storms prevail over the hills bounding the plain on the north and east, and electric flashes lighten the sky at night, more or less, continually; whilst on the plain prevail hot winds of greater or less severity and activity, interrupted for a few hours, at intervals of ten days or so, by violent storms, accompanied by thunder and rain.

Dews. During April and May, and September and October, the nights are generally clear; and, more or less, heavy dews fall.

Earthquakes. Earthquakes are of frequent occurrence, and more so during the hot months. At Murdan I recorded the following during 1862, and in each instance, without being violent, the shocks were very distinct, viz. on 18th April, 6th May, 18th June, 8th July, 31st July, 10th August, and 26th August. In all the general direction of the wave appeared to be from north-east to south-west, or *vice versa*. The direction of the shock was determined by the rising of water against the sides of a tub.

Of the hills. The climates of Swat and Buhnair, though differing from that of the Yusufzai plain, are described as resembling each other in

Buhnair and Swat.

most points. In these districts the hot weather sets in later than on the open plain, but is more oppressive and continuous, owing to the mountains around preventing the free circulation of the winds. The frequent storms that burst over these hills do not cool the air; but, on the contrary, produce a hot, steamy atmosphere in the valleys below.

Unhealthy.

Both districts are unhealthy in summer, Swat especially so; for, owing to the extensive surface there under cultivation of rice, malaria is exhaled in great abundance. This circumstance has given the country an unenviable notoriety for its peculiar and obstinate endemic intermittent and remittent fevers, which affect all ages alike. The malaria, it appears, is of universal distribution throughout the valley, and very poisonous in its effects. It has impressed its mark on the people, who, in their general physical condition, are more or less fever stricken and unhealthy.

Autumn.

During the autumn months the atmosphere of these valleys is close and oppressive, and swarms with myriads of midges and musquitoes. Buhnair and its tributary Chamla valley, are not so unhealthy as Swat; but the coarse, gravelly soil composing their levels, becomes fervently hot during the summer months, and, radiating its heat during the night, makes the air very close and oppressive. In the spring and autumn, malarious exhalations rise from this porous soil, and fevers become very rife during both these seasons.

Winter.

In both Swat and Buhnair, shut in as they are by lofty snow-clad mountains, the winter is a milder season than on the open plain; for the air is less disturbed by winds, and the frosts are also less severe. Snow does not always fall on the lower levels. At intervals of three or four years, the valleys everywhere receive a coating of snow; but it seldom remains longer than a week or ten days. On the whole, from what I can learn, the winter in these valleys is a less severe season than in the plain country; but it is more prolonged, and the atmosphere is much more humid, and persistently so, than on the open plain.

Highlands of Ghorband.

The country bordering the Indus eastward of Buhnaïr, consisting as it does of a number of narrow, dark, deep, and winding valleys and gorges, of which the largest are known as Puran, Chakaisar, Kana, and Ghorband; enjoys an agreeable temperate climate for nearly half the year, though, during the two months of the rainy season, the air is described as close, damp, and unhealthy.

Winter.

The winter lasts nearly five months, and for two of these snow covers the surface everywhere except on the immediate banks of the river.

High mountains.

The highest mountains in this tract, such as Mahaban, Dumah, Ilam, Dosirra, Gâdwâ, and Ghorband, are more or less deeply covered with snow from the end of October to the middle of May; but only on their northern slopes during the latter part of this period.

Elevation.

Their heights are supposed to range between 7,000 and 11,000 feet above the sea. The valleys enclosed between them are supposed to lie at an elevation varying between three thousand and five thousand feet above the sea.

Malizai.

The climate of the Malizai country which lies north of Swat, and comprises the several valleys draining to the Panjkora river, viz. Turmung, Oshairai and its branch valleys of Nihag and Karoh, Tâl Lamotai, Dir, Barawal, and Maidan, as well as of the Bajawar plain and its tributary valleys of Otalai, Babakara, and Chandûl, which all adjoin the Malizai country on the west, is described as differing very much from that of the districts already noticed.

Summer.

The summer, it is said, is a temperate and healthy season compared with that of the other districts. Excesses of heat during this season are moderated by oft-recurring thunder-storms and showers of rain. The former are accompanied by violent electric disturbances, and are sometimes of terrific force, the hurricanes uprooting lofty forest trees, and hurling huge rocks from their natural resting places; whilst the clouds pour down torrents of rain, or volleys of destructive hail stones.

Winter.

The winter season in Malizai is described as a severe one; snow lies everywhere for nearly three months, except on the banks of the Panjkora river and on the Bajawar plain, from the surface of which it disappears after a few days. On the higher ranges of mountains in this tract, as Larram, Lahorai, Asmâr, Kamoji Kistoji, Hinduraj, Lajbok, Shalkandi, &c., snow lies from two to four or five months. Throughout the highland tracts on the north and east of the Yusufzaï plain, the several valleys and glens are constantly

Fogs.

overhung by heavy drenching mists and drizzles from the middle of November to the end of March. They gather during the night; and, settling at the bottom of the valleys, disperse about noon, or an hour or two later. In the plain country morning fogs appear occasionally between November and March. They rise from the surface at daylight and quickly disperse a few hours after sun-rise. They are very different from the mists of the highland valleys, are much rarer and less humid, and lie less heavily on the ground.

Seasons.

Amongst the Yusufzais, the year consists of two principal seasons of equal duration, viz., the winter, or *zhimi*, and the summer, or *ori*. The former consists of three distinct seasons, and the latter of two. Their commencement and duration vary in different parts of the country, but in the Yusufzai plain their names and times are as follow:—The winter, or *zhimi*, of six months, commences with the *mani*, or autumn, which lasts during October and November, and ends with the *sparli*, or spring, which lasts during February and March. The intermediate months of December and January constitute the winter proper, or *zhimi*.

Winter seasons.

The summer, or *ori*, of six months, from April to September, inclusive, comprizes also the intercurrent rainy season, or *parshakâl*, which lasts during July and August, or June and July. The two months preceding the *parshakâl* are termed *ori*, and the two months succeeding it *ori mani*. Of these seasons, the *zhimi* and *sparli* are considered the most healthy. In the *ori*, boils and furuncles are epidemic both amongst men and cattle. In the *parshakâl* they are still more rife, and small pox also becomes epidemic in this season. In the *mani* intermittent fevers are epidemic; and, from this circumstance, the period is often termed the "fever season."

Summer seasons.

The varieties of climate noted in the preceding pages have their due influence on the flora and fauna of the several tracts to which they are more definitely confined. Thus, on the Yusufzai plain the vegetation, scanty and poor as it is, is characterized by plants common to the tropical rather than to the temperate climate; for, in the mixture of both kinds, the former appear to be the most numerous. Of the common plants met with on the uncultivated wastes, where they are exposed to excessive heats and droughts, and are dependent for subsistence on a hard

Flora.

On the plain.

arid soil, often of a saline nature, the following are the most noteworthy :—

English Name.	Botanical Name.	Pushtu Name.
Wild Rue, ...	Peganum harmala,	Spailanai.
Muddar, ...	Asclepias gigantea,	Spalmai.
Jujube tree, ...	Zizyphus sp., ...	Bairra.
Camels' thorn, ...	Hedysarum alhagi,...	Zôz.
Tamarisk, ...	Tamarix orientalis,	Ghwhaz.
Glasswort, ...	Salsola kali, ...	Khorakhai.
Glasswort, ...	Salsolaceæ, ...	Zmai.
Glasswort, ...	Salsolaceæ, ...	Lânâ.
Sensitive Mimosa ...	Mimosa sensitiva, ...	Zhand.
Gum Acacia, ...	Acacia modesta, ...	Palosa.
Absinth sp., ...	Artemisia sp., ...	Mastiara.
Wormwood, ...	Artemisia sp., ...	Tarkha.
Fleawort, ...	Plantago sp. (3), ...	Spighol.
Prophet flower, ...	Arnebia echioides,	Sulaimani gul. Paighambari gul.
Leafless caper, ...	Capparis aphylla, ...	Kirrarra.
Lac gum tree, ...	Butea frondosa, ...	Palai.
Figwort sp., ...	Scrophularia sp., ...	Parharbuti.
Sage sp., ...	Labiata sp., ...	Khardag.
Clustered fig, ...	Ficus racemosa, ...	Gular.
Wild Colocynth, ...	Citrullus sp. (2), ...	Maraghuni.
Caltrops, common, ...	Tribulus terrestris,	Mâlkundai.
Malcomia sp., ...	Malcomia sp. (3), ...	Kharor.
Wild Chamomile, ...	Anthemis sp. (2), ...	Krichi.
Common Spurge, ...	Euphorbia sp., ...	Zaghâgha.
Mallow sp., ...	Malvia sp., ...	Panirak.
Mallow sp., ...	Althea sp., ...	Sonchal.
Fumitory, common, ...	Fumaria officin, ...	Pâpra.
Fenugreek, ...	Trigonella sp., ...	Malkhozai.
Trefoil sp., ...	Trifolium sp., ...	Pashtarai.
Purslane, ...	Portulaca sp., ...	Warkhârai.
Calendula, common, ...	Calendula officin., ...	Ziarguli.
Wild safflower, ...	Carthamas sp., ...	Kâriza.
Common vervain, ...	Verbena officin., ...	Shamuki.
Thorn apple, ..	Datura fastuosa, ...	Toradana.
Common cleavers, ...	Chenopodium sp., ...	Bushkha.
Trefoil sp., ...	Trifolium sp., ...	Spaishtai.
Indian hemp, ...	Cannabis Indica. ...	Bang.
Common dock, ...	Rumex sp., ...	Shalkhai.
Variegated tulip, ...	Tulipa sp., ...	Ghântol.
Wild rape, ...	Sinapis sp., ...	Joâwân.
Wild mustard, ...	Sinapis sp., ...	Aorai.

Trees.

The trees commonly met with on the plain about the villages, near water-courses, and around irrigation wells, are the following, viz. the date palm (*khajûr*), the mulberry (*tût*), the sissu (*shiwa*), the melia sempervirens (*draig*, or *bukaian*), and the willow (*walai*). Of these, the first and last are much less common than the others.

On the hills.

On the low hills bounding the plain, and on the spurs projecting on to it from them, the more common trees are the following:—

English Name.	Botanical Name.	Pushtu Name.
Malabar nut, ...	Adhadota vasica, ...	Bahaikar.
Straight randia, ...	Randia stricta, ...	Gandaichar.
Oleander, ...	Nerium odorum, ...	Gandairai.
Persian Salvadore, ...	Salvadora Persica, ...	Plaiwan.
Bog Myrtle, ...	Dodonæa Burman:	Ghorâskai,
Bignonia sp., ...	Tecoma undulata, ...	Raibdun, or Raidawân.
Reptonia sp., ...	R. Buxifolia, ...	Gurgura.
Olive, common, ...	Olea sp. (2), ...	Khoan.
Leafless Periploca, ...	P. Aphylla, ...	Barrarra.
Travellers' Joy, ...	Clematis orient: ...	Praiwatai.
Wild Indigo, ...	Indigofera sp., ...	Ghwaraiza.
Edible celastrus, ...	C. edulis, ...	Karko.
Carounda, ...	Carissa sp. (2), ...	Grûnda.
Spiny carissa, ...	C. Spinarum, ...	Surazghai.
Thorny astragalus, ...	Astragalus sp.,	Spinazghai, or Paishkand.
Purging cassia, ...	Cassia fistula, ...	Lândais
Asparagus sp., ...	Asparagus officinalis,	Mârchob.
Asparagus sp., ...	Asparagus sp., ...	Raizakai.
Withiana sp., ...	Withiana coagulans,	Shâprânga.
Withiana sp., ...	W. somniferum, ...	Kutilâl.
Castor oil tree, ...	Ricinus sp., ...	Arhand.
Chaste tree, ...	Vitex negunda, ...	Marwandai.
Staff tree, (?) ...	Catha sp., ...	Mumânri.
Peppermint, ...	Mentha sp., ...	Wailanai.
Myrabolan sp. ...	Emblica sp., ...	Khadang.
Dyers' rottlera, ...	R. tinctoria, ...	Kâmbaila.
Thorny shrub, ...	Red berry, ...	Ilanai.
Poplar sp., ...	Populus sp., ...	Tâgha.
Silk cotton tree, ...	Bombax sp., ...	Badarkand.

English Name.	Botanical Name.	Pushtu Name.
Jasmine sp. ...	Jasminum sp., ...	Râchâmbail.
Asiatic grewia, ...	G. Asiatica,	Pastaoni or Shikari. maiwah.
Sebesten tree, ...	Cordia sp., ...	Lâshora.
Dyer's wood, ...	Granatum sp., ...	Dâtki.
Mountain ebony, ...	Bauhinia sp., ...	Kohliar.
Banyan tree, ...	Ficus Indica, ...	Bargat.
Large-leaved fig, ...	F. Glomerata, ...	Ormul.
Moonseed sp., ...	Cocculus sp., ...	Chinjanwali.
Bael fruit tree ...	Œgle marmelos, ...	Balâghund.
Acacia sp. ...	A. Arabica, ...	Kikor.
Climbing mimosa, ...	M. scandens, ...	Kulmawali.
Cowitch, ...	Mucuna pruriens, ...	Surpalai.
Box-leaved ehretia, ...	E. buxifolia, ...	Shamshâd.
Embelia sp., ...	E. ribes, ...	Bâbrang.
Pomegranate, ...	Granatum sp., ...	Anâr.
Myrobalan sp., ...	M. sp., ...	Bahaira.
Ditto do., ...	Emblica officin., ...	Awlâ.
Ditto do., ...	Teminalia sp., ...	Haraira.
Grislea downy, (?) ...	G. tomentosa, (?) ...	Dâtki.

Plants specially localized.

Most of the plants above-mentioned are more or less generally distributed on the lower hills throughout the Yusufzai country. Some others are confined to special tracts, as the cypress *(sarwai)* to Dir; the dwarf palm, a species of chamœrops *(maizarri)* to the Ranizai country; the horse chesnut *(banj)* to the hill tract east of Buhnair, &c., &c. In Swat and the valleys to its north and west are found the plane *(chinar)*, the white poplar (*spaidâr*), the sirrus (*srîkh*), the mulberry (*tût*), &c., &c.; also the ash (*shwâai*) and alder (*girra*), &c. The two last named also grow in Buhnair and the country to its eastward. In the Malizai country, and that of the Tarkilanris, besides the above-named, are found both wild and cultivated the grape vine (*kwar*), the plum *(alucha)* and (*kishtai*), the peach (*shaftalu*), the apricot (*khubâni*), the quince (*tâṅgwân*), the apple (*maruza*), the pear (*naspâtai*), the wild plum (*mânrû*), the lime *nîmbû*), &c.

The following trees also are mentioned as grow-

On the higher mountains.

ing on the higher hills, more or less, generally throughout the country :—

English Name.		Botanical Name.		Pushtu Name.
Longleaved pine,	...	P. Longifolia,	...	Nakhtar.
Edible pine,	...	P. Webbiana,	...	Zalghozai.
Pine, sp.,	...	P. sp., or Abies, sp.,		Pihuch.
Larch, sp., (?)	...	Larix, sp.,	...	Surûp.
Deodar,	...	Cedrus deodara,	...	Diâr.
Wild grape vine,	...	Vitis vinifera,	...	Kwar.
Horse chesnut,	...	Castanea Indica,	...	Banj.
Mountain ash,	...	Fraxinus, sp.,	...	Shwâai.
Alder, sp.,	...	Alnus, sp.,	...	Girra.
Date plum,	...	Diospros, sp.,	...	Amluk.
Walnut,	...	Juglans, sp.,	...	Ghoz, or Akor.
Wild Almond,	...	Amygdalus, sp.,	...	Bâdâm.
Common sloe,	...	Prunus spinosa,	...	Mânrû.
Lotus tree,	...	Zizyphus, sp.,	...	Makhranai.
Barberry,	...	Berberis, sp. (2),	...	Korai and karoski.
Blackberry,	...	Rubas vulgaris,	...	Karwara.
Raspberry,	...	R. sp.,	...	Achu.
Bramble,	...	R. sp.,	...	Gorach.
Bilberry,	...	R. sp.,	...	Baganna.
Pœony,	...	Pœonia, sp., (?)	...	Mâmaikh.
Arum,	...	Arum, sp.,	...	Nuralam.
Common fig,	...	Ficus, sp.,	...	Inzar.
Yew,	...	Taxus baccata,	...	Kharoa.

Others.

The above list comprises the more common of the plants growing on the higher hills, whose names I have been able to ascertain. There are many others whose names even are unknown to the people of the country, though some of them are used as pot-herbs or domestic medicines by the mountaineers in whose vicinity they grow.

Fanna.

Of the plains.

The fanna of the Yusufzai country has also like the flora a special distribution in the different tracts of country. Thus in the plain and valleys the more common species met with are the following :—

English Name.	Latin Name.	Pushtu Name.
Wolf,	Canis lupus,	Sharmukh.
Jackal,	C. Jacalus,	Gidarr.
Fox,	C. Vulpes,	Lûmbarr.
Hyæna,	Hyæna vulgaris,	Kog, sartîta.
Wild cat,	Felis lynx,	Parâpush.
Mungoose,	Mangusta, sp.,	Naolai.
Rat and Mouse,	Mus, sp., (5 or 6)	Magakh.
Grave digger,	Viverra, sp.,	Gorkhakh.
Otter,	Lutra potamophil :	Sanglâo.
Porcupine,	Hystrix cristata,	Shkunr.
Hedgehog,	Echinus, sp.,	Shishkai.
Pangolin,	Manis pentadact,	Kishor.
Ravine deer,	Antilope gazella,	Osai.
Hare,	Lepus, sp.,	Soya.
Vulture, dusky,	V. cinereus,	Gargass.
V. Egyptian,	V., sp.,	Ganjai.
Common kite,	Milvus, sp.,	Tapus.
Common Harrier,	Circus, sp.,	Bâd-khor.
Harrier,	Circus, sp.,	Shaindai.
Owl, desert,	Strix otus,	Gûngai.
Owl, barn,	Strix, sp.,	Goâtki.
King-fisher,	Alcedo, sp.,	Mahikhorak.
Common Tern,	Sterna, sp., (2)	Bâbozai.
Mina, common,	Eulabes Indicus,	Tutkhoraka.
Waterwagtails,	Motacilla, sp., (2)	Spinak ; ziarak.
Sparrows,	Fringilla, sp., (2)	Chanchanr.
Hoopoe,	Upapa epops,	Mulla chargak.
Starlings,	Sturnus vulgaris,	
Raven or crow,	Corvus corax,	Kâgha.
Jay,	Garrulus cyanoco rax,	Sarkhakha.
Larks,	Alauda, sp.,	Kharâra.
Rooks,	Corvus frugilegus,	Kargha.
Sand grouse,	Tetrao, sp., (3)	Khrai kâotar.
Quail,	Coturnix, sp.,	Mraz.
Partridge,	Perdix, sp.,(2)	Tanzirai.
Francolin,	Francolinus, sp.,	Zarka.
Sissi,	F. sp.,	Sissi.
Pigeons,	Columba, sp., (3)	Kâotar.
Bustard obara,	Otis houbara,	Kharmor.
Bustard, little,	Otis tetrax,	Sâri.
Common peewit,	Venellus, sp.,	Tittâri.
Koulan,	Ardea koulan,	Kulang.
Black crane,	Ardea, sp.,	Ding.
Snipes,	Scolopax, sp., (2)	Karak.
Sandpipers,	Calidris, sp., (4)	Tamtil and Kablaí.
Common coot,	Gallinula, sp.,	
Wild ducks,	Anas, sp., (10 or 12)	Ilai.
Tortoise,	Testudo Indica,	Shamshatai.
Iguanas,	Iguana, sp.,	Ghârandûni.
Thick-tailed lizard,	Ecphimotes, sp.,	Samsarai.
Snakes, various,	Anguis, sp., (8 or 10)	Mar.
Frogs and toads,	Batrachus, sp.,	Chindakha.

Of the hills.

To the hill tracts are confined the following :—

Ibex,	...	Capra ibex,	...	Markhor.
Wild goat,	...	C., sp.,	...	Gharsa.
Wild sheep,	...	Ovis, sp.,	...	Daghra gada.
Chamois,	...	Ibex; sp.,	...	Zba Sârânai.
Leopard,	...	Felis leopardus,	...	Boârgai.
Tiger,	...	Felis tigris,	...	Zmarai.
Bears,	...	Ursus, sp., (2)	...	Mailu.
Monkeys,	...	Cercopithecus,	...	Shâdû.
Barking deer,	...	Moschus, sp,	...	Ghawara.
Tree marten.	...	Mustela, sp.,	...	
Wild pigs,	...	Sus scropha,	...	Sarkuzai.
Peregrine Falcon,	...	Falco comm,	...	Bâz.
Merlin,	...	F. asalon,	...	Charagh.
Golden eagle,	...	Aquila, sp.,	...	Bâtur.
Pheasants,	...	Phasianus, sp.,	...	Munal, Mor.
Parrots,		Psittacus, sp.,	...	Toti.
Magpies,	...	Pica, sp.,	...	Shâm.

Others.

Besides the above, there are a number of other species. especially of the feathered tribes, such as of accippitres, falcons, hawks, harriers, &c.; of passerinæ fly-catchers, orioles, thrushes, minas, chats, swallows, larks, tits, finches, &c.; of scansores, there are no common species; of the gallinæ there are the sand-grouse, partridge, francolin, quail and pigeon families; of the gralla, there are bustards, plovers cranes, herons, snipes, sandpipers, and coots; of the palmipede there are terns of two kinds; the swan is sometimes seen on the Swat and Panjkora rivers; geese are plentiful, and ducks in great variety, during the cold weather.

Reptiles.

Reptiles, such as lizards, in great variety, and iguanas, as also eight or ten kinds of snakes, are common all over the country. The black hooded cobra is common on the plain, where I have obtained speci;mens of six other kinds. Two of these possess poison fangs one is barred with black and white rings in alternate succession; the other is brindled with yellow, green, and brown patches. Both are small varieties, have capacious square jaws, and are undoubtedly poisonous.

Minerals.

The principal mineral products of the Yusufzai plain have been already described in the first chapter of this report. Iron is produced in the Malizai country and Barawal. Antimony and green vitriol, and mica clay, are also found in Swat and the hills to its north. A list of the more common minerals will be given in the Appendix attached to this chapter.

Diseases.

Prevalence.

Nature.

Tabular returns.

The climate of the Yusufzai plain, as experienced at Murdan, is on the whole a very healthy one. The most prevalent diseases are of the zymotic class. Those of its miasmatic order come first in frequency; next follow diseases of a local nature, such as affections of the digestive and urinary organs, and these in a great measure are merely the advanced forms or sequela of the miasmatic diseases. Diseases of the skin are common; but those that are not of a parasitic nature are confined to a few common forms, and are as much, if not more, dependent on the personal habits of the people, as on the effects of climatic influences. The annexed tabular statements of the diseases treated in the Regimental Hospital of the Corps of Guides, from 1857 to 1863, inclusive, and in the Murdan Charitable Dispensary, from 1860 to 1863, inclusive, very well illustrate the relative proportions and frequency of the different forms of disease met with in this country. The absence of any special epidemic is noteworthy. In the first mentioned tabular statement the returns for the year 1857 are included, as they serve to shew the differences produced by a change of climate and the exposure and hardships of active service in the field.

Return of Diseases treated in the Murdan Charitable Dispensary (of both In-door and Out-door Patients) for four years, from 1860 to 1863 inclusive.

		Years.	1860.			1861.			1862.			1863.		
		Average daily sick.	46			46			45			50		
Class.	*Order.*	DISEASES.	*Cases.*	*Died.*	TOTAL.	*Cases.*	*Died.*	TOTAL.	*Cases.*	*Died.*	TOTAL.	*Cases.*	*Died.*	TOTAL.
I.	1	Febres, ...	338	6		435	0		248	1		153	0	
		Variola, ...	0	0		0	0		0	0		0	0	
		Tonsillitis, ...	2	0		0	0		4	0		5	0	
		Opthalmia, ...	178	0		122	0		129	0		143	0	
		Erysipelas, ...	2	0		0	0		1	0		1	0	
		Furunculus, ...	0	0		0	0		19	0		55	0	
		Influenza, ...	48	0		52	0		58	0		45	0	
		Dysenteria, ...	54	3		151	3		68	1		33	2	
		Diarrhœa, ...	62	2		66	1		54	0		68	2	
		Cholera epidemic, ...	1	0		0	0		1	1		0	0	
		Rheumatismus, ...	132	1	817	113	0	939	99	0	681	133	0	636
	2	Syphilis, ...	76	0		42	0		44	0		57	0	
		Gonorrhœa, ...	54	0		55	0		23	0		40	0	
		Bubo, ...	0	0		0	0		4	0		0	0	
		Orchitis, ...	8	0		8	0		6	0		0	0	
		Strictura urethra, ...	2	0		6	0		4	0		4	0	
		Lepra, ...	19	0	159	2	0	113	6	0	87	7	0	108

Years.			1860.			1861.			1862.			1863.		
Average daily sick.			46			46			45			50		
Class.	*Order.*	DISEASES.	*Cases.*	*Died.*	TOTAL.	*Cases.*	*Died.*	TOTAL.	*Cases.*	*Died.*	TOTAL.	*Cases.*	*Died.*	TOTAL.
I.	3	Scorbutus, ...	21	0		16	0		17	0		30	0	
		Purpura, ...	0	0		2	0		0	0		1	0	
		Bronchocele, ...	14	0	35	1	0	19	2	0	19	1	0	32
	4	Apthæ, ...	10	0		4	0		3	0		0	0	
		Porrigo, ...	46	0		22	0		7	0		0	0	
		Scabies, ...	25	0		1	0		0	0		5	0	
		Vermes, ...	22	0	103	7	0	34	3	0	13	0	0	5
II.	1	Anœmia, ...	0	0		10	0		0	0		25	1	
		Anasarca, ...	9	0		8	2		7	2		9	2	
		Carcinoma, ...	4	1		1	0		3	0		10	0	
		Lupus, ...	1	0	14	0	0	19	6	1	16	2	0	46
	2	Scrofula, ...	17	0		3	0		5	0		5	0	
		Phthisis pulmon, ...	1	0	18	2	1	5	3	0	8	3	0	8
III.	1	Paralysis, ...	5	0		1	0		8	0		6	0	
		Mania, ...	1	0		1	0		3	0		1	0	
		Dementia, ...	0	0		0	0		0	0		0	0	

Class.	Order.	Years.	1860.			1861.			1862.			1863.		
		Average daily sick.	46			46			45			50		
		DISEASES.	Cases.	Died.	TOTAL.	Cases.	Died.	TOTAL.	Cases.	Died.	TOTAL.	Cases.	Died.	TOTAL.
III.	1	Convulsir, ...	0	0		1	0		2	0		1	0	
		Neuralgia, ...	32	0		97	0		94	0		87	0	
		Cœcitas, ...	10	0		12	0		9	0		5	0	
		Otitis, ...	25	0	73	16	0	128	23	0	139	42	0	142
	2	Carditis, ...	1	0		3	0		4	0		1	0	
		Morb. Valv. Cordis, ...	1	0		0	0		2	0		1	0	
		Varix, ...	0	0	2	2	0	5	1	0	7	1	0	3
	3	Laryngitis, ...	16	0		3	0		0	0		1	0	
		Bronchitis, ...	136	2		83	1		66	2		28	2	
		Pleuritis, ...	22	0		17	0		15	0		13	0	
		Pneumonia, ...	10	0		2	0		0	0		0	0	
		Asthma, ...	45	0	229	11	1	116	12	1	93	61	0	103
	4	Gastritis, ...	4	0		1	0		12	0		4	0	
		Obstipatio, ...	46	0		0	0		10	0		3	0	
		Hernia, ...	2	0		0	0		2	0		0	0	
		Dyspepsia, ...	211	0		169	0		155	0		157	0	
		Colica, ...	109	0		124	0		103	2		95	0	
		Hœmorrhois, ...	14	0		20	0		11	0		15	0	

Years.			1860.			1861.			1862.			1863.		
Average daily sick.			46			46			45			50		
Class.	*Order.*	DISEASES.	*Cases.*	*Died.*	TOTAL.	*Cases.*	*Died.*	TOTAL.	*Cases.*	*Died.*	TOTAL.	*Cases.*	*Died.*	TOTAL.
III.	4	Fistula ani, ...	0	0		2	1		1	1		1	1	
		Splenitis, ...	35	0		11	0		20	0		33	0	
		Hepatitis, ...	21	0		2	0		5	0		0	0	
		Icterus, ...	15	0		10	0		7	0		5	0	
		Ascitas, ...	9	0	466	0	0	339	1	0	327	1	0	314
	5	Nephritis, ...	2	0		16	0		7	0		12	0	
		Diabetes, ...	0	0		6	0		5	0		5	0	
		Hœmaturia, ...	5	0		4	0		1	0		0	0	
		Calculus Vesicœ, ...	9	2	16	4	0	30	16	4	29	9	0	26
	6	Hydrocele, ...	0	0		1	0		2	0		0	0	
		Hysteritis, ...	0	0	0	0	0	1	4	0	6	0	0	0
	7	Contractura, ...	7	0		0	0		1	0		0	0	
		Ostitis, ...	25	0		0	0		3	0		0	0	
		Caries dentis, ...	86	0		26	0		78	0		109	0	
		Necrosis, ...	6	1	124	1	0	27	4	0	86	9	0	118
	8	Eczema, ...	1	0		2	0		5	0		2	0	
		Herpes, ...	11	0		42	0		29	0		39	0	
		Psoriasis, ...	5	0		22	0		27	0		71	0	

Class.	Order.	Years.	1860.			1861.			1862.			1863.		
		Average daily sick.	46			46			45			50		
		DISEASES.	*Cases.*	*Died.*	TOTAL.	*Cases.*	*Died.*	TOATL.	*Cases.*	*Died.*	TOTAL.	*Cases.*	*Died.*	TOTAL.
III.	8	Phlegmon, ...	10	0		9	0		7	0		16	0	
		Abscessus, ...	67	0		86	0		81	0		99	0	
		Ulcus, ...	176	0	270	63	0	224	72	0	221	145	0	372
IV.	4	Asthenia, ...	46	0	46	17	1	17	51	0	51	49	0	49
V.	1	Ambustio, ...	6	0		1	0		3	0		2	0	
		Luxatura, ...	3	0		2	0		2	0		5	0	
		Fractura, ...	9	1		5	0		23	0		16	0	
		Contusio, ...	97	1		57	0		94	0		53	0	
		Vuln. sclopet, ...	2	0		0	0		3	0		3	0	
		„ incisum, ...	46	1		21	2		16	4		25	1	
		„ contusum, ...	43	0		81	1		39	0		82	0	
		Morsus sanguis, ...	0	0	206	2	1	169	0	0	180	1	0	187
		TOTAL, ...	2578	21	2578	2185	15	2185	1963	20	1963	2149	11	2149

During the year 1862, epidemic cholera was very prevalent and fatal in the adjoining district of Peshawur. Beyond a few exceptional cases the Yusufzai plain entirely escaped infection.

Return of diseases treated in the Regimental Hospital of H.. M.'s Corps of Guides stationed at Murdan, in Yusufzai, for six years, from 1858 *to* 1863 *inclusive.*

Years.			1857*.			1858.			1859.			1860.			1861.			1862.			1863.		
Average daily strength.			768.			830.			960.			1016.			878.			906.			677.		
Average daily sick.			103.			42.			35.			31.			53.			41.			29.		
Class.	*Order.*	DISEASES.	*Cases.*	*Died.*	TOTAL.	*Cases.*	*Died.*	TOTAL.	*Cases.*	*Died.*	TOTAL.	*Cases.*	*Died.*	TOTAL.	*Cases.*	*Died.*	TOTAL.	*Cases.*	*Died.*	TOTAL.	*Cases.*	*Died.*	TOTAL.
I.	1	Febres.	1117	3		379	1		352	0		568	1		778	1		438	1		232	1	
		Erysipelas, ...	1	0		2	0		0	0		1	0		1	0		1	0		0	0	
		Influenza, ...	35	0		29	0		85	0		107	0		79	0		76	0		32	0	
		Tonsillitis,...	13	0		4	0		1	0		8	0		10	0		12	0		4	0	
		Ophthalmia, ...	38	0		30	0		36	0		50	0		67	0		51	0		37	0	
		Dysenteria, ...	83	2		23	0		27	0		37	0		58	1		32	0		107	1	
		Diarrhœa, ...	76	3		46	0		75	0		68	0		53	0		42	0		29	0	
		Furunculus, ...	7	0		2	0		0	0		0	0		52	0		111	0		43	0	
		Rheumatismus, ...	55	0		45	0		80	0		94	0		119	0		83	0		47	0	
		Cholera spasmod, ...	45	14		0	0		1	0		1	0		2	2		2	0		0	0	
		Variola, ...	1	0	1471	11	5	571	4	0	661	0	0	934	7	2	1226	2	0	850	0	0	531
	2	Syphilis, ...	39	0		26	0		10	0		15	0		14	0		19	0		5	0	
		Bubo,...	13	0		12	0		10	0		4	0		2	0		15	0		3	0	
		Gonorrhæa, ...	48	0		22	0		20	0		10	0		24	0		23	0		13	0	
		Orchitis, ...	3	0		5	0		8	0		5	0		5	0		5	0		2	0	
		Equinia, ...	1	0		0	0		0	0		0	0		0	0		0	0		0	0	
		Rabies, ...	1	1	105	0	0	65	0	0	48	0	0	34	0	0	45	0	0	62	0	0	23

* The returns for the year 1857 are added, to shew the difference produced by the corps being on active service at Dehli.

Years.			1857.			1858.			1859.			1860.			1861.			1862.			1863.		
Average daily strength.			768.			830.			960.			1016.			878.			906.			677.		
Average daily sick.			103.			42.			35.			31.			53.			41.			29		
Class.	*Order.*	DISEASES.	*Cases.*	*Died.*	TOTAL.	*Cases*	*Died.*	TOTAL.	*Cases.*	*Died.*	TOTAL.	*Cases.*	*Died.*	TOTAL.	*Cases.*	*Died.*	TOTAL.	*Cases.*	*Died.*	TOTAL.	*Cases.*	*Died.*	TOTAL.
	3	Scorbutus, ...	3	1		3	0		3	0		3	0		4	0		1	0		0	0	
		Purpura, ...	0	0		3	0		0	0		4	0		1	0		0	0		0	0	
		Ebriositas, ...	0	0	3	0	0	6	1	0	4	0	0	7	1	0	6	0	0	1	0	0	0
	4	Scabies, ...	12	0		13	0		5	0		14	0		17	0		4	0		0	0	
		Vermes,...	6	0	18	10	0	23	0	0	5	0	0	14	3	0	20	2	0	6	0	0	0
II.	1	Anœmia, ...	4	0		3	0		2	0		8	0		17	0		5	0		7	0	
		Anasarca, ...	1	0	5	2	0	5	0	0	2	1	0	9	4	1	21	0	0	5	0	0	7
	2	Phthisis pulmon, ...	0	0		4	1		2	0		4	1		7	0		2	0		1	1	
		Hamoptysis,...	2	1	2	2	0	6	3	0	5	0	0	4	0	0	7	0	0	2	1	0	2
III.	1	Apoplexy, ...	1	0		1	1		1	0		1	0		3	0		0	0		1	1	
		Mania, ...	1	1		1	0		0	0		0	0		1	0		0	0		0	0	
		Neuralgia, ...	2	0		7	0		13	0		26	0		50	0		32	0		9	0	
		Otitis, ...	10	0	14	12	0	21	7	0	21	10	0	37	0	0	54	4	0	36	7	0	17
	3	Pneumonia, ...	2	0		3	0		0	0		3	0		0	0		4	0		2	1	
		Pleuritis, ...	4	0		20	0		33	0		22	0		19	0		22	0		5	0	
		Bronchitis, ...	35	4	41	22	1	45	27	0	60	5	0	30	10	0	29	6	0	32	11	1	18

Years.			1857.			1858.			1859.			1860.			1861.			1862.			1863.		
Average daily strength.			768.			830.			960.			1016.			878.			906.			677.		
Average daily sick.			103.			42.			35.			31.			53.			41.			29.		
Class.	*Order.*	DISEASES.	*Cases.*	*Died.*	TOTAL.	*Cases.*	*Died.*	TOTAL.	*Cases.*	*Died.*	TOTAL.	*Cases.*	*Died.*	TOTAL.	*Cases.*	*Died.*	TOTAL.	*Cases.*	*Died.*	TOTAL.	*Cases.*	*Died.*	TOTAL.
	4	Hepatitis, ...	2	1		1	1		4	0		0	0		4	0		3	1		0	0	
		Icterus, ...	2	0		1	1		1	0		0	0		0	0		4	0		2	0	
		Dyspepsia, &c., ...	29	0		32	0		28	0		39	0		41	0		72	0		11	0	
		Colica, ...	18	0		15	0		36	0		44	1		60	0		42	0		52	0	
		Splenitis, ...	2	0		1	0		13	0		4	0		6	0		2	0		2	0	
					53			50			82			87			111			123			67
	5	Nephritis, &c., ...	3	0		0	0		13	0		4	0		18	0		7	0		5	1	
					3			0			13			4			18			7			5
	7	Ostitis, &c., ...	4	0		4	0		0	0		0	0		0	0		0	0		2	1	
		Caries, ...	3	0		6	0		1	0		0	0		0	0		0	0		1	0	
					7			10			1			0			0			0			3
		Urticaria, &c., ...	8	0		10	0		36	0		12	0		21	0		17	0		25	0	
		Abscessus, &c....	77	0		95	0		111	0		110	0		86	0		21	0		38	0	
		Ulcus, ...	73	0		103	0		71	1		61	0		58	1		34	0		38	0	
					158			208			218			183			165			72			101
V.	1	Accidents,...	375	52	375	94	2	94	123	1	123	189	0	189	164	0	164	132	0	132	116	4	116
		TOTALS, ...	2255	83	2255	1104	13	1104	1243	2	1243	1532	3	1532	1866	8	1866	1328	2	1328	890	12	890

Productions.

Of the productions of Yusufzai, those termed natural have already been noted as far as concerns the ones more usually met with. It remains now to notice those which are the result of man's industry. These are altogether, with but few exceptions, of the agricultural class, that is, products of either the fields or flocks. Throughout the country agriculture is of the most primitive kind. In most parts the seed is cast on to the ground without further preparation than the superficial scratchings of the plough; but near the villages manure is always used, and, wherever it is practicable, the fields are irrigated also. There are two principal crops, viz. the spring and the summer.

Agricultural.

Spring crops.

Cereals.

Mustard.

The spring crop, termed *rabbi*, or *oarai*, is the great cereal harvest. Barley *(oarbushi)* and wheat *(ghanum)* and mustard *(sharsham)* are sown during all *Asû, Kâtak, Magar, and Poh,* or from September to December, inclusive, and are reaped together, first barley and then wheat and mustard, during *Baisâk* and *Jait*, or April and May. At the same time, with the above are sown and reaped the chick pea or *cicer arietinum (chanai)*, the lentil or *ervum lens (nask)*, and the haricot bean, or *dolichos sp. (lobia.)* The straw of the cereals, and the dry leaves and stalks of the pulses, &c., are stored in stacks as fodder for the cattle during the winter. The latter, however, are most frequently expended whilst still fresh, and are considered a very nourishing diet. The straw of the former is termed *bûs*, and the fodder of the latter *katti*. The other crops

Pulses.

Beans.

Fodder.

Vegetables.

cultivated during the rabbi season are the following:—In February *(Pâghan)* onions and other pot-herb vegetables are sown; they are gathered during June and July. In March *(Chaitar)* are sown tobacco *(tambâku)* and egg-plant (*batinganr*), and are gathered, the former in June (*Hâr*) and the latter in May *(Jait)*. At this season also are sown coriander *(dannia)*, anise *(kaga)*, poppy *(khâshkhâsh)*, and capsicum *(sura murch)*, and a few other spices and medicines.

Sugar-cane.

The sugar-cane *(ganni)* is only cultivated in some particular tracts where there are facilities for irrigation, as in Hashtnaggar and Swat, &c., for the plant requires regular and free supplies of water. The cuttings are put in during February and March, and the crop is cut during all October, November, and December.

Autumn crops.

Cotton.

The autumn crop, termed *kharîf*, or *manai*, is the busy season of the cultivators. During April and May *(Baisâk* and *Jait)* the cotton crop is sown; it ripens, and the wool is gathered, as it forms, during all August, September, and October (or *Badro, Asu,* and *Katak)*.

Millet.

During June and July *(Hâr* and *Pashakâl)*, Indian millet, or *holcus sorghum (nari joar,* or *wâra joar,* or *niki joar)*, and in some districts Italian millet, or *Panicum Italicum* (*ghokht,* or *kaokan*) are sown; they are reaped during September and October, and are independent of water from artificial sources.

Maize.

During July and August, maize, or Indian corn, or *zea mays* (or *makki,* or *joâr,* or *ghatt joâr*) is sown and reaped in October. This crop requires water, and is, therefore, mostly sown where such is available.

Straw.

The stalks of maize and Indian millet, termed *tântai,*

are used as fodder for cattle; and, for use in the winter, are stored in the villages. During July is sown spiked millet, or *holcus spicatus (bajra)*, but only on light, sandy soil, and where water is available. The plant is cut, and yields three successive crops during September and October. Though a very remunerative crop, this grain is not much cultivated in this country, owing to its stubble being useless as fodder for cattle, the means of subsistence for which are as much to be provided for as are those for man; for the country, unaided in this respect, cannot pasture a tithe of the cattle reared in it. In July, or during August, the kidney bean, or *phaseolus aconitifolius* (*mot*), the rayed kidney bean, or *phaseolus radiatus* (*mai*), and hairy-podded kidney bean, or *phaseolus max* (*mâhai*), are sown, and during October they are reaped. The seeds are the common pulses, so essential an article in the diet of the natives; the stalks and leaves serve as fodder for cattle; and, in the fresh state, are considered very nourishing. At the same times with these pulses is sown and gathered the common sessame, or *Sesamum Indicum* (*kanzali*), from the seeds of which is expressed the common sweet oil, or *til*, of the country. The seeds are sometimes eaten roasted.

Bajra.

Fodder for cattle.

Sessame.

During September are sown carrots (*gâzari*), radishes (*mulai*), turnips (*tipar*), and other vegetables; also fenugreek (*malkhozai*), beet (*pâlak*), common dill (*soa*), and other pot-herbs; also indigo (*wasma*), and *lawsonia inermis* (*nakriza*, or *hinna*), used as dyes for the hair and hands, respectively.

Vegetables.

Included with the *kharíf* are the *parshakâl*, or rainy season crops. They are sown in April (*Baisakh*) and gathered in June and July (*Hâr* and *Parshakâl*). They

Rainy season crops.

consist of the different kinds of musk-melon, or *kharbuja*, and water-melon, or *tarbuja*. Of the former, the common kind is the *khataki*, and of the latter the *hindwâna*. Several kinds of cucumber also are cultivated, as the common cucumber, or *badrang*, the luffa, or *turai*, the *kakri*, the *kaddu*, the *khîra*, &c., &c. All these crops require a light, sandy soil and regular irrigation, and are, therefore, generally found only near the villages.

Melons.

Cucumbers.

The above are the common crops cultivated on the Yusufzai plain. In Swat the principal crops are wheat, maize, and rice; barley is only grown in the western end of the valley. Lucerne and clover *(shotal)* are grown generally throughout the valley as fodder for the cattle and horses. Two kinds of pea, termed *matar* and *krâk*, are also largely cultivated in most parts of Swat. Cotton and the sugar-cane are cultivated largely; but bajra, nari joâr, and kunzali, are not cultivated at all either in Swat or Bajawar, or Malizai and Panjkora.

Cultivation in Swat.

In these tracts, except Swat, already described, the chief crops are wheat, barley, rice, maize, cotton, mustard, lucerne, and tobacco. Besides these a great variety of pulses and beans are very generally cultivated; those of the spring crop are termed *matar*, *krâk*, and *nask*; those of the autumn crop are termed *kalol*, *kulat*, and *lobia*. The following kinds of millets also are pretty extensively cultivated, viz., *ghokht*, *kârâ*, and *ghadan*.

In Malizai.

In Buhnair and the hill tract to its eastward, the cultivation in the main is the same as that of Malizai; but they cultivate more wheat and maize, and less rice, barley, &c.

In Buhnair.

In Mandaur.

In the Yusufzai plain most of the cultivation is confined to the immediate vicinity of the villages where there are wells and other facilities for irrigation; but a considerable portion of the *mairah,* or waste tract, is also brought under the plough. The crops raised on it are wheat, barley, mustard, maize, sesanum, and the common pulses. Though not very remunerative, owing to its entire dependence on the skies for water, this kind of cultivation, or *lallam,* as it is termed, has greatly increased during the past six or eight years. In most parts the surface soil of the mairah is light and porous, and of medium strength. The crops raised on it, without either water or manure, are described as in the proportion of one to two as compared with those raised on *abi* lands, where both water and manure are used; that is to say, a maund of wheat sown on *lallam* land yields twenty maunds, whereas the same quantity sown on *abi* land returns forty maunds, in round numbers, for both.

Unirrigated.

Irrigated.

Canals for irrigation.

In former times, there is reason to believe that the present extensive waste between Mandanr and Hashtnaggar was irrigated by means of canals. The remains of a very extensive one are still traceable in some parts of the plain between Abazai and Pirabad. It was led off from the Swat river, a little below Jûd Baba Ziarat, and crossing the Jaindai ravine, by means of which no signs remain, flowed past Gandairai southwards on to the plain. The canal is now filled up and in ruins; but its course is easily traceable at short intervals for many miles. At a comparatively small cost, this water channel might be cleared out and made useful. It would fertilize about two

Former existence.

hundred square miles of, at the present time, waste land, and would certainly in a few years repay any expenditure incurred in its repair. The produce in grain alone would be, at the lowest estimation, twenty times more than it is at this moment, and might be increased to a hundred times as much.

Present want.

Besides the cultivated crops mentioned in the preceding pages, the Yusufzai plain and its bordering hills produce a number of wild herbs, edible fruits, grains, and grasses, which are used by the natives as articles of diet, some only in seasons of scarcity or famine, and others at all times as ordinary food. Of the wild herbs used as ordinary vegetables or pot-herbs, termed *sāg* in the vernacular, the more common are the following :—

Uncultivated fruits and pot-herbs.

ENUMERATION.

ENGLISH NAME.	BOTANICAL NAME.	PUSHTU NAME.
Common purslane, ...	Portulaca, 2 sp., ...	Warkhârai.
Mallow, sp., ...	Malva, sp., ...	Sâochal.
Mallow, sp., ...	M. rotundifolio, ...	Panîrak.
Wild rape, ...	Sinapis, 2 sp., ...	Aorai.
Wild mustard, ...	Sinapis, sp., ...	Joâwân.
Fenugreek, ...	Trigonella, F., ...	Malkhozai.
Trefoil, common, ...	Trifolium, sp., ...	Spaishtarai.
Common sorrel, ...	Rumex vesicarius, ...	Tarûki.
Solanam, sp., ...	Solanum, sp., ...	Kachmâchu.
Trefoil (?)	Trifolium, (?) ...	Laiwani.
Buckbean, (?)	Menyanthes, (?) ...	Chalwairai.
Common orache, ...	Atriplex, sp., ...	Sârmai.
Spinach, (?) ...	Spinacia sp., (?) ...	Bibi Painsai.
Cyperus grass, ...	C. tuberosus, ...	Dila.
Millet grass, ...	Panicum frument: ...	Shâmukha.

Of the above, the two last named are grasses. Of the *dila*, only the tuber, or *ghotai*, is eaten, and generally roasted. Of the *shâmukha*, of which there are three

Wild millet.

varieties, only the seed is eaten. It is considered a nutritive and wholesome food; and, boiled with milk, is eaten by Hindus on certain fixed religious festivals. For cows giving milk it is considered the best food. This grain forms the principal diet of the present Akhûn of Swat, for whose use it is cooked with milk in a variety of palatable forms. *Shâmukha* is cultivated for the Akhûn's special use in Swat, and it is said has formed the chief diet of "His Holiness" for more than thirty years. Of the other pot-herbs, only the leaves and leaf-stalks are used. The favorite kinds are *warkhârai*, *sâochal*, *panirak*, *malkhozai*, and *sârmai*. *Aoraî* and *joâwân* are bitter to the taste and are looked on as preventives of flatulence. *Tarûki* is considered cooling, and all are considered preventives of scurvy; hence, probably, their very general use in the absence of other fresh vegetables.

The Akhûn's diet.

Pot-herbs.

The wild fruits and berries commonly used as food or medicines, are the *bair* (three kinds), the *kirrarra*, the *gurgurra*, the *mumânri*, the *krûnda*, the *karko*, the *balâghund*, the *surazghai*, the *mânrû* or "sloe," &c. &c. With the exception of the two first named, none of these are found on the plain, but all are to be found on the lower spurs and at the foot of the hills bounding it on the north and east; and in these localities they are gathered by natives of the neighbourhood and sent for sale into the villages on the plain. Their English names have been given in the list of plants mentioned as characterizing the flora of the lower hills bordering on the Yusufzai plain.

Wild fruits.

Next to their crops the Yusufzais are occupied in the care of their cattle and flocks. In these they are everywhere rich. On the plain are kept cows, buffa-

Cattle.

Of the plains.

loes, and sheep. The two first are for the most part kept only for their milk, but that of the sheep is also used and is considered good for making ghî with. It is a valuable product, and collected in considerable quantity. Oxen are in great abundance; they are used at the plough and irrigation wells, and generally as beasts of burden—ponies, mules and donkeys being not so numerous, whilst horses are only used for riding. In the hill tracts buffaloes are more numerous, and cows and oxen less so than on the plain; the same holds as regards ponies and mules, whilst sheep are almost wholly replaced by goats.

Of the hills.

Means of subsistence.

On the plain country the flocks and herds are frequently hard pushed for pasture during the summer droughts and winter frosts, and suffer greatly at such seasons from epidemic diseases. When thus deprived of their natural pastures, the cattle subsist on the dry stalks and straw of the various grain and pulse crops which are stacked in the villages for the purpose of meeting such contingencies. Occasionally this diet is varied, and for a few days they receive "oil cake," or the bruised seeds left after the expression from them of their oily matter; but this cake is generally reserved for the milch cows and buffaloes. Mustard, sessanum, and cotton seeds are the common components of the "oil cake." Sometimes the dry leaves of the *bair*, which are gathered and stored for the purpose, are given; they are considered very wholesome and nourishing food.

Diseases.

Cattle diseases are often epidemic and very destructive. They prevail mostly in the spring and autumn months, and rapidly spread over extensive tracts of country. They depend either directly on atmospheric changes or else on the changes in the pasture-diet of the cattle, produced by them. The common epidemics among cows, oxen, and buffaloes, are the following:—

Scurvy.

Ghûndârai and *Gôdwâ.* These appear to be rapidly fatal forms of scurvy. The animal is suddenly struck ill and sometimes dies in less than twenty-four hours, and always within eight or ten days. Few it is said ever recover. The gums become spongy and bleed; the bowels discharge thin, stinking, and bloody motions; the hair falls off, and large mortifying sores form on all parts of the body.

Rheumatism and fever.

Chârmaikh and *tâkû.* These diseases appear to be forms of rheumatic fever. They generally occur in the rainy season. The animal becomes attacked with spasms across the chest, is unable to move or eat, and withers to death in a few days; but they sometimes recover.

Dysentery.

Loai ranz. Epidemic dysentery. It kills in a few days, and is seldom recovered from.

Of sheep the destructive diseases are these:—

Gripes.

Hamídai. Dysentery and gripes; an epidemic of the spring season, and mostly fatal in two or three days, though often in only a few hours.

Small-pox.

Nannakai. Small-pox; an epidemic of the rainy season; and very destructive; described by shepherds as the same disease as the small-pox in man.

Apoplexy.

Warkhârai. Inanition and sun-stroke; an epidemic of the hot months, and very destructive during unusual droughts. The animals droop and expire in a comatose state.

The only fatal epidemic common to goats is termed *bûddai.* It is a kind of epilepsy, and is commonly prevalent only in the hot months.

Cure.

For none of these diseases have the natives any certain or recognized mode of treatment. Salt, mustard-oil, assafœtida, and the common spices, with all sorts of herbal drugs are administered, according to the fancy of the owner or the advice of his friends; charms, and pilgrimages to the ziarats in the vicinity, if practicable, are never omitted.

Pasture food.

The natural food of the cattle on the pastures of the plain country comprises a variety of herbs and grasses, of which the most common are the following :—

Hurtful.

Wholesome.

The last named, or *dadam,* is considered bad for cattle, and is supposed to cause several of their diseases. All the others are reckoned good food, and are often gathered and given to stall-fed cows, &c., to increase their milk. The *ziarguli, shâmukha, sarbagga,* and *sargarai,* are especially valued on this account.

Manufactures.

As before stated, the care of their fields and flocks constitutes the main occupation of the Yusufzais. Beyond the ordinary industrial arts for the supply of

PLANTS.

ENGLISH NAME.	BOTANICAL NAME.	PUSHTU NAME.
Mallow, ...	Malva, 2 sp., ...	Panirak, sâochal.
Trefoil, ...	Trifolium, ...	Spaishtarai.
Ditto, ...	Ditto, ...	Spaistai.
Ditto, ...	Ditto, ...	Laiwanai.
Calendula, ...	C. officinalis, ...	Ziarguli.
Fleawort, ...	Plantago, 2 sp., ...	Spighol.
Chamomile, ...	Anthemis, sp., ...	Krichi.
Dandelion, ...	Taraxacum leon, ...	Joulakai.
Malcomia, ...	M. 3 or 4 sp., ...	Kharor.
White lily, ...	Convolvulus, sp., ...	Praiwatai.
Caltrops, ...	Tribulus terrestris,...	Mâlkundai.
Safflower, ...	Carthamus, 2 sp., ...	Kârîza.
Goosefoot, ...	Chenopodium, ...	Orbushki.
Wild oats, ...	Avena sativa, ...	Jâodar,
Thread grass, ...	Agrostis linearis, ...	Kabbal, dûp.
Panic grass, sp., ...	Panicum, sp., ...	Shâmûkha.
Ditto, ...	Ditto, ...	Shama, drab.
Ditto, ...	Ditto, ...	Sarbagga.
Cyperus grass, ...	Cyperus, 6 sp., ...	Dila, wîga.
Ditto, ...	Ditto, ...	Malai, mota.
Ditto, ...	Ditto, ...	Malanga &c.
Dogs' tail grass, ...	Cynosurus, 2 sp., ...	Ghûndwagai.
Ditto, ...	Ditto, ...	Mândarû.
Millet grass, ...	Milium, 2 sp., ...	Sargarai, &c.
Andropogon, ...	A. 2 sp., ...	Dadam.

their own domestic requirements, they have no manufactures. To describe the common trade arts would extend this report beyond the intended limits ; but the principal materials used in them will be found in the accompanying Appendix of the various productions of the country (not already described) and their uses.

Trade.

Though not a manufacturing people, the Yusufzais carry on an extensive (considering their state of society) and varied trade with the countries around, and especially with those on the south-eastern border.

Timber.

Thus from Swat, Malizai, and the valleys east of Buhnair, by means of the Swat, Panjkora, and Indus rivers, respectively, are exported various kinds of timber, and these are stored in the depôts at Attock, Nowshaira, and Hashtnaggar. At the Nowshairah depôt are also collected the timber from the Kabul country, which has a rival timber trade of its own, by the channel of the Kabul river. These several depôts supply the wants of the Peshawur and Dairajat frontier with timber for building purposes. The common timbers brought down to the depôts are the *pinus longifolia* (*nakhtar*), *cedrus deodara* (*diâr*), and *juglans regia* (*akor*). Of the deodar the finest timbers are felled in the Tâl Lâmotai district of Malizai, and the Tâl Dardiâl district of Swat ; but they can only be got down to the market in short lengths on account of the natural obstacles to their free carriage presented by the narrows, rapids, and falls of the Swat river in its passage through the Hatmânkhail hills. The timber trade of Yusufzai is entirely in the hands of a few wealthy families of the Mian fraternity settled in the Hashtnagger and Khattak districts. Owing to the disturbed state of the country generally, this trade is attended by many risks and vexatious delays. It can never successfully compete with that of the Kabul country on account of the irremediable obstacles to carriage for timbers of the larger dimensions.

Iron.

From Malizai, Barawal, and Bajawar, the staple export is iron. It all goes to Peshawar to the consignment of merchants of the Mian class. The metal is obtained by smelting the sands of mountain torrents in the Bârawal, Maidan, and Oshaizai valleys. It is said to be of superior quality, and easily managed by native artizans. On its way to Peshawar most of the metal passes direct through the Momand hills, but a considerable quantity comes through Swat and the Yusufzai plain. The carriage is altogether by land upon bullocks and mules; the former return with salt, sugar, indigo, spices, cotton, &c., &c., but the latter are mostly sold in the Peshawar market.

Rice.

From Swat is exported rice for the Peshawar market. It all comes by mules, camels, or bullocks, over the Malakand and Mora passes into the Yuzufzai plain, and on to Peshawar by the Hashtnaggar (Charsadda) and Khattak (Nowshaira) routes, respectively. By this route, also, come ponies from Shukalam; hawks and precious stones from Kashkar; also fruits, as the walnut, *amluk* (diospyros) apple, apricot, &c., from Swat itself, and all the country northward to the foot of the Hindu Kush.

Ghî or Butter.

Buhnair and the country to its eastward exports only *ghî*, or prepared butter. Small quantities of this article also come down from Swat and all the country to its north as far as Kashkar. Honey also comes from Swat and Buhnair.

On the Yusufzai plain, the depôt for the Malizai trade is Charsadda in Hashtnaggar; for the Swat trade Lundkhwar in Baizai; and for that of Buhnair, Rustam Bazar in Sudhum.

Imports.

In return for their exports the hill tribes take back salt, indigo, spices, sugar, cotton fabrics, Multan silks, and Kashmere shawls, &c., &c. From Kabul, Nangnahar and Kunar they receive, in return for their fruits and iron, arms and ammunition, such as guns, swords, &c., nitre and sulphur, &c.

Plain.
Cattle and corn, &c.

The trade of the Yusufzai plain is almost entirely with the Peshawar market. They export oxen, sheep, ghî, grain, sheeps' wool, and latterly cotton, also oil, and a few horses. In return they import cotton fabrics, indigo, salt, sugar, spices, drugs, &c., &c.

People.

The Yusufzais, whose country, history, manners, and industry have been described in the previous pages of this report, as far as space permits of, are a fine, healthy, hardy, and brave people. Of the diseases met with in the plain country, the tabular statement of the diseases treated in the Murdan Dispensary during the past four years will convey a correct idea. Of the hill country, as far as I have been able to ascertain, the characteristic diseases are fevers of the intermittent and remittent types with their sequela, as enlarged spleen, indurated liver, abdominal dropsy, &c., syphilis and leprosy, bronchocole, cataract.

Diseases.

I 3

(in Swat especially, where it is often congenital), stone in the bladder, pulmonary diseases, phthisis pulmonalis, and parasitic and other diseases of the skin, &c.

Doctors.

The Yusufzais, in the hills especially, have no regular educated class of medical or surgical practitioners. In the hill countries both the *hakim* and the *jarrah* are alike unknown. And the *tabib*, or general practitioner, who is enterprizing enough to trust himself amongst them, is always looked on as an oracle, and flocked to by numbers of the sick and wounded, all expecting an immediate and perfect cure of their several various ailments, whether real or imaginary.

Practice.

The old adage "experientia docet," however, here comes into play; and these hardy mountaineers, whether comparatively successful or not, are fertile in their resources for preventing or curing diseases and injuries. Their first appeal is to the priests and holy men, on the efficacy of whose charms and prayers they place implicit reliance. Their next resource is the long list of drugs and superstitious ceremonies which by long usage have become familiar domestic remedies. To follow these is not worth while, but the annexed appendix will shew the drugs and the purposes for which they are chiefly used, together with other articles of indigenous production, and the purposes to which they are commonly applied.

FINIS.

APPENDIX.

INDIGENOUS PRODUCTIONS OF YUSUFZAI, AND THEIR USES, &c.

ENGLISH NAME.	PUSHTU NAME.	REMARKS.
Adamant, ...	Kurund, ...	From Swat and Kabul. Powdered and combined with other ingredients, used as "razor paste" for polishing swords, &c.
Antimony, ...	Rânja, ...	From hills north of Swat. Powdered and used as a dry collyrium for strengthening and ornamenting the eyes. Hindustani name is *surma*.
Arsenic, ...	Hartâl, ...	Orpiment. From hills north of Swat, used as a yellow dye by dyers, carpenters, and scribes. Used as a medicine in skin diseases and syphilis, &c.
Clay, mica, ...	Matai, ...	From Swat. Used as an ornamental plaster on the cornices and walls of rooms, &c.
Clay, red, ...	Sura khaora, ...	Red ochre. Found in Lundkhwar, and used by potters.
Clay, white, ...	Spina khaora,...	Chalk. (?) Used as a medicine for heart-burn; also by school boys for writing on tablets.
Lime, nodulated,	Krût kânri, ...	*Kankar*. Sometimes burnt for lime by dyers, &c. All over Yusufzai.
Millstone, ...	Maichanagatta,	Gneiss. In the Malandarra hills. Used for the manufacture of millstones.
Mortar-stone, ...	Sil silâta, ...	Sand-stone, marble, or amygdaloid. Used as slabs or bowls for grinding spices on, &c.
Nitre, ...	Khora, ...	Saltpetre. On Yusufzai plain. Used as a medicine and in the manufacture of gunpowder. The extraction is limited in the British territory by licence.
Slate, ...	Khazai kanri,...	Ranizai, Khattak, &c., hills. Used as head-stones over graves, tablets, &c.
Potashes, ...	Sijji, ...	Prepared in the Yusufzai plain for the use of soap-makers, dyers, and washermen.
Sand, black, ...	Tora Shiga, ...	River Indus. Washed for the gold it yields. In Yusufzai the gold washers earn from four to six annas a day on the average.

English Name.	Pushtu Name.	Remarks.
Sand, red, ...	Sura Shiga, ...	Indus and hill streams. Used in the composition of "razor paste," and also mixed with lac gum for making grinding wheels, termed *sarkh*.
Sand-stone, ...	Bilâo, ...	Firm, fine, and compact grained. Mahaban hills, at Kadra, Dakâra, &c. Used as hones and razor strops, &c.
Sand-stone, ...	Barjokanri, ...	Firm, coarse, and loose grained. Low hills of Yusufzai and Buhnair. Used for sharpening swords, daggers, &c.
Soap-stone, ...	Shâokânri, ...	Soft, grey steatite. Used for the blow holes of furnaces and for baking-trays, termed *tâira*, or *taba*. Is indestructible in the fire.
Iron, metallic, ...	Ospana, ...	Procured by smelting the sands of mountain torrents in Barawal, Maidan, and Malizai. Exported to Peshawar.
Iron, sulphate, ...	Kâhi, ...	Green vitriol. Found in hills of Swat, and in Chingli, &c. Used by dyers as a mordant.
Alum, red, ...	Patkarai, ...	Both red and white are met with, and are said to come from Malizai.
Lizards' dung, ...	Sams-arai ghul,	In the Yusufzai plain. Applied to the eyes in ophthalmia.
Mummy wax, ...	Momiai, ...	A dark, musty, greasy compound. Found in caves, and supposed to be produced by mountain deer rubbing their sides against the rocks. Some specimens I have examined proved to be cakes of bats' dung. It is supposed to be an universal specific, but is especially prized as a remedy for fractures, bruises, strains, &c. It is said to act as a stimulant and anti-spasmodic, taken inwardly.
Pangolin, ...	Kishor, ...	The scales are applied round the necks of children and pregnant women as a charm against the evil eye, &c.
Calculus vesicœ,	Gitai, ...	Stone of the human bladder or urinary calculus. Prized as a medicine for those suffering from stone in the bladder; taken internally in powder. It is supposed to act as a stone solvent.
Acacia modesta,	Palosa, ...	A common tree about grave-

English Name.	Pushtu Name.	Remarks.
		yards. The wood is used for ploughshares. The gum, or *chinr*, is used as a medicine, and supposed to possess restorative properties.
Anise com. ...	Kâgâ. ...	Cultivated in gardens. Seeds used as a carminative medicine; fresh plant used as a pot-herb, and believed to counteract tendency to flatulence.
Apricot, ...	Ashârai, ...	In Swat and Malizai. Cultivated and wild. Decoction of preserved fruit combined with other herbs, used as a laxative and refrigerant in fevers, &c. The plain decoction is used by goldsmiths to clean and brighten their metals.
Berberry, ...	Korai, ...	In the hills of Swat, Malizai, and Buhnair. The fruit is given in electuary as a cooling laxative for children. The stems, *chitra*, are given in decoction as a diaphoratic and laxative in rheumatism; the root, *ziar largai*, is used in decoction as a remedy for mucous discharges from the lungs and bowels. The fresh fruit, termed *zirishk* in Persian, is wholesome food, and makes good preserve; the extract of
Dil, common, ...	Spairkai, ...	Cultivated on the plain; used as the preceding.
Dock, common,...	Shalkhai, Zagûki.	Leaves used as a pot-herb; applied as dressing to sores, burns, &c.
Diospyros, ...	Amluk, ...	Hills of Swat, Buhnair, and Malizai. Fruit, an article of diet, generally cooked with rice or eaten plain; an ingredient of several medicinal sharbats.
Fennel, Indian,	Tor ranja, ...	Common about the base of the hills. The seeds are given in warm milk as a remedy for colic.
Fœnugreek, ...	Mâlkhozai, ...	Two kinds are common weeds all over the plain. The fresh plant is a favorite pot-herb. The seeds are used as a remedy for colic and flatulence.
Fleawort, ...	Spighol, ...	A common weed. The seeds are demulcent, and are added to many medicinal sharbats; steeped in water they produce a cool-

English Name.	Pushtu Name.	Remarks.
		for diarrhœa, and externally for bruises and strains, &c.
Calotropis, ...	Spalmai, ...	Common all over the Yusufzai plain. The milky juice and leaves are used to raise blisters and dissipate chronic tumours; the silky cotton attached to the seeds is used to stuff pillows with; the fresh root is used as a tooth-brush for the cure of tooth ache, and the fresh juice is used in the preparation of catgut.
		cathartic. A cultivated variety is used as a vegetable.
Hemp, Indian, ...	Bang, ...	Flowers and leaves mashed into pulp are applied as a cataplasm to hœmorrhoids and other painful tumours; sometimes used for purposes of intoxication. Common on the lower hills.
Hinna, ...	Nakrîzi, ...	Is sparingly cultivated; used for dying the hands and feet and the beard preparatory to the application of indigo, or *wasma*.
Jujube, wild, red,	Aslai baira, or Karkanna, ...	Common all over the plain. Berries are eaten; leaves gathered as a nourishing and milk-producing fodder for cattle; thorny stems used as fences for sheep-folds, &c.
Ditto, wild, white,	Bada baira, ...	A small tree, in most parts of the plain, in the vicinity of grave-yards, &c. Fruit eaten as plums; leaves given as fodder to cattle. The leaves stirred in in water produce a lather and are used by women to wash their heads with.
Ditto, lotus, ...	Sowa baira, or Unnab, ...	Cultivated in Swat and Buhnair, &c. Fresh fruit eaten as plums; preserved or dried, they are added to medicinal sharbats as demulcent and laxative.
Liquorice, ..	Khwâga-wali, ...	In Hashtnaggar. The root is added to purgative sharbats; and, powdered and mixed with black pepper, is a remedy for colds and coughs.
Malabar nut, ...	Bhaikar, ...	Common on lower. hills and their base. Leaves in mash used as a cattle medicine; in infusion taken as a remedy for rheumatism; fresh flowers bound over

ENGLISH NAME.	PUSHTU NAME.	REMARKS.
		decoction is emetic; the oil from the flowers is used in liniments for rheumatism.
Convovulus, ...	**Tarbad,** ...	On the plain. Infusion of stems demulcent and attenuant; an ingredient in several purgative sharbats.
Coriander, ...	**Dania,** ...	Cultivated. Fresh plant used as a pot-herb; distilled water of seeds carminative.
Cress, Chinese,	**Halam,** ...	Grows on the edges of cultivation on the plain. The seeds boiled in milk are given to produce abortion.
Cummin, ...	**Zankai,** ...	Grows wild in Swat and Malizai. The seeds in decoction are given as a cure for colic; the fresh leaves are cooked as pot-herbs to correct flatulence.
		the root is the *rasaut* of the bazars, and prized as an ophthalmic remedy.
Bauhinia, (?) ...	**Kohliar,** ...	Grows in the hills around Yusufzai.
Ficus, sp., (?) ...		The bark is used as an astringent by curriers and dyers; strips of the inner bark are used as fusees for the matchlocks of the mountaineers, and is termed *pat.*
Bengal beet, ...	**Pâlak,** ...	Cultivated with the autumn crop. A favorite pot-herb; fresh leaves used as an application to burns and bruises, &c.
Bengal quince,	**Balaghund,** ...	In the Malandarra hills. The fresh fruit is eaten raw and roasted as food, and as a remedy in bowel complaints. The dried gum resin is termed *bail kath,* and sold in the bazars as a remedy for dysentery; the ripe fruit shells are manufactured into snuff boxes, and tastefully carved at Peshawar.
Butea downy, ...	**Palai,** ...	In the northern and eastern hills of Yusufzai. The flowers in decoction are given to sheep as a medicine for hœmaturia; and are used by dyers to produce a yellow dye; the gum in electuary is used by puerperal women to hasten recovery; also

English Name.	Pushtu Name.	Remarks.
		ing mucilaginous drink used in fever cases; the seeds roasted and mixed with sugar are a very common remedy for diarrhœa and dysentery.
Fumitory, ...	Pâpra, ...	Common in cultivated tracts. The whole plant in decoction is used as a diuretic and laxative for heat of body and dryness of skin. Is an ingredient of most cathartic sharbats.
Gourd, colocynth like, ...	Maraghunai, ...	Common on the plain and low hills. The fruit is termed *kâkora*, and is given to horses as a purge. A few grains of the pulp mixed with warm water is a common remedy for constipation and colic; the powder of the dried root is used also for the same purpose. The fresh root is used as a tooth-brush.
Gourd, bitter, ...	Tarkha Torai,...	At the foot of the hills round the plain. The seeds mixed with black pepper are given in warm water as an emetic and
Caltrops, ...	Mâlkundai, ...	The fresh plant bruised and stirred in water makes it viscid; this is drank as a cure for impotence; women eat the seeds to ensure their fecundity; an infusion of the stalks is used as a remedy for gonorrhœa. Common in Yusufzai plain.
Cassia absus, ...	Sakhkû, ...	Grows along the base of the hills; the powder of the seeds is blown into the eye, or mixed into a paste applied over the lids in ophthalmia.
Cassia fistula, ...	Lândais, ...	In the hills round Yusufzai. The pod, pulp, and seeds bruised are combined in decoction or electuary with other drugs, and given as a laxative; the root is used in decoction as a tonic and febrifuge.
Castor oil, ...	Arand, ...	Grows wild in ravines and borders of the fields; infusion of flowers and seeds used as a laxative for children; the seeds, to six or eight, are eaten as a purge for adults.
Chamomile, ...	Krichi, ...	Common. Infusion of flowers and leaves is aromatic, tonic, and febrifuge; a strong

English Name.	Pushtu Name.	Remarks.
		the eyes in ophthalmia.
Mallow, round leaved, ...	Panirak, ...	Common. Leaves, a favourite pot-herb; seeds demulcent, and added to purgative and expectorant sharbats; the root, or *risha khatmi*, is laxative and diaphoretic.
Mallow, small flowered, ...	Saonchal, ...	Common. The fresh leaves are used as a pot-herb; in other respects as the last.
Mimosa, climbing, ...	Kulmawali, ...	In the hills of Buhnair and Swat. The stem is used in decoction as a tonic and febrifuge.
Mulberry, ...	Tut, ...	In the hills everywhere. The wood is used in making ploughs, &c; the fruit eaten; on the plain the tree is grown near the villages.
Mustard, wild, ...	Aorai, ...	Common in ditches and fields, &c. Used as a pot-herb when young; seeds used as a demulcent in medicinal sharbats; the cultivated mustard is also used as a pot-herb when young; the seeds are often roasted and eaten with parched wheat. The crop is cultivated for the oil yielded by its seed.
Myrabolans, ...	Bahaira, ...	In the hills of Swat and Buhnair. The covering of the fruit is used in decoction or powder as an astringent and tonic in mucous discharges from the bowels or the lungs.
	Haraira, ...	Hills of Totai and Buhnair. (?) Covering of fruit is very astringent; is used in combination with other drugs as a purge in cases of diarrhœa or dysentery; by dyers it is used mixed with alum to produce a yellow colour, and mixed with ocre to produce a black colour; used also in making ink.
	Aola, ...	Hills of Buhnair. Fruit and flowers used as purgative drugs, and generally mixed with the last.
Oleander, ...	Gandairi, ...	In ravines and at base of hills. The powdered leaves used as an errhine in neuralgia and cephalalgia.
Olive, ...	Khoan, ...	Common on base of hills and lower heights. Wood used for ploughshares, cotton machi-

English Name.	Pushtu Name.	Remarks.
		nery, &c. The fruit is not eaten; oil is sometimes extracted as medicine.
Pæony, (?) ...	Mâmaikh, ...	Hills of Buhnair, Swat, &c. Root in powder given as a cattle medicine to render them prolific; mixed with powdered turmeric, barberry root, and sugar is a favorite remedy for bruises, strains, &c.
Pine, sp., ...	Nakhtar, ...	All the higher mountain ranges of Yusufzai. Yield crude turpentine; used in slips of the wood as candles and torches, or *shontái*; timber exported, cones roasted, and fruit eaten; is not the true edible pine. Bark used by curriers for tanning leather.
Poplar, ...	Tâgho, ...	In Swat, Buhnair, &c., and lower hills. The wood is used to make charms to avert evil eye, &c., from man and brute.
Pursalane, ...	Warkhârai, ...	A common pot-herb. The fresh leaves bruised are applied as a cataplasm in erysipelas; seeds in decoction in fevers as demulcent and diuretic.
Rape, wild, ...	Joâwân, ...	A common weed. Fresh young leaves used as a pot-herb; seeds in powder are given for flatulent colic; the oil is applied to the skin in a variety of its affections in man and brute.
Rue, wild, ...	Spailanai, ...	Common everywhere. Seeds burnt as incense to drive away evil spirits, &c., at night, and to avert evil eye and other calamities from the sick, &c. Seeds are masticated for cure of colic; decoction of the leaves is a remedy for rheumatism; the powder of the root mixed with mustard oil is applied to the hair to destroy lice, &c.
Salsolaceæ, ...	Khorakai, ...	Common all over the plain country. Burnt in heaps for
	Lâna, ...	potashes. *Lâna* is used by wo-

English Name.	English Name.	Remarks.
	Zmai, ...	men to wash the head with; the fresh fleshy leaves of *zmai* are applied, mashed, as a poultice to the eyes in ophthalmia.
Safflower, ...	Kârîza, ...	Common on the plain. Seeds eaten roasted; yield an oil used medicinally; is never cultivated here.
Sessamum, ...	Kunzali, ...	Cultivated on the plain only. The seeds yield a sweet oil; are eaten roasted; the stálks of the plant are useless.
Silk cotton tree,	Badarkand, ...	Not a common tree. Grows in Chinglai, the gum resin, termed *badarkand*, is used combined with *bail kath* as a cure for diarrhœa and dysentery; the root is considered to possess aphrodisiac properties; the wood is used for sword-sheaths, &c.
Sissu, ...	Shiwa, ...	Not common. About villages and in the islands of the Indus, the wood is used for the general purposes of carpentry.
Sloe, ...	Mânru, ...	In the hills of Swat and Malizai, &c. The fruit is eaten, and used in various medicinal sharbats as a laxative.
Sorrel, ...	Taruki, ...	Common in the hills. Used as a common pot-herb.
Succory, ...	Kâshnî, ...	Common in waste places. Sometimes cultivated; seeds used in medicinal sharbats.
Tamarisk, ...	Rghaz, ...	In sandy wastes on the plain and about the villages. The galls termed *mâhî*, are used by dyers to produce a drab, or *khaki* color, generally combined with oak galls; the timber is used in the wheels of wells, &c.
Thorn apple, ...	Datura, ...	Common in waste places. Leaves applied to ulcers and painful tumours, &c.; seeds used as a remedy for asthma and chronic pulmonary diseases; smoked with tobacco; used as a poison, but seldom.
Verbena. ...	Shamûki, ...	Common on the plain. Fresh